six months backwards

First Published in Great Britain 2018 by Gatito Publishing

First edition: 2018

A copy of this work is available through the British Library.

ISBN: 978-1-719991-47-6

six months backwards

mix amylo

For F

the end...

The fire of the sand burns my eyes as they follow the heavy trudge of my soaked sneakers. Opalescent pebbles glare at me, smoothed lava stone glowers blacker than black. The sky retches its blue over an overturned world. My sight in turn fogs and clears to a new, malevolent vividness. A pure clarity, a retina-scorching assault of every colour and hue.

And the sea. This piece of glorious, gleaming, glistening sea to my right. These tumbling, playful aquamarine waves, sparkling and winking at us even as we stumble into utter darkness. Such is its power, its majesty, that it didn't even notice, didn't blink a wet eye as one of its tendrils ensnared and extinguished one of us. I had never seen it more beautiful.

As I am protectively pulled along, I pull my gaze upwards and left to the cliff top, where throngs gawp, the sunlight silhouetting their curiosity. As my eyes drop the orange-clad men and one woman surround, but fail to hide from me, his blanketed form, lying on a stretcher. Briefly the thought of running to him, lying fully on top of him as on so many other days, and not letting go, flickers through the space where my mind used to be, but I know he has already gone. He is just a shell. He is not him. We will never lie like that again, rubbing noses like two moonstruck cats, scratching each other's neck, burying our hands in hair, inhaling that unique oneness, comforted by compounded years of being strangely drawn to one another.

I walk past him. Beyond him. Beyond us.

unearthed

31st March 2017, Órgiva, Spain

Echoing through me as it echoed through summer days,
the musicscape you created returns and replays,
filling my new rooms with shadowy shimmers of string and sound.
I am as destroyed as I was spellbound.

Did you know that like the power that floated so free,
you'd be floating high and leaving me?

Melodies soaring as you made those harmonics sing,
layering the static air with your everything.
I remember you trying to capture that perfect phrase.
I yearn for your soul, I pine for your ways.

Did you think that when you titled the track with that word
that you would be the one to be unearthed?

Now as I numbly walk down all the streets where you held my hand,
I reach out to nothing and cannot understand
how somebody like you with such an energy
is now just memory.

Now there's just me.

normalising

Sometimes something fills too many of your waking breaths with a horror that eats you from the inside out. You dread it so much that you tremble. You feel sick to the core, and incapable of facing it head-on.

And then you do it, you make yourself do it, and it is curiously fine. You are calm, you are mostly detached, you don't think too much; you are not the frightened, helpless you that was expected to show up that day.

Someone said to me recently that the human spirit is amazing, that it is incredible how it can heal. I suppose, eventually, you reach a point where things you believed impossible can be overcome.

Perhaps pre-empting it in my mind, going over and over what might happen, every step, every possibility, every detail, how I might feel, how I might break down, actually made me live through it then, and not when it came to the feared moment.

I'm talking about going back to Las Negras, where it happened, where I lived for seven happy months before that day; I'm talking about returning to the place that took F from me, from us, and packing up my stuff in order to move it to a different part of Spain, to a different life.

How could I ever be capable of doing this? And why was I even going to try? My thoughts threatened to destroy me, demolish me. Because of a wonderful friend, M, who had boxed up practically everything I own, the process was already so much easier. But then there was the journey. How could I drive there? Apart from the obvious angst of revisiting the village, and the feeling of getting closer and closer to the place, noticing signs, seeing the macabre Mediterranean to my right almost all the way there, it would be the first time I had driven in over six months. Somehow, however, it felt quite normal, and I drove as if the enforced hiatus had never happened. With another close friend, B, at my side, I was numbly unaffected as we ascended the hill to my old apartment. I tried not to gaze down at the sea below, but even when I did dare to look, nothing ripped my guts apart, nothing exploded in my brain.

That word, 'normal'. Normalising. Making sense of terror, of torment, of insane grief. I'm not sure I can truly say that I have made peace with Las

Negras in going back there, but maybe I am one cell closer. The last time I was there it seemed evil. Intrinsically evil. There was a blackness over it, in it, from it, which seeped into me. This time it was just a village. A small fishing village, its white houses surrounded by big cliffs and moonscape mountains. It was just a place where people live. Where I lived. Where people go on holiday. An epic, beautiful place. My studio flat was just a studio flat. A room. With all my worldly possessions in it. Where memories lingered in the air, but more good than bad. Even the sea, dare I say it, appeared normal. A body of water. Blue stretching all the way to Algeria. Just water. What makes up most of the planet and most of us.

I just couldn't put what I was seeing together with what happened; it resembled a dream, and in my haze I was not even sure if the dream was then or now. Either way, I'm grateful to whatever part of me that managed to normalise this return, for my spirit which has healed enough to have made the journey possible, and for the new life I'm about to attempt to start.

haven to home

Impenetrable white below, sun rays blinding me as they bounce off the flimsy silver wing a metre to my right, as I gaze over plains of soft snow into pure blue. I'm going home, I suppose, and, despite everything, the heat on my skin and the incredible light are trying to lure me back towards a place of happiness. The intense weight of the last months, at least in this moment, is lifting.

England, and its endless winter, has been nothing but a haven. In its housing of so many people I love and who I needed to be with, it had to be the place that nursed me back to at least rudimentary health. The boundless kindness of others has meant I haven't needed to worry about how to navigate the mundane, about survival, what to eat, where to sleep, how to be. In its familiarity and indoor cosiness, in its chilly woods and sodden greens, its currency and slang, pubs and charity shops, in its self-deprecating humour and sense of irony, its weather obsession and apologetic pavement shuffling, it has protected me in a comfort blanketed cocoon.

But now, perhaps, as I travel to an old yet new life, I am ready for my own space in my chosen country, and whatever unknown paths lie ahead. Journeying back to the south of Spain seems like the right move. Accompanied by my great friend B and a bucket load of apprehension, I fly from Manchester to Málaga and on to Órgiva, the town that was my home for five years. I will be there again, renting a new place, with memories snapping at my heels, but it's a new beginning. Looking through the clouds at these lands below I feel actual, though transient, euphoria.

Much of the anxiety before boarding was due to the memory of the last flight I took, glued to my brother, 'Biglittlebro', like a broken limpet shell, hollow, empty, tiny, nine days after it happened. I imagined being transported back there, to the blackest of many black days, and finding myself unable to breathe, trapped in my own mad head, clawing at the walls and causing chaos; this, incredibly, does not happen. As we touch down safely my fears stay strapped into seat 21F, and I carry on my journey very much lighter.

And now – let's see.

the hunter of small happinesses

28th March 2017, England

Just in time. Just before I leave my English refuge to fly back to Spain, my piano and strings album 'the hunter of small happinesses' is finally completed, almost exactly six months since that unimaginable day.

It has been a five month journey, on three pianos, where each note was composed in his memory. To say it has been therapeutic would be an understatement; from the first, tentative, fragile pressings of notes, to the formation of the idea to write an album for him, the gradual evolving of a suite of seven piano pieces, and the adding of a string quartet, it has been at once an escape and a confrontation.

To play certain combinations of notes that would trigger certain emotions; to feel, truly feel, everything I have lost in a melody, a phrase, a chord; to lose hours, tears, sleep as I find inspiration from who knows where; this has been an unbelievably necessary, profoundly healing process.

I have to thank my dad number two, 'Papa Dos', for the title. In his many emails to me throughout this time, as he combined spiritual thoughts with practical advice, funny stories and virtual hugs, his idea for me to be the hunter of small happinesses, even as all seemed impossible to bear, struck home. When he wrote that, I found it incredibly difficult to imagine ever being able to be happy again, but as weeks and months passed, tiny moments have brought me tiny joys, and they are growing in size, bit by bit. I find I have to redefine happiness, just as I have had to redefine sadness, having experienced a depth, weight and volume to it previously inconceivable. Without doubt, an appreciation for those miniscule moments that otherwise might have passed me by can now be rebranded as a happiness. Not fading away into non-existence myself, still being here every day, surviving somehow, has to count as a happiness. Many things that in those far-away times brought me joy now bring me the memory of joy, and that has to suffice, for now. Until happiness becomes what it used to be, if ever, I will keep redefining, and keep hunting.

i miss you

27th March 2017

i miss you i miss you i miss you i miss you i miss you i miss you i miss you i miss you
i miss you i miss you i so miss you i so miss you i miss you i miss you i miss you i miss
i miss you i miss you i miss you i miss you i miss you i miss you i miss you i miss you
i miss you i miss you i miss you i miss you i miss you so much i miss you i miss you
i miss you i miss you i miss you i miss you i miss you i so miss you i really miss you
i miss you i miss you i miss you i miss you i miss you i miss you i miss you i miss you
i so miss you i miss you i miss you i miss you so much i miss you i miss you i miss you
i miss you so much i miss you so i so miss you i miss you i miss you i miss you i miss you
i miss you i miss you i miss you i miss you i miss you i miss you i so miss you i miss you
i miss you i miss you i miss you i really miss you i really miss you i miss you so much
i miss you i miss you i miss you i miss you i miss you i miss you i miss you i miss you
i really miss you i miss you i miss you i miss you i miss you i miss you i so miss you
i miss you i miss you i miss you i miss you i miss you i miss you i miss you so much
i miss you i so miss you i miss you so i miss you i miss you i miss you i so miss you
i miss you i miss you i miss you i miss you i miss you i miss you i miss you i miss you
i miss you i miss you i really miss you i miss you i miss you i miss you i miss you so
i miss you so much i miss you i miss you i miss you i miss you i miss you i miss you
i miss you i miss you i miss you i miss you i miss you i miss you i miss you i miss you
i miss you i miss you so i miss you i miss you so much i miss you i miss you i miss you
i miss you i miss you i miss you i miss you i miss you i miss you i miss you i miss you
i miss you i miss you i miss you i miss you i miss you i miss you i miss you i miss you
i miss you i miss you i so miss you i so miss you i miss you i miss you i miss you i miss
i miss you i miss you i miss you i miss you i miss you i miss you i miss you i miss you
i miss you i miss you i miss you i miss you i miss you so much i miss you i miss you
i miss you i miss you i miss you i miss you i miss you i so miss you i really miss you
i miss you i miss you i miss you i miss you i miss you i miss you i miss you i miss you
i so miss you i miss you i miss you i miss you so much i miss you i miss you i miss you
i miss you so much i miss you so i so miss you i miss you i miss you i miss you i miss you
i miss you i miss you i miss you i miss you i miss you i miss you i so miss you i miss you
i miss you i miss you i miss you i really miss you i really miss you i miss you so much
i miss you i miss you i miss you i miss you i miss you i miss you i miss you i miss you
i really miss you i miss you i miss you i miss you i miss you i miss you i so miss you
i miss you i miss you i miss you i miss you i miss you i miss you i miss you so much
i miss you i so miss you i miss you so i miss you i miss you i miss you i so miss you
i miss you i miss you i miss you i miss you i miss you i miss you i miss you i miss you
i miss you i miss you i really miss you i miss you i miss you i miss you i miss you so
i miss you so much i miss you i miss you i miss you i miss you i miss you i miss you
i miss you i miss you i miss you i miss you i miss you i miss you i miss you i miss you
i miss you i miss you so i miss you i miss you so much i miss you i miss you i miss you
i miss you i miss you i miss you i miss you i miss you i miss you i miss you i miss you

clocks forward

In a few days it will be six months since it happened. Six whole months. How surreal. How impossible.

And tonight the clocks go forward, and spring is officially here. And I'll be angry at myself if I don't try, really try, to live, to create, to love, to appreciate what is left around the gaping chasm he has left... if I don't try to find beauty, make beauty, and attempt to make it count, even in the smallest way... if I don't attempt to seek out new adventures, feel new feelings, climb mountains and walk through unknown streets in unfamiliar cities... if I don't start conquering my fears and taking chances again, like I used to do...

Otherwise there is nothing.

Finding my way out from this long, long winter has been the hardest thing I will probably ever have to do. Being with me, supporting and loving and trying to make sense of it, has without a doubt been the toughest of times for my family and close friends as well. I feel scared sometimes about leaving them; so soon I'll be back in Spain, the country I have lived in for nearly nine years, and this nest I have nestled in for endless months will be flown.

I can never underestimate what they have taken on, these beautiful beings that have surrounded me with such care; they have protected me, sheltered me, calmed me, loved me, smoothed me, carried me, so much and so often that I can never begin to thank them enough. I also know they don't want my thanks, and that they only want to try to help to take away the pain. And I hope that they know that I would do the same for them. Nevertheless, what I am feeling today more than anything is gratitude; how anyone gets through something like this without the circle of love I've had is utterly beyond me.

grief is...

25th March 2017

Grief is snide; creeping around the side of a rare, snatched joy it sticks barbs into my fragile flesh and pulls my hair, hides behind unexpected photos and old songs and leaps out to brutally shove me down stairs and into an airless cellar.

Grief is fierce; pummelling my body repeatedly with raging fists, kicking, scratching, punching me furiously, and shrieking, screaming, yelling in my ears, telling me it is my fault.

Grief is lonely; sitting in a darkened room, hunched up and immune to kind gestures, numb to embraces, deaf to loving words, it cannot absorb others but instead quietly digs, using a tiny rusted spoon, and tunnels inward.

Grief is bitter; sweetness is gone, love trampled, and the sour knowledge of the injustice of it all hovers over me, spitting vinegar and snarling in strange tongues.

Grief is unease; unsettling visions tilt my night-times, as my waking hours are infiltrated by fears: the fear of more dying, yet also of too much life pulsing unbidden around me, of travel, of fire, of traffic, of loud noises, of enclosed spaces, of responsibility, of being alone.

Grief is endless; grief is endless.

Grief is liquid; the place where a spine once resided is now inhabited by wretched, tepid fluid, my face pours and my pores leak misery.

Grief is heavy; layer upon layer of enforced, concreted facts and information flatten dreams and the possibility of it all being a mistake, as I am pressed soundlessly, wordlessly into the ground.

Grief is counting; time passes and is noted and mourned, moments since you left are calculated, months without us are ticked off, the first or the last time we did this or that marked indelibly into my veins.

Grief is movement; the rubble of memory and the scree of erased futures cascade incessantly through my days and my weeks, pushing aside the solidity of assumption and the serenity of habit.

Grief is stillness; molecules thicken and congeal, hugging themselves around my fallen figure, freezing me there, with only the anxious rise and fall of my chest marking me as alive as silence crowds in and my mind shuts down.

Grief is empty; all is grey space, with no horizon, no east or west, and the vessel I once was, full of frantic sparks, endless textures, and jumbled colours, lies vacant and cold.

Grief is endless; grief is endless.

Grief is growth; a sordid springtime of opening buds revealing forgotten shards of pain, of forest floors coated in forget-me-nots, of the creeping vines of awareness that this is a reality.

Grief is animal; as primal instincts of fight or flight grip tightly, wrenching back time in horror-filled shapes, the survival that is unwanted in the beginning begins, somehow, to seem important.

Grief is constricting; as my chest contracts and my throat refuses to swallow food or air, its form writhes and tightens around my voice, so that its squashed sound only spews out banalities.

Grief is holding on; clinging to the ledge even as the drop seems the only way, clutching onto thoughts and drifting, shifting, theoretically uplifting recollections, grabbing the offered hands that haul me upwards and calm me down.

Grief is letting go; the string that lengthens daily, and cuts into my fingers as I hold so tightly, could be released and I could watch as the balloon of you rises gently through storm clouds and atmospheres, leaving me behind, too small.

Grief is resignation; you are gone, you are lost. I can search but will not find, not ever, except perhaps in hopeful signs: the cat's gaze at something behind my right shoulder, the bird that lingers in the garden, the murmuring shadows on all the shelves of my brain, and, sometimes, in my dreams.

Grief could be endless. I will not let it be.

transformation

24th March 2017

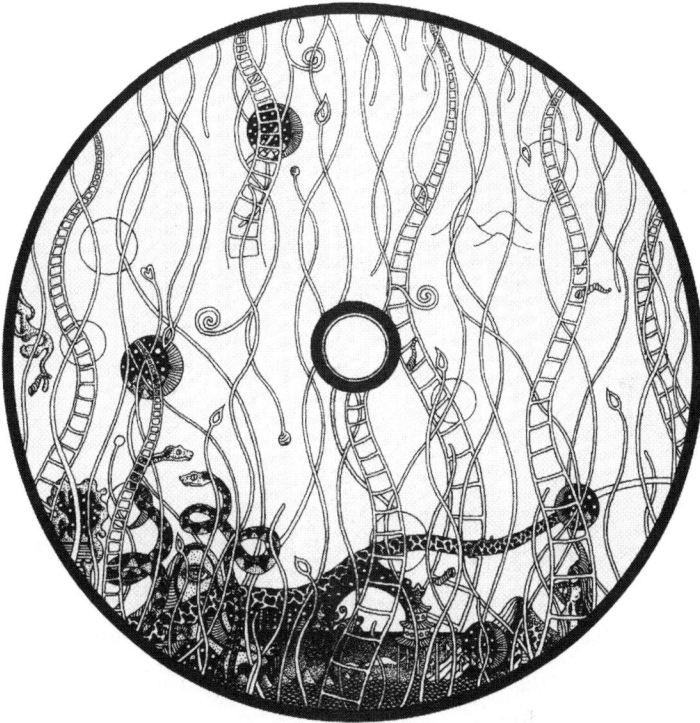

I'm in the beginnings of a drawing for a close friend, SP. Because of the amount of time 'the hunter of small happinesses' has consumed, I haven't been drawing much in the last couple of months. I wanted to have completed this by the time I moved back to Spain (looming ever nearer), but, as always, time never decides to stretch itself enough for me to fit in everything.

Drawing creates a good space for me to be in. It has always, always, taken me to a meditative place, where the world disappears and only the next dot or line matter. It numbs me, soothes me, and makes me feel safe. Hours and hours can pass, as I hardly move, and my fingers start to seize up; 'just one more bit',

I say; 'I'll just shade this in' as another sixty minutes fly by. Not much of a cardiac workout; and my body won't thank me, but my mind does. It has been the only thing that can tranquilise my itchy brain and "quiiick!" mentality. Yes, music transports me, but in the transporting is emotion; as I move between this world and that, I feel it pulling at me, clawing feelings out of me and inserting them back in anguished or joyful pushes. It's a healing of a different kind.

As with the piano, I never thought I'd draw again. When my brother suggested I packed my pens and drawing pads on the day we left my flat in Las Negras to come back to England, it felt like he was telling me to pack a pair of wings, so unlikely was I to use them. I couldn't contemplate being able to embrace art and saw no point in its existence. How lucky to have so many wise people around me, who can see ahead, and know me better than I knew myself in those first weeks.

I had asked SP for any themes or feelings that I could bear in mind as I set to work on her drawing, in order to create something personal that would, I hoped, resonate with her; she told me that present in her thoughts at that time were transformation and clarity.

As I write now, I am thinking about transformation. How events transform you. How you can transform yourself. Wondering about the level of control you really have over who you are, when life kicks you onto the floor. Do you spend all your time and energy simply trying to regain old ground, and get back to where and who you were before it happened? Or does your path now follow a different course without you knowing it; do you climb and climb, getting higher each day, only to realise the mountain you stand upon is a different one and the view utterly new? How much of this trying to transform yourself back to what you were is habit? The patterns that are engrained in you, concerning how you live, how you perceive life, how you relate to others, how you give and receive; is it just a search for our comfort zones? Shouldn't you accept that you will be a different person, and just hope that this new being is one you can live with?

In fact, this speculation only makes me think that none of this is conscious at the time. I haven't spent months pondering how I will be transformed; rather I have simply been dealing with the residue of events. I haven't thought too much about who I will become, and if I will be changed; my priorities have been existing, going through the motions, learning to eat and sleep and laugh again, conquering fears, until I found myself recognising elements of my old self.

Looking back, I realise I have tried to transform myself many times. I have officially changed my name, and surname, twice. I shed the skin of environment when moving from school to music college, and from college to London, and from London to Spain. I wanted to metamorphose in all my other habitats along the way, whether I lived in them for weeks, months or years. It felt important to be new, to start again in a sense. Did it work? There are things about yourself that are a lifelong battle to change, and you wonder whether it's worth the effort. Sometimes I think I haven't evolved much at all from the teenager I thought I'd left behind.

I will have to see how I am transformed after losing someone so close to me. If and how I have changed, now that there is only a space where he used to be. I think of all the ways we related to each other, in person or simply by knowing each other so well that we could predict the other's reaction to something without them even being there. The hearing of his voice almost every day. The knowledge that there was a bond between me and someone else, whether that cord travelled from one side of the bed to the other, or across thousands of kilometres. The feeling of being loved, needed, supported, desired, cared for. The shared language, the private jokes, the implicit understanding.

Will that hole that housed him push the rest of me outwards, so that everything I was before still remains, but further away from the core of me? Given the enormity of his presence in my life, I'm going to be the size of the world.

piece number six

I am in the last stages of practising for my piano album. There is a sadness in leaving this friend that has accompanied me through the darkest of times. I am already pre-empting feeling bereft, lost, adrift. It has consumed my days for months, particularly the last three. Most of it was written before Christmas, but it has evolved since then, with many alterations and additions, and the writing of parts for violin, viola, cello and double bass, and I don't feel ready to let it go.

The positive side of me, however, knows that there will be another idea snapping at its heels. As always. In fact, I can think of at least nine incomplete or ready-to-start projects in my pipeline; the vault is bursting with unfinished business, and my head swirls with too many thoughts and concepts. I've never not known what to do with my time. My problem is being realistic; given how long each artistic adventure takes, ten lifetimes would not provide enough moments in which to complete them all. This is the endless dilemma of time management; to concentrate on one, and only one piece of work until it's done, or to dilute the days dipping into one then another as the mood takes me? I haven't discovered the answer yet.

I found it fascinating, looking from the outside in, if that is truly possible to do with yourself, how the innate need to create has regrown, and in fact how quickly it came back, despite everything. Why is that; how is that?

What is it that drives me, that pushes me to write, draw, play, paint, compose, construct, record constantly?

I have no boss telling me what to do, no deadlines drawn in the sand by others. I could float, relax, do nothing, except make enough to survive. In the case of these last six months, I think I know why I am driven; left to its own devices, my mind would derail me. The tigers would strike. Losing myself in a drawing or on the piano lets them become a blur on the peripheries for a while; the pen strokes and the chord voicings silence their howl and I become only what my essence has always been.

I have had longer to become familiar with this composition, due to my gypsy roaming and studio availability.

Six pieces on the album are written and recorded, which will be numbers one to five and seven in the running order, but last time I was in Manchester we only had time to put down the piano and record the string players for those six; this one was left for later. So in theory, given the amount of practising I've done on it, I should be more at ease when the red light goes on, but I'm actually more nervous about it than all the others. Too much time to think. And I haven't yet got through it all without a mistake...

It took a while to find this one. As with all things creative, you never know how or why some ideas just pour out of you, without thought or planning, while others have to be prised out inch by painful inch...

I was a little stuck. I had more or less written the other six pieces that would all have a string quartet accompanying the piano, and had decided this one should stand alone as a solo piano piece. Perhaps it was that that blocked me.

I asked my youngest brother, 'Littlebigbro', who isn't a musician, to give me three notes that would kick off the piece.

He played a very low F, an A above middle C, and a low G. Not the normal go-to notes you would pick to construct a melody; not hugely hummable. But it worked; using them to dictate the key, (F major), they led me on to other notes, as notes do, and I could feel some direction at last, as it flowed towards F minor. It also seemed to lend itself, if only for a few bars, to a baroque style, which was something I hadn't tackled before.

I was incredibly struck by the serendipitous nature of these three notes and what they gave me. It blew my mind that I had already been thinking that the piece would be in that key, and that some of it might be baroque in style, and here it was, given to me in a random game with a grin on my Littlebigbro's face. These two things, the key and the style, were in my mind because of the first piece of music I tried to play in late October, even as I thought I would never, could never, play again; it was a Domenico Scarlatti sonata (K466/P501/L118 for aficionados).

It is in F minor, and the simple beauty of it wrenched tears from me as I tried to pick it out. I was in Biglittlebro's recording studio in Manchester, feeling spirits at my back and an unshakeable ache everywhere else, and it had taken a long time to get me there. Biglittlebro had only just ordered the book of Scarlatti's music just before 'it happened', and it was as yet unopened. He encouraged me to try, to take the book to the studio, to see if I could distract myself for a moment. For some reason I chose this particular sonata. As I touched the keys, and discovered the perfect melody and harmonies, two hundred and sixty-one years old, I also began to tentatively rediscover myself, and how the power of music can heal. Trite as that may sound, it is nothing but true.

From the bottom of despair there is the bottom rung. Climb up to that one, and there is another. And another. The diameter of the circle of light at the top of your personal well increases. I was at the bottom of everything, as never before, and yet... here I was back home, back playing my favourite instrument that I have played since I was seven, and I knew right then that it could save me.

parklife

22nd March 2017

Walking through the gates
of Longford Park, sensing the
strength of earth below.

The day surrounds me
with luscious air and pure smells;
blithe daffodils nod

as I pass them by,
stepping around yesterday's
puddles with care.

Squirrels bound up oaks
and across pathways with no
shyness in their bounce.

Tree trunks hold up the
fresh green weight of unfurling
possibility.

I am held high by
the rare sighting of a new
positivity.

My ache is inside,
as always lurking, but at
this moment it could

be someone else's
pain; all is outwards, around
me, feeding my soul.

the hauntings

It can be anything...

A moment in a film, a throwaway phrase, running water, a glimpse of a drama from a car, the scent of a stranger...

Being in the bathroom, a faraway siren, a weeping child, a gust of wind...

An article in a newspaper, an empty park bench, the eyes of a dog, lying on the floor, the shape of a shadow...

There is a spool that, seizing on any trigger, begins to rewind, slowly but surely at first, then accelerating wildly, throwing a sequence of images and memories at me even as I try to stem the flow, and regain the now.

I spent weeks, months being haunted in this way; it has lessened, as all things seem to thankfully do.

I decided to try to combat it one day, by walking round and around a bus stop listing, out loud, all the flashbacks that kept monopolising my brain, and putting them in order from the most disturbing to the least.

(The worst kind of travel guide – 'Top Haunts' for the mind tourist...)

I realised there were seven hauntings.

Five were remembered visuals.

One was the memory of the thinking about something as it was actually happening.

And one of them I had imagined; although it *had* actually happened, I didn't see it. I had claimed it as my own, as I suppose one can do upon hearing about any traumatic event that doesn't involve you.

But this one photo that surged at me at all hours was constructed by *me*, not reality, which felt important to realise. It didn't take away the fact that it had happened that way. It would never erase the truth. But given the length of my spool, and the depth of my misery, I felt that at least this particular image could be cut out.

I was unsure as to whether circling the bus stop on a cold winter's day, and reaching inside for the things that I normally tried to run from, would help or hinder, but I somehow instinctively knew I had to do it.

I needed to solidify them, know them, and acknowledge their power, in order to release them, to let them be, and to know that they would visit and revisit but that they would always pass.

Papa Dos, that wise owl, had told me the same thing (and I'm paraphrasing him here); that these thoughts are like tigers, you have to let them roar. Don't oppose them, or they will get sly and devious, and linger longer; let them get bored and tired, and they will sleep.

And in fact something did lift after I verbalised these hauntings.

I also came back and told Biglittlebro, and this two-pronged exorcism managed to at least mould the spool of images into a tangible form, and made me capable of placing them into a box that only I had the key to. Without doubt they could always escape, but I could always put them back in and turn the lock, and strangely those tigers have seemed to become wearier as time unfolds.

Of course they are still there, whether they sleep or growl.

And I have no doubt that they will always be with me, hiding under foliage, waiting to pounce when I least expect it.

But the ever-growing distance from the actual happenings and now, occasionally allows me to see them from afar; from time to time, as in a dream, I gaze at them, puzzled, and wonder what they have to do with me.

everywhere, nowhere

20th March 2017

A tucked-in corner in an alehouse.
Roughed-up burgundy leather, darkened wood.
A striped old kitten, swollen with babies too soon,
sprawled on a nearby table against the dregs of a pint,
amber eyes slowly blinking.
Old soul filtering through invisible speakers.
The smell of years, of barrels, of forgotten smoke.
Two elderly men playing chess, two others backgammon.
Three women whispering, clinking glasses.
A few more like me, further down the bar. Sitting heavily alone,
clutching their liquids, gazing at those around them unselfconsciously.
The rain coming down,
the wind serving it in aces towards the windows,
lobbing it underneath the awning.
Cars trudging by, wipers on double, hugging passers-by with sodden arms.

The music changes, to one of his favourite songs.
And there it is.
The moment falls away.
I can't escape.
I am nowhere, he is everywhere.
I think I can hide, bury myself away in a place he has never been,
and be still for a small while. But no.
The corner, the cat, the drinkers, the rain, the cars; they are full of him.
They shout him at me.
The air breathes him in and out.

I drink up and go.
To another place, it doesn't matter which, where he will be everywhere,
and I will be nowhere.

slowly vanishing

19th March 2017

He is in hospital, critical, but conscious. I am not allowed to see him; it's now Monday, and he has been there since Friday. No one will tell me anything, or let me in to be at his side.

A long, agitated queue finally forms, writhing with people going to see patients. I spot S and G up ahead, and join them. I am beyond angry. Why has no one told me what is going on?

We never reach him, but instead are shown a video. In the film, he is sitting in a hospital garden. There are others, all younger than him, all male, all dressed in orange, milling around. He is alone on a bench. Completely still. Wrapped in something white, with more white in the form of a huge cloth wrapped around his head.

So pale.

He is not there.

A bell sounds, and the orange-clad boys leave.

He is left, sitting there, slowly vanishing.

My dreams are torture; my wakings no better.

This is just one of the many parallel stories that have pushed me out of sleep.

But whether chimeric or true, the story ends the same way.

ghost bear

When we were kids, my two brothers and I each had a pocket money bear. Carved out of wood, they stood on top of the piano in our living room, guarding weekly gifts of double-your-age-and-add-ten (pence).

This weekend I'm with my mum and Papa Dos in their house near the northeast coast. Although the days of the pocket money bears bearing coins are long gone, they have kept their place in the home. The house has changed and the piano has gone, but they still stand together, on a shelf near the fire.

And now they have a new companion. Papa Dos found a glass bear, and thought it could represent the spirit of our lost one. He placed this ghost bear next to mine, to watch over and take care of me. When he told me, and showed it to me, the whole of me whirled and the hole in me yearned. My insides caved in, my eyes streamed, but my heart was lifted somehow by this beautifully sad creature.

painful paradox

17th March 2017

I want to stop the fading... the evaporating... the dissipating... of him.

I need to force myself back towards who he was, who we were, as he disappears into blurred breezes and muddied memory.

But that means facing the last moments of his life, as much as the recollections of his living essence.

I have to talk about him, as hard as that is for me and for others to do, to keep him near.

But that means, it seems, revisiting the times that puncture and slash me, the parts that stab the most, the things that bring anger or intense despair.

Happy anecdotes do not trip lightly off my tongue right now, and amusing stories, from the mouths of the few others who manage to verbally remember, render me frozen, far from entertained on the inside despite my attempts at a smile.

It's not a laughing matter! I want to scream.

I suppose I'm just not ready.

And this is the paradox: I am so glad that these others can talk in this way about him. Glad for them, glad for his memory.

I want people, family and friends, to feel able to do that in front of me. To talk about the hole he has left, or the space he occupied.

But the former usually makes me teary, as much as I want it, causing them to stop and back off, and the latter, as I say, seems to involve the kind of memories that I can't handle, and often have nothing to do with how I related to him – and this is making the endlessness of silence lengthen, and the pieces of me descend into confused, anxious territory.

This painful paradox: of feeling him fly further and further away, and wanting to shout louder and louder to bring him back to me, and discovering I have no voice, no strength, and my pathetic whispers in the night do not so much as tremble the air molecules around me or the spider's web above my head.

balancing

Piano recorded a couple of weeks ago in an intense long weekend, violin, cello and viola in the week after, double bass the other day. Apart from piece number six, which is just piano, all the notes are recorded. The thousands and thousands of notes. And now we, Biglittlebro and I, are balancing the instruments to create the sound that has been in my head for so long. I'm often too much of a perfectionist, and we don't have all the time in the world to spend on it, but it's all coming together; the emotion in the string players' playing matches my own, and at times I almost feel detached from the composing of it, and only open to the feelings it brings.

balancing: the walking of a tightrope strung between despair and determination, high from recognisable ground, blown by dark winds.

balancing: juggling the confronting of what has happened with the dream that it didn't.

balancing: using anything to hand to calm my mind, to smooth my scars, to stop myself tipping over the edge.

balancing: feelings of unfairness and injustice measured against the impartial force and power of nature.

balancing: the years I had with him versus the years before him or the ones ahead of me.

balancing: wedging myself between the strength of those around me and my own lifeforce, weakened but surely still there underneath.

balancing: finding equilibrium and peace, somehow, somewhere, someday.

perfect

15th March 2016

There is a tendency, understandably so, to put someone on a pedestal after they're gone. Any faults are swept away, and they are glorified. I imagine it is normal to remember the good things first about someone you loved and lost. The lack of them, and the upheaval and trauma of their passing, makes the missing of everything you adored about them, and the mourning for the relationship you had, turn them into perfect humans.

I'm conscious of not wanting to do that. It wouldn't be real; a false worshipping of him would blur the truth.
He wasn't perfect. And neither am I.
Who is?

We all have our foibles, our moods, our weaknesses, our failures, our annoying tics, our misjudgements, our egos, our jealousies, our stupidities, our cruelties, our blinkers, our bad habits, our petulancies. Our imperfections.
We don't like to think we do. But we do.

Perfection is not the point, is never the point. What is perfect anyway? An abstract construct, largely fed to us poor sponges by the incessant pushing in the media of how we should be, act, look, achieve, feel, behave, love.

I can't in all honesty, no matter how much I miss him and yearn for him, turn him into someone who was *everything* I wanted or needed. And I'm sure he would say the same about me, if he could. Alongside his funny, charming, easy-going, silly self, he could be very stubborn, extremely moody. Occasionally being selfish, intolerant, resentful, or unfriendly in company were traits of his personality as much as those qualities of his such as kindness, affability, sweetness, generosity, and humility. He was sometimes impossible to fathom, his logic, priorities or decisions planets away from mine. The whole deal was not perfect; the situation, as in the geographical madness, certainly wasn't, but also probably what we took from and gave to each other wasn't always enough. There were, as in any relationship, angsty days and difficult times, misunderstandings and sulks, tears and anger, and the fact that he isn't here anymore doesn't make those memories erasable.

The good, the bad and the ugly; the rough and the smooth, the fabulousness and the frustrations; the entirety of such a long time with someone can never and should never be put into a box and labelled. It was not one thing; he was not one thing; I am not one thing. The multitude of variables in any human being, and their bonds and connections with others, is such that to sum someone up in a few words will always do them a disservice.

The point, the *only* point, is that I loved him, and he loved me. For a long time. Without stopping. As we were. The real us, not a glossed-up, sanitised, eulogised version. And that's perfect enough for me.

there you are

There you are... in my dream.
Still existing.
It's the only place you are, at least in your known human form,
and I see you.
You see me, sometimes.
Sometimes I'm watching you from afar.
Occasionally we interact.

You were playing guitar, along with someone else, and along to a pre-recorded instrumental track. It was for a video, I think. After a minute of miming, you put down your guitar and hared off into fields, surrounded by others, running fast and gleefully, kicking a ball, the sun pouring down on you, happy.

I lost sight of you, but the feeling of seeing you has remained, etched in my daytime tears, engraved into my addled consciousness, carved into my emptiness.

There you are.

That's what you always said when I picked up the phone to you. There you are. After you'd tried to get hold of me once, twice, and finally we spoke. There you are. That's what you said when we met, at airports, stations, the houses of family or friends. After you said you could breathe again, now that we were together after our time apart. Before we nuzzled and stroked, and inhaled and touched, and whispered in our private language. There you are.

There you are. Where are you?

objects

Objects. Things. Stuff. Items. Material possessions.

What do they mean?

What's the point?

We go, they are left, cluttering up the world.

Material things don't mean much to me. I don't put great stock in possessions. I own no furniture; my many musical instruments are functional, not objects for objects' sake. I rent the place where I live; my car is an old banger. Clothes and jewellery come and go.

But wait.

I cling onto photos, to cling onto the past. Onto cards and letters, to reread forgotten words. Onto concert programmes for gigs I don't want to forget, whether I performed or watched. Onto found objects: fossils, shells, stones, that conjure up memories of places and times. Onto trinkets I don't love but that were given to me by someone I love. Onto small, quirky or beautiful things that had attracted me from a shop shelf on a needy day. I guard my books fiercely, because they transport me to other worlds. I surround myself with other people's art, because you should. I hold onto CDs, even though everything now flies through digital air.

And now, now he has gone, I wonder at my need for something of his. Something tangible, something more than memory. More, even, than the music he left behind. Something he had next to his skin.

His sister J has, from time to time, sent me a package of a few of his things. Apart from one well-worn black jumper, there was nothing more I felt I needed that had belonged to him; I *did* feel something approximating happiness when that arrived back in my life. It was something he had worn over years and years, on countless occasions, and the one thing I playfully tried to steal from him from time to time. To be able to wear it now brings a dark irony I can barely contemplate. And I couldn't think, with my clouded mind, of anything else that represented him, that would make me feel in any way better, that I wanted to have. Heavyheartedly opening the parcels, with the opposite of childish Christmas glee, the first sensation was smell. His clothes, still carrying his essence; a very real trace of him, months after he had gone. I suppose in reality, and unromantically, it was the washing powder he used, but that was how he smelled, clean, and the jolt of recollection knocked me down every time. There were shirts, scarves, jumpers, even socks. Watches, photos, glasses, a framed drawing I had done of him. And, hard though it was to confront them, I was so glad, in the end, that J had sweetly taken the time to choose and post these things.

But then there it was. The thing I had forgotten that I had actually mentioned to J in the first month but that she hadn't been able to find. The thing that meant something. There it was: a carved wooden scarab beetle, on a leather bracelet. A handcrafted gift from Papa Dos to him a few years ago, after he had admired the one PD was sporting. A gift he wore for months, years, until the strap broke. A gift that could now be passed on to me, repainted, the strap fixed and tightened to fit my wrist. A gift that I wear all day, every day, as he did, and in doing so feel somehow connected to him.

Objects. Things. Stuff. Items. Material possessions.
Sometimes they do mean something.

facing it

Not quite the Mediterranean. Not as dramatic, not as blue, not as scary to me. Probably just as dangerous, under the wrong circumstances, but a different animal. Nevertheless, here was the sea, and a sort of beach, right in front of me for the first time in nearly half a year.

Overlooking the Thames estuary at Southend, eating fish and chips and braving the view with close friends, the horror my last proper sighting of the ocean brought me had dissipated. I chanted within "it's only water, it's only water." "Look, it's beautiful. It's only water." I drank wine and relied on one of my best friends in the world, SD, to keep an eye on me. She had suggested I do this when I arrived yesterday, as a small step towards facing what I have to face in about two weeks, when I go back to Spain and to Las Negras to collect my things; strangely I had had the same thought. I knew I could run if I needed to. I knew she would whisk me away and ply me with hugs, love, and more wine. I knew it wasn't the same sea, that it wouldn't have the same effect on me. And I thought I was ready. Maybe.

The water was still, calm, and very far away. Silvery, unreal. The mud flats stretched for what seemed like miles; the strip of sea was innocuous. As we talked, and looked at each other rather than out beyond us, the water moved in. It moved so fast it seemed impossible, as suddenly it had reached the railings by the road. That frightened me, and reminded me of its insistent power, but I kept sitting there. "It's only water."

After lunch we moved towards the pier, and the area where all the amusement arcades reside. Some slot machine action was deemed necessary, and an ice cream, and then we decided to try sitting on the wall by the beach.

This was now more like the sea I dreaded seeing again. This was up close and personal.

I lasted ten minutes before the flashbacks started in earnest. They had been hovering, cackling to themselves, waiting to strike, but I was ready for them. I gave SD the look, and we left; that was enough.

And I was plied with hugs, love, and more wine, and that was enough.

paradise

11th March 2017

In those bygone days, before the seemingly unbreakable thread that bound us was snapped, snipped with watery scissors, I adored the sea. I saw paradise in those shorelines, peace in those waves. I remember a trip to Sardinia one warm November, strolling along the whitest of sands alone, feeling as if the beach would be my final destination. I imagined having an incurable illness, and asking to be brought and laid by the ocean, to gently slip away to the sounds of the tides.

Although the sea is now the very opposite of paradise for me, it will remain so for others. I am wondering what will happen if or when, in some unimaginable future, I find myself back in the place that is the idyll for most people. I envisage the reason would be performing, having plucked up the courage to accept a gig somewhere I used to play. I might be observing the clientele sipping on cocktails and enjoying our live music in a pretty terrace bar next to the sand, the intense blue stretching out beyond, and the salty happiness in the air. Would I break down? Would I run?

I would be battling it from within, and questioning how the perfect, relaxed, beautiful holiday environment can be the stuff of nightmares for someone else. But who knows what story all the people there might be carrying; who could see what demons or sadness they had to bear? You can never tell from the outside what the inside looks like. Maybe they would be battling too. There we would be, all of us in our personal microcosms, feeling or pretending that we were in paradise.

The word 'paradise' always takes me back to the moment when I and my two friends S and G, barely able to stay upright, were walking away from the beach, through the many people who had gathered to watch, and a woman I knew from the village asked me what had happened. After I told her, (as best I could, as I didn't, couldn't comprehend what I was saying), she said she was there for me, whenever and however, and that I had to remember that he died in paradise.

I still don't know what to make of that statement. Is it better that someone dies somewhere beautiful, as opposed to somewhere ugly? A place where, in general, people are happy, as opposed to where they are generally not? What difference could that possibly make? Was she saying that if you die in 'paradise', you're closer to the next paradise, that it's less of a journey?

I have no idea, but I know what she said came from the very best place, and I can still feel her enormous hug on my skin.

underpinning

Today Biglittlebro recorded the double bass for 'The Hunter of Small Happinesses'. The last string instrument to put down, the last notes except for piece number six, it completed the four-part harmonies that accompany the piano, and the soundtrack in my mind.

Such an amazing musician, I was so proud to have him play on this project that means everything to me. He has been such a huge part of all of this, so much so that I am afraid to leave his side when I make the move back to Spain next month. Whilst being completely empathetic, and able to both feel my feelings and express his own, he also has a gift for making me feel lighter, for making me laugh, for making me able to be silly and surreal, for making me feel almost like myself again. Like the double bass underpinning the string quartet, he has underpinned my falling debris and grounded my flailing sadness. As violins sob and cellos weep, they do so knowing the bass is underneath, a solid certainty, a warming resonance, a force.

The base of me; the bass of me; the core of me.

He, and my other brother, and the rest of my wonderful family, have provided ground level support, something to crash down upon, a soft, smooth cushion for my raw, bleeding spikes. And if friends are the new family, I have two incredible families, and am so relieved. And so lucky, as I have said before, and will continue to say, because even though the worst thing has happened, and the impossibly huge wound stretches and screams and sometimes seems like it can never even begin to heal, my base, my bass, are there for me.

frozen sound

The clock is ticking like a curse.
Outside a slow cold writes its words.
You disappear, we search the universe
for traces, spaces where your voice was heard.

Icy phrases ink my body.
Losing you is plain to see.
My face tattooed with Nature's sorry.
The lines of this song etch to bleed.

The air around us blackens me
with nothing and with everything.
This air was once your poetry,
our rhyme before the frost got in.

You were there, somehow not anymore.
We were here, but now I'm on the floor.
You've been moved from around me
and the frozen sound of you leaving
fills my world and empties my core.

soul stealing

It's over five months since it happened, and for the last two or three I haven't been able to look at photos of him. In the beginning I had a pile of them, hastily and numbly torn out of albums in my flat in Las Negras to throw into suitcases to be flown to England; they were propped up against anything I could find in the bedroom I was using in Biglittlebro's house; they gazed at me from the bedside table; I kept them inside books and in bags; hundreds were printed and collaged; he was everywhere. I looked at them, unable to grasp even a sliver of the truth. I needed them; I needed him; I wanted him around me. This seemed a tangible way to keep him next to me. But as time ticked on, and days turned to weeks and to months, and I needed him ever more, these images of him seemed to hurl the terrible truth at me in incrementally crueller throws. It was him, but he is no more. It wasn't him; he was a flesh and blood human, not a printed piece of paper. It was him; I remember that day, that instant, those feelings. It wasn't him; maybe time has erased the remembering and turned it into something else. It was him; look into his eyes – that's how he looked, that's how he looked. It wasn't him; he was posing for the camera – the actor in him taking over.

It was him; it wasn't him.
He was there; we were there.
He was; we were.
He's not here; we're not here.
He isn't;
I am, without him.

I've always found photos strange. They solidify a moment, a millisecond, and usually a self-conscious one at that. The pose, the pout, the affected camera face, the angling of the head, the cheeky grin or the studied serious stance, the fluffing of the hair, the sucking and tucking in of extraneous flesh. The image we want to project; the way we want to be remembered. The way we'd like to be. But the photos often do not tell the real story. The forced smile can hide all manner of emotions lurking beneath; an apparent camaraderie and bonhomie could be telling lies about the fissures or pressures in a group. Of course it doesn't have to be that dramatic; most photos of you and your close ones say that yes, you are close, yes, you are happy to be here now, in this place, with this person, with these people. But there is something that itches at me, despite my love of photos in general, and my hoarding of them; is the past what we have told ourselves it is? In the same way that we hold ourselves differently when the lens is pointed at us, have we edited our lives to suit us, to make a better story?

I always wondered about childhood memories. Which ones were my actual memories, and which were merely memories of the photos I had pored over so many times, and the almost folkloric stories that accompanied them? My mum is a great photo album maker, and one of our favourite things to do whenever we visit her is to look through the latest one, and without fail delve back into a few more. I love that she has documented our lives, and in such a warm, creative way, cutting the photos into shapes, writing little comments, always with her impeccable sense of design and colour. Leafing through the pages and contemplating all of our intertwined lives gives a real sense of pleasure, and a feeling of belonging.

The last time I was there, just before Christmas, I didn't dare to look inside the albums. I couldn't see his face; I couldn't bear to confront the unconfrontable. But in recent days I have brought him out again, out from the plastic bag that was at the bottom of the bed, back onto the shelves, into my line of sight. There he is. With me, or looking at me as I took the picture, or with my family and friends. It's both uncomfortable viewing and completely normal; these images are ones I have seen hundreds of times over many years, and their familiarity is not jarring, though the context in which I regard them is. It's surreal, bizarre. But somehow warming too. The memories buzzing around each photo, whether true or edited, or even invented, fill me with some kind of – happiness? not exactly – sadness? definitely – but somewhere between the two is a need to cherish what we had.

So when I visit Mum and Papa Dos in a week or so, those albums might just get opened.

getting it

I wrote the parts, but as A sight reads them flawlessly it's like I'm hearing the phrases for the first time, as they blend and soar with the piano, and with the violin that was recorded the other day. I am constantly amazed by that intuition possessed by many musicians, that instinctive feel, that 'getting it', that on occasion seems impossible. A had never heard these pieces, had no idea of the style, tempo, key, dynamics, anything, but from the first notes I knew she was feeling it the same way as I felt it, and as I would have played it had I played the cello. There were subtle rallentandos, miniscule crescendos, slight pauses, hesitant accelerandos, and somehow, magically, she knew where they would fall. What connection, what affinity, what bond; how can two people who have never met somehow feel groupings of notes in exactly the same way?

It touched me. She touched me, so much so that my emotions that I was trying very hard to keep in check throughout the whole process started pouring out, and threatened to flood the day. I felt at once apart from and totally immersed in what I was hearing; a curious sensation. A beautiful sensation. A terrible sensation. A letting go, a taking hold of. A remembering, an acknowledgement, a deep abyss, a true sadness. A pure loss. A reality, a dream, both. An incomprehension, a confusion, a bewilderment. A plummet, a plunge, a profound pain. A confrontation of why these notes had appeared, an awareness of who they represented, a fierce kick in the stomach to remind me, if I needed reminding, that this wasn't just a project I had decided to put together randomly; this was my saviour, this was my therapy, this was my ode to him. My ode to us.

end of you

6th March 2017

What are you now?
What am I left with?
Here in my head I don't know what you've become.
What was our time
if now it's over?
I don't know what to feel about your love.

And weakly I try to keep hold of you,
my hands reaching out and finding nothing.
Images flash of before and after,
but the after lingers longer than before.

Is this what will stay?
Is this what will remain?
Just the end of you.
Just the end of you.

Who are you now?
You are out in the distance,
disappearing further day by day.
Who can I be?
This veil that stops me feeling
lies heavily and buries me in grey.

Is this what will stay?
Is this what will remain?
Just the end of you.
Just the end of you.

the lonely one

There's an image I keep drawing or painting, over and over again. I've done it for nearly ten years. It might be me, it might not; it's a sitting, hunched, solitary female figure, and she appears in most of my work somewhere. In almost all of my recent drawings she is there in the centre, surrounded by circles, which are in turn surrounded by a complex jumble of life forms; flora and fauna and naked girls entwine in surreal universes; glimpsed through gaps in parallel worlds, or leaping out from the background, each reality exists alongside the other in detailed chaos.

It started with a project in the art school in Barcelona where I studied for a year. I posed for some photos, and the only posture I wanted to represent was this; I wasn't sure what it meant, or why it had to be that, but it seemed right. This translated into an image I could cut out, and use in an installation. It became, while not exactly a trademark, a recurring theme. Even in my house, in the town where I am going to live again in Spain next month, I stuck the image above each light switch, so I could see where to press in the dark.

Now – and I know I am reading into it, as I am reading into everything – I am struck by it. I am saddened by it. I wonder if it was a premonition. That lonely girl, sitting, desolate, surrounded by black, but also by a circle of love, with the stuff of life pulsing and pulsating around and beyond her.

Out of reach.
Alone, apart.
Enclosed in nothingness.
The lonely one.

golden nuggets

4th March 2017

"I'm mewing," he said. This was one of our words that meant being in pain, physically or emotionally.

We stood outside a bar where I'd just been doing a gig, our arms wrapped around each other.

"Why?"

"It's never felt so hard to leave you before. It has never hurt so much."

Although we were holding each other tight, and close, he seemed detached, apart. So thin, as if I could crush him. His colour, even that of his clothes, was slightly faint, slightly faded.

"Where are the golden nuggets?"

"The what?" I had forgotten what that meant; it must have been a phrase of ours that I somehow couldn't remember.

"You know; the golden nuggets. The nice things, the treats that make up for being apart from each other for so long."

He faded a little more, became even thinner.

"I'm not sure I can take this anymore," he said.

This was my dream last night.

note to self

Sitting nursing a hot chocolate in a Chorlton cafe. Utterly, crushingly exhausted. Today we recorded the violin, the first of the strings to be added to the piano on the album. H was fantastic, and brought that extra emotion to what is already pretty up there in the emotional stakes. I was writing the final violin part up to the moment I left the house for the studio, and from the early hours this morning, in the usual last minute panic. I haven't slept well for weeks, and my stress (pointless, but it was very present), to get it all written, arranged and ready for the string players has been huge. It's been such a project, over months and months – so how can I still be rushing to finish it at the eleventh hour? It's not even over; I still haven't completed all the cello and bass parts, there's the viola, cello, and double bass to record, and then piece number six on the piano. But somehow, as someone else started to play what only I have played up until now, it felt like it was done, and I'm coming crashing down. Doing this album has propelled me forwards, lifted me up, and helped me immeasurably. And now I feel empty, yet still agitated.

Thinking about stress; knowing how damaging it is, in every way. Aware that it is almost always, in my case, self-inflicted.

When you live by creativity, and unless you're lucky enough to have some kind of 'audience' or 'public' out there, breathlessly waiting for your latest offering, it's hard to accept that no one really cares *when* (or even *if*, but that's too depressing to go into now) you throw yet another album into the world, or proffer an etching, or print a stream of words. It's difficult to acknowledge that there are no deadlines, or that no one else is stressing while waiting for you to finish your project. So you manufacture your own deadlines, you grow your own stress. The deadline part can be useful in reining-in an otherwise endless ramble through whatever medium you are using; the stress is never, ever good.

And you'd think I would have learned, if nothing else, how ridiculous it is. You'd think the message of carpe diem would have been hammered into my hazy head enough times in the last months for me to never feel stressed again. How can anything matter that much, when this has happened? But I can't seem to help myself; I want everything I do, I suppose, to be good; great, even. (Or at least as good and as great as I can make it, which is not the same thing at all.) Especially with this; it's for him, to him, in memory of him; this has to be the best it can be. To give my all to whatever I'm in at the time seems the only way to be, but when I end up worried, sleepless, shaking and anxious I have to wonder about my own logic.

goodbyes

I find I cannot say goodbye to him. It seems impossible that I would have to. It seems incredible that I can't pick up the phone to him, connect through the airwaves, talk and then say goodbye in the happy knowledge that we will say hello again within twenty-four hours. I experience another terrible, miserable day, and want to tell him about it, want to hear his take on it, want him to ground me, smooth me over, have him gently laugh at me and put it into context. His number is still in my phone – how can it not be? How can I ever erase it? That would make the truth undeniable. When I go to type in an email address beginning with his initial his email comes up as a suggestion. Yes, thanks Yahoo, I would love nothing more than to write to him and have him reply, but if he IS somewhere nearby, in the particles floating around me, I'm not sure he would use that method to contact me. In Messenger he has stopped being in my 'favourite contacts'; thanks Facebook, for reminding me that we haven't been in touch that much recently. Which is worse: that he is still there, inscribed in the virtual world of communication, or that he has been moved to the back of the queue, even erased?

I can't say goodbye. It still doesn't seem real. I don't, can't, won't feel that he has truly gone. That it hasn't all been a hideous joke. It seems ridiculous that I won't be driving to a nearby airport to pick him up, that we won't be holding each other again, spending time in our bubble, then saying goodbye, being teary, but already looking ahead to the next time. People say the funeral is the time to say goodbye; that was four months ago, and I didn't say it then. I was too busy trying not to collapse. And I haven't said it since. Will I ever?

Is everything just another goodbye in the end?
Goodbye to the womb,
to breast or bottle,
goodbye to innocence,
to naivety,
goodbye to dependence,
to the family home,
goodbye to youth,
goodbye to first friendships,
to lovers,
to childhood icons,
goodbye to dreams,
goodbye to hopes,
goodbye to those you should never have to say goodbye to.

Or is it hello?
Hello to the world,
to wonder, freshness,
hello to knowledge,
to wisdom,
hello to independence,
to exploration,
hello to adulthood,
hello to lasting friendships,
to real love,
to inspiring discoveries,
hello to different dreams,
to amended hopes,
hello to...
No, that one I can't turn around. It's still goodbye.
Whether I say it or not.

narcissus

Of course it is only the beginning of March, in a bleak windswept corner of northern England, and I am aware I was hoping for too much. The silver birch tree my family, friends and I planted in his memory, in the dale where I spent most of my childhood, near to the village where my dad, 'Papa Ping', lived for decades, in a lonesome field on a bare, barren, but incredibly beautiful hillside, is just a stick. No sign of life, no burgeoning leaves, no growth spurts; just a stick. It has been there for nearly four months now, through a relatively mild winter, protected by a plastic tube, a wooden frame, and wire to keep animals from nibbling. I hope it is alive; I imagined I spied a tiny bud, although perhaps it was wishful thinking. I want so much for it to be okay, I need it not to die. I have placed too much pressure on its tiny form, but because it represents him, how could I not?

On the, literally, brighter side, the daffodils that S and G brought to plant around it are coming up, and starting to sprout. There is life, there is beauty. I won't be around this area again for quite a while, so I will miss their full bloom, but I will know they are there, surrounding his tree, and the idea of him, in splendour and style.

After the walk across, down, and back up muddy fields to check on the tree and its yellow friends, Papa Ping and I made our way to the local pub in the village; a newly formed habit. How we love our rituals! This was the inn we all decamped to in early November on the day of the planting, to dry off, warm up, and be together. The last time I visited the birch in January, I and Ping ended up by the same fire, under the same oak beams; it felt right to repeat. Now it is a mandatory part of the pilgrimage. In June, on his birthday, I have a plan to come back here, with whoever would like to join me, and picnic by the stick. Who knows, perhaps by then it might resemble an actual tree. And no doubt we will descend afterwards to the same, obligatory drinking hole, and raise a glass to him in the place he never set foot in that has, along with many other unexpected places, strangely come to represent him and his part in our lives.

bechstein phantasm

The door is locked. I have the keys. There is no one here but me. There is no other way in.

So why do I constantly feel I am not alone? Why am I so spooked?

As I play the piano, finally recording the pieces for 'The Hunter of Small Happinesses', I feel something behind me: a creaking, a thickening of the air, a silent whisper. I turn sharply, too often, sure I will see someone. I stomp loudly across the studio floor, swearing at myself for being utterly ridiculous, down the little corridor to the front door and back, checking pointlessly for an intruder, for unwanted company. Of course there is no one, and I return to the control room to erase what I have done and try again.

I have channelled him, as some might say, in the most emotional way possible, through every note I have composed, but I can't believe that if he was really here that he would want me to feel this scared. It can't be him, causing me to stop every few bars; it can't be him making my heart race, my palms sweat, (not great when you are trying to play), my spine tingle with fear. So, then, what is it? Why, when I should be feeling safe, secure, happy to be finally let loose in Biglittlebro's studio, to record these pieces on his lovely Bechstein, do I want to run from here? Shaken and stirred, I want to rush into my brother's hug and not spend any more agitated time alone, feeling tiny and afraid.

Somehow I kick myself an adequate amount of times, slap my own face sufficiently, and shout at my pathetic demons to pipe down forcefully enough that I manage to be there, in those rooms, just me and the Bechstein, from ten in the morning to ten at night. More importantly, in those twelve hours I got done what I wanted to get done, and, aside from my mysterious unease, it felt good, and as I locked up the studio in the slanting rain and walked back to the house, the relief was such that I danced between drops and lifted my smiling face to the darkened sky.

Many people have asked me if I have sensed him, felt his presence around me. They often ask in such a way as to presume that of course I have. I hate to have to say no; as much as I would give anything to say yes, I just haven't. I just haven't. It's not for lack of trying, or wanting, and attempting to force my eyes, mind, heart, and being into seeing, but I suppose it doesn't work like that. Those who seem to feel these things are lucky, and few. The strange thing is that he was like that; he often sensed ancient souls, presences, ambiences that passed me by completely. Maybe I thought he would pass on his gift to me; maybe I hoped he would open those doors for me, and transmit some kind of understanding, higher perception, a way to make sense of all this. But no. I am left, as ever, with only the tangible. And the lack of him. And the hope that there *is* more, and the desire to find it. And inexplicable impressions of things beyond me, and a heightened awareness of that which is behind me.

unminced legacy

Last chance to practise my pieces before recording tomorrow, and as usual I am cursing my floppy, sloppy discipline. I feel as if I have been living with these notes for so long and yet they are not all under my fingers as I want them to be. I haven't been lazily lying around, no thumbs have been twiddled; I have been writing this album constantly, and playing it a lot. Maybe it is simply that I am not as good a player as I should be by now.

How many musicians say the same; how many recognise how far they still have to travel, no matter how long or hard their road has been; how many blow the minds of listeners, yet cringe inwardly as they fluff the phrase they intended to play, or are annoyed at themselves for saying the same thing twice? How many drop the ball for a second, a second in which no one but the keenest of ears would pick up its fall, and dwell for the rest of the evening on that tiny moment, rather than enjoy the memory of the notes that didn't tumble down the hill? How many are certain and sure in their technique and knowledge in the comfort of their own homes, but crumble under the gaze of others, are distracted and disturbed by the pressure of a crowd?

I don't include myself in the tribe of mind-blowing musicians, as much as I would like to be in that gang. But today I was thinking about how amazing *he* was as a musician, and believe me I am not just saying that because of who he was to me, as anyone who has heard him play guitar will affirm. He really *was* in that tribe, he really *did* blow people away with his feel, sound, technique and improvisation; musically he was incredible, and not just as a guitarist, but as a writer, producer and arranger too. And yet, how he doubted himself and how he continually strove to be better; his mantra was that the bar is set so high these days, he felt he wasn't good enough. To me, and to many others who knew him well, he was humble, modest; I saw the fragile side of him, the insecure side of him, the side that couldn't sleep at night for worrying about whether or not he could pull off his latest project, be it a video, recording or a live gig. I saw his oscillating faith in himself, his fluctuating confidence. Funny how he could come across as arrogant to those not au fait with his ways, when he really wasn't; he just sometimes appeared aloof, or over opinionated, or both. He didn't mince words, whereas I am a consummate mincer, and was squirming slightly the first time I met him; his brutal honesty in a band situation made me cringe, however right he was. And that was the thing; he told it how it was, which was hard to take, but he was almost always right. He had a clear, strong vision of how the music should or could sound, and was impatient when it didn't. He occasionally put people's backs up, but it was because he was passionate about it sounding good. Many was the time he critiqued something I had done, whether musical or artistic, (he was also a great artist); I was always excited to show him, and wanted his opinion, but his bluntness left me sulking like a small child. Weeks, months or even years later, however, I realised he had been right about whatever it was, and I had learned from him, and improved. He was a great teacher, whether or not he pandered to the sensitivities of us creative creatures, and I am indebted to him for the many things he taught me, or made me aware of. He leaves us not just a legacy of fantastic music, but the gift of insight and knowledge through unminced words.

these are for you

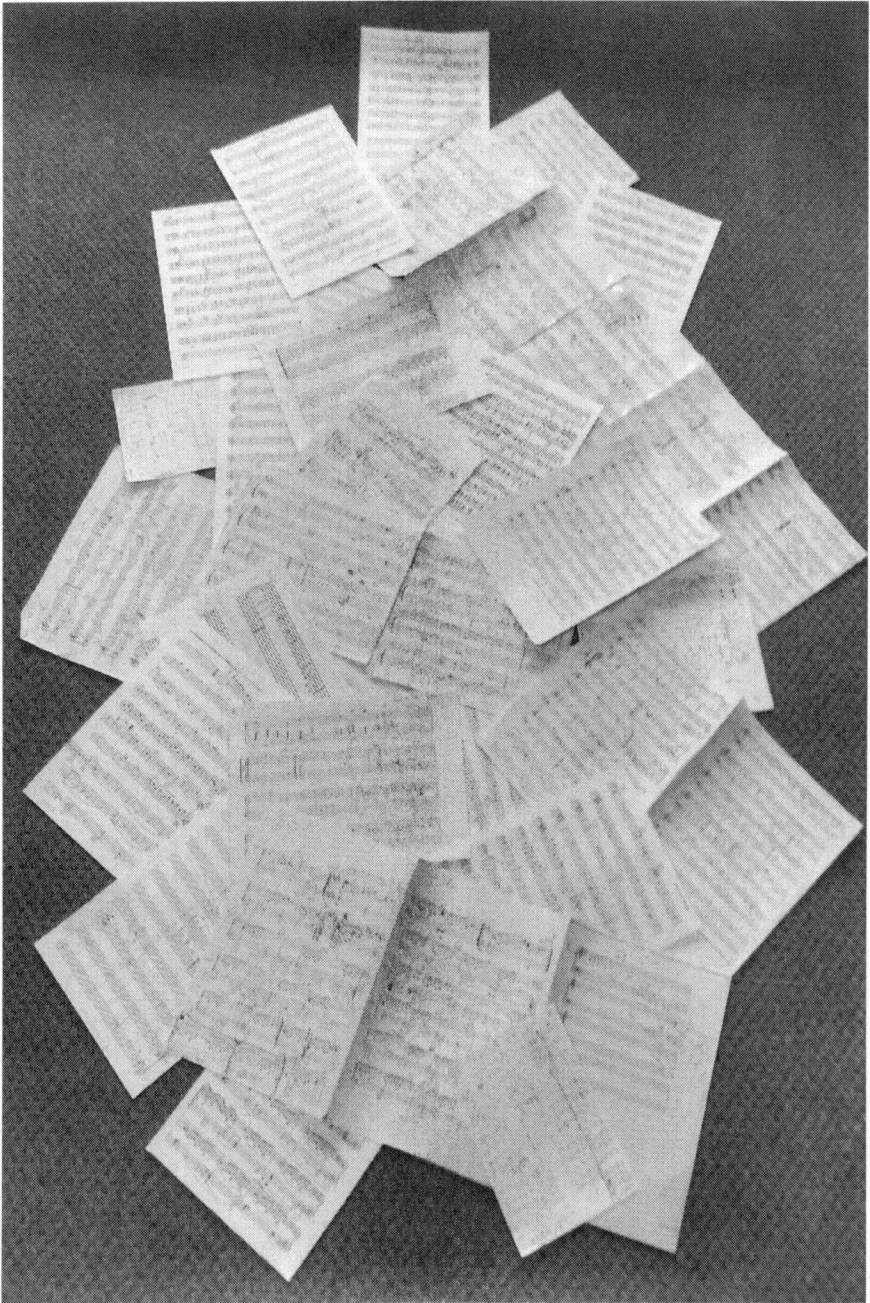

dependence day

25th February 2017

I was always bemused when some people expressed their astonishment that I could live life jumping from one place to another, in varying states of monetary disrepair, without any kind of safety net. I didn't understand when their own fears about doing the same made them tell me I was brave. I leapt. I never thought I'd fall; I never doubted that it would be alright. It wasn't a big deal. I had faith that wherever I went, I would make it work somehow. Not that I changed countries incessantly, or continent-hopped exactly, but I suppose I have lived or had a long stay in about thirty or so places since I left college, in a few different countries. There was a lot of moving around in London, and then a couple of apartments in both New York and Florence, but they were just temporary, to study, or to hustle. I dipped into France for a few months, but on the back of a complicated moment and a brotherly offer. I have called at least eight places home in Spain. Sometimes it involved a mere shifting of a kilometre or two, a packing of bags and boxes and a drive, with a plant-filled windscreen, across a city. Sometimes it was crossing borders, hiring vans, completing paperwork, arriving in unknown territory to who knew what. Either way, it was never something I questioned; it was just the next move, the next step of the journey. I had chosen it, and it would be okay, and anyway it was nothing, certainly nothing courageous as far as I was concerned.

There have been times in my life when I have landed in a place where I knew no one, or virtually no one, had no friends, no contacts in terms of work, and simply decided that it would work out. I have travelled alone, with only a few books, a diary and a camera for companions. I have sat in bars, cafes, restaurants, people watching and wondering. I have perched on hills overlooking bays with only thoughts at my side, wandered through museums, galleries and bookstores proffering books in another tongue without anyone speaking to me, walked over mountains, down trails, and through parks talking to myself. I was lacking a connection, a mutual experience, a companion in those moments, but I embraced those times anyway.

Now, in these times of being surrounded by the best of people, but also by utter, desolate loneliness, I cannot imagine how she was, that girl, who took planes, trains and automobiles to whatever destination drew her; who pored over maps and Googled dreams; who decided to change tack or follow an impulse. Now, in these times of dark dread, of paranoid paralysis, of apoplectic angst, I don't relate to her at all.

I have lost my nerve; I am needy, pathetic, clingy, and can't contemplate striking out on my own, as I did so easily before. Will I get it back, that nerve I used to call my own? I am planning on moving back to Spain in about a month, and at this moment it seems an impossibility. I only want to stay in familiar armpits, nestle in cosy and protected environments, not have to make any decisions. I was so independent, but now my dependency on others knows no bounds.

I suppose that I did it all, always, on my own, without him. I followed my own dreams, drew my own lines in the sand, wished upon my own stars. Our thing was such that we lived around that; he worried often, or so he said, about me, and my restlessness, and how on earth I was going to survive in whatever situation I had hurled myself into without any money. He couldn't, not even for a moment, imagine doing the same; he would never contemplate the upheaval into uncertainty, the plunge into uncharted territory, the risk that change brings. But wherever I ended up, he would be there, amused that I had done it, amazed if I made it work, and then becoming a part of the new life I had found, or the new memory I had made.

Which makes me, despite all of the hideousness, ever so slightly hopeful. I was able to function and travel and make decisions all my life; why should it be any different now? I was never reliant on him, financially, geographically, domestically. I was never, actually, dependent upon him.

Well... I was. I was dependent emotionally, romantically, in a million ways. Yes, I can go and live anywhere I want to. I can start a new life, and indeed I have to, I don't have much choice in that; I can't depend on others to take me into their lives and homes forever. I can plough on through my days, doing what I do, hoping to find some kind of meaning, and happiness, in the creating of whatever I create. But he was such a constant, for a hundred years, in my life. I depended on him to be there, to be there for me, to be there as part of us. And now he's not there, and I don't know how to depend upon myself to get myself through.

default setting

24th February 2017

This is my default setting,
my default setting,
no blood-letting, no therapy getting,
just letting the fact of your sun setting settle.
It gets lower and lower as each day goes by,
old I feels like storming mountains and shooting sky,
but instead new me hardly moves,
hardly looks at the world.
I'm sure it unfurls itself every morning
and hurls its curveballs and miracles at all of your lives,
but I stay inside,
I hide,
I slide down further and further into numb.

This is my default setting,
my default setting,
no point betting on bettering my mood,
unfettering my gloom,
my room keeps letting in the dark.
It gets harder and harder to keep on leaving the space
I can face for that outside place
and the race
and the chase to embrace normality,
when reality kicks you in the face
and screams its profanity,
swearing the truth, the whole truth,
and nothing but the hole where you were
is the proof that forever I am changed,
rearranged,
and the pain stains every day.

the stories that shouldn't have to be told

23rd February 2017

The story of him, and us, is in these seven piano pieces. Words have not come so easily. Sentences, paragraphs, phrases, have spooled out of me in the form of key changes, counterpoint, leitmotifs. Our tale is told, but for the worst of reasons, and in a wordless fashion.

I'm sad he will never hear all these notes. I would have liked to tell our tale at some point, in a happy way. I would also have liked to write an album for him one day – but not this one. Not one in his *memory*! No, one that we could have listened to together, one that almost certainly wouldn't have been a classical piano and strings affair. One that we could have shared, talked about, one he might have loved, and at least been happy that someone would do that for him; proud of me, even.

This story shouldn't have to be told. Right now he should be finishing off his second, undoubtedly incredible, solo album. He should have settled into his new job, or the way it was going, jobs, as guitar tutor in a couple of great music colleges. His musical star should have continued to rise, as his own music overtook his teaching and playing of other people's. He should have been spending time with his sons, being a dad. He should have bought a new car, or a guitar or three, as was his wont. He should have travelled, with me, or with bands. His stress of the last year should have dissipated; we should have had amazing times together, wherever we were. But here I am, just left remembering, and the word 'should' is impotent.

I read another story yesterday. Another story that shouldn't have had to be told. A book that had been waiting for me, should I ever feel I wanted to read it, since it happened; a book in Biglittlebro's care, given to him by a close friend, SP, who had read it and thought it might, one day, help me. I read it faster than any other book I have read in recent memory; I couldn't stop. Biglittlebro was anxious, scared it would tip me over into an even worse place, but it didn't. I had demanded it late at night, after a few wines, knowing that that was the moment I had to find out what was inside. The book is 'All at Sea' by a Guardian journalist, Decca Aitkenhead, who tells the story of how her partner drowned. It is her story, and yet it is mine too. Although of course not completely the same, there are so many similarities it was uncanny; I related to not just the events, but how she described the aftermath, the emotions, the whirlwind, the shock, and the many, many aspects she had to try to deal with. Was it because of our shared stories that I was mesmerised, drawn into her world unstoppably? It is a compelling story, and so well-written, but perhaps also I felt a connection to someone else, who would understand utterly and completely how I was feeling. I feel so strongly that I want to meet her, such is the bond I feel with her, this stranger, after reading her searingly sad, brutally honest chronicle.

Our story shouldn't have to be told. But it is.

la distancia

22nd February 2017

A yoyo of togetherness: a bungee jump of a union.
String stretched taut between countries;
string snapping back into place upon reconnection.
Endless elastic.
Extra rope required as one or other of us travelled to further flung places;
we kept it afterwards to wrap around ourselves,
to hold us tighter together.

My maths isn't what it was, and it was always pretty bad, but I reckon there must have been a quarter of a million kilometres travelled to be together over the years, mainly by him; it's a good job he wasn't hodophobic.

We modulated between being over two thousand kilometres apart, (by road; less if the proverbial black bird had flown it), or joined, fused together with no space separating us.

Even for our many years in London we were always about twenty miles away from each other; his roots stayed firmly embedded in outer suburban soil, whereas I had severed mine long before, and dipped in and out of about twelve different inner boroughs. But each time we met, the distance was forgotten, and the time together was all.

As technology revolutionised our world, (strange to remember that mobile phones had only just become popular when we first met), la distancia shrunk. Texts or expensive international calls became cheap conversations and then completely free video chats. We spoke almost every day, sometimes many times, and were intertwined in virtual space when not sharing a geographical location.

How far is he from me now?

Some might say, and I'd like to be among them, that it is no distance at all; he is within me, a part of me.

Some might say that when he ran into the sea he ran beyond the realms of this reality, and the distance is incalculable.

Some might say he is nowhere.

Others, everywhere.

I only know that I still sometimes feel his imprint upon me, as if he has just pressed me to him, and kissed me deeply, but then I remember, and something tears him away, wrenches him from my grasp, pulls out my insides with brutal fangs and throws them to the wind, where they twist and turn in malevolent air, and fly further than I can see.

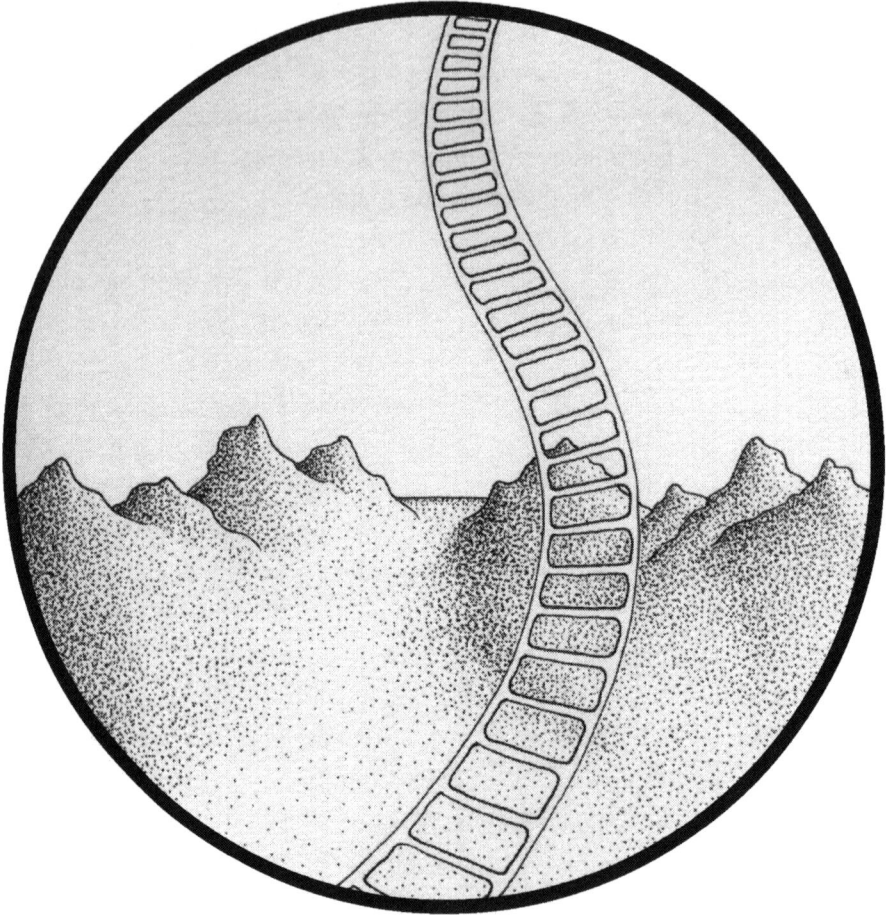

eskimo kissing

21st February 2017

At the kitchen table watching the rain and feeling drenched inside. How it rains here; I had forgotten how many months could be sodden and downtrodden, the earth mulching and the pavements streaming. Trees bend in reverence to their persistent life blood, stone shines silver. A stark contrast to the arid, orange dust of the part of southern Spain I lived in before; the rare showers there burst dramatically to make up for their sparseness and the cacti gulp them up.

Stanley the cat seems more interested in bedding down upon the viola parts I am writing. I turn away for a second, and he has made a nest between pen and ruler, exactly on the part of the page I am trying to finish. His being there warms my soul and indeed my cockles, and I find something, anything to do at the table so as to leave him there, sleepily serene on top of the alto clef. We nuzzle from time to time, rubbing noses and sliding fur against hair, and the contact with this handsome being is one of the best moments I have had in a long time.

I am learning to spend hours alone again, and yet my eye is always on the clock, counting the minutes along with it until someone will come home. I don't want to be this child, but it is proving difficult to grow up. So Stanley is the perfect companion on these rainy afternoons, impervious to the hour, only interested in pleasure and repose, and pleasure in repose. He calms me, as does his brother, Angel, whose incredibly slumbersome nature and amazingly fluffy presence makes me want to take to my bed as often as he, as long as he is there alongside me.

Many animals have calmed me in these last months. I have always loved cats, but even dogs I have spent time with in the houses of friends have utterly melted any wariness, and brushed away the slight discomfort I might have had in their presence before. It's a new feeling, and I love it. Gum love! I never thought I'd get it. (I call dogs 'gums', after their (sometimes) weird, black, hanging, drippy, well, gums, which used to slightly bother me. I take it all back.) The only gum I had grown to adore before this time was one of the dogs belonging to my wonderful landlady and lord in Las Negras. And he's a story for another day.

Cats don't always possess that famous unconditional love that dogs give out, but they tap in, I am convinced, to emotions. Stanley can be aloof with some people, but as soon as I arrived here off the flight from Almería, broken, barely functioning, he approached me and we bonded as never before. The gentle head butting and smoothing each other quickly became what we always did when we passed each other on the stairs. Angel sometimes even got on my lap on the sofa, something he's never done with me previously; he slept on my bed for many nights, and they both slept there by day. They seemed to sense my need. At S's place in London, the night before the funeral, one of her cats, Harry, shared a moment with me that will stay with me forever; I was lying on my bed there, distraught, empty, in a ball, and he came and lay in my curl, putting a paw on my arm and staying there as I sobbed.

Although it is undoubtedly the worst time for me to take responsibility for any living creature, and anyway impossible right now, all I want is a cat. I really do. A ball of fluff, a purring noserubber, a cute spirit by my side. It would not make everything else magically disappear, but I'm certain it would make things so much better.

lost footage, crumbling foothold

20th February 2017

Thinking back to just over a year ago, January 2016. I was staying for a month in a cute studio flat in the old town of Alicante, that my niece Mrs Cole was renting for her year abroad, the third year of her language degree. She wasn't in it at that time; I was floating, so she offered it to me.

F came to stay for a few days, and we wandered, explored, ate and drank in various hostelries, acted like complete tourists. One day we decided to go up to the castle on the hill overlooking the city. To get up there, unless you take a *very* scenic route that I hadn't quite figured out, you walk through a tunnel into the centre of the mountain, and take a lift up to the top. My claustrophia exploded in a fountain of panic, and a few metres into it I was on the verge of running out. He calmed me down in his usual way: logical, dismissing my fears, laughing not quite condescendingly but enough to make me snap out of it. We made it up to the castle, although I can't say I really enjoyed being inside a mechanised contraption encased by rock. On the top of the battlements, I filmed him making a mini travelogue, describing the spectacular views all around us. It was him at his best: witty, extravagantly silly, cute, confident, and it made me laugh beyond belief.

I played the video to Mrs Cole the next week, when she arrived back in Spain. We both agreed it was a gem, and I promised to send it to her. A week later, both my camera and my laptop that I had backed it up onto got stolen, and the footage was gone. I was, and am, gutted; I would give a lot to see that again.

So strange though, that I can watch him any time I want. He is on so many YouTube videos; sometimes playing gigs, but more often he is talking about guitars, guitar gear, guitar techniques, or breaking down another guitarist's song and improvisation in order to teach it. Not my usual preferred viewing, not being a guitarist, but because it was him of course I watched them all as they came out. And he is still there, talking, playing, interviewing others, being interviewed. Being him. Like photos, but more so, the capturing of someone for all time is a curious thing. And I can hardly ever bring myself to watch him. I braved one today, and had a meltdown as soon as it started, as he joked about looking a hundred and three years old. His strange mixture of assuredness and slight awkwardness; his passion for what he did; a quick flash of his huge smile that when it came, blazed through the air between him and the recipient. He looked so beautiful I fell in love with him all over again, and I couldn't, can't, fold my pulverised mind around the fact that he is gone. My foothold on reality has crumbled, and I don't know what to stand upon that will not also disintegrate into the void.

falling years

19th February 2017

The years keep falling away... time loops backwards... and forwards again...
flashes of instances, chinks between history's rocks...
A decade is peeled back... shedding old skin... revealing younger days...
A few even earlier years bounce before me, confusing in their carefreeness...
the remarkable things, the mundane...
the calm moments, the tempestuous times...
the misunderstandings, the bumpy landings...
the undefined, the crystal clarities, the in between...
the pivotal points, the decisive dates, the changes, the constants...
the heartbreaks, the mendings... the returns, the sendings...
the beliefs, the doubts... the frustrations, the adoration...
Everything, all things, the whole caboodle, the whole shebang...
A smell sends me somewhere... a word somewhere else...
Memory flutters over frontiers
and falls upon familiar and unfamiliar lands...

I bounce upwards to the top of a twin tower four months before its demise...
I ceaselessly play 'which would you rather' in a transit van
up and down the M1...
I crawl into damp, stalactite-riddled French caves...
I sway to a singer-songwriter whose top half is hidden
in the tiniest London venue...
I lie on my bed holding hands and watch a bad film with good wine...
I watch the swifts dart and stream above my head,
gazing at Sierra de Lújar, watching out for the first star...
I sneak glances across the stage, smiling secretly, looking too much...
I devour so much spicy jalfrezi I should never eat again,
and laugh a lot across the table...

I punch the air upon reaching a shelf of a mountain in the Pyrenees,
and imagine jumping down onto clouds...
I groan as I miss the clear shot into the far pocket...
I drive through typical English country lanes,
sip a glass in a typical English country pub...
I relax with friends and play the YouTube game, choosing music in turn...
I wait outside the airport in the freezing rain, searching for a car...
I stare at Michelangelo's ceiling, explore Roman remains,
tramp up Gaudi's stairs...
I hit a ball over the net and expect to see it again all too soon...
I perch on a stool in a Dubai pool and order mojitos...
I hang out with family as we film ourselves crazily dancing in pairs...
I eat Brick Lane salmon and cream cheese bagels in the small hours...
I feel my stomach skip sideways as I spy a long black leather coat...
I leap to get a piggyback, nuzzle into neck, and feel like I'm home...

Snippets, fragments, mind films, photo stills, seemingly endless bits of life.
I say I, but it was we, of course.
All these things and more are what we shared.
They haven't gone forever,
though they were the past as soon as they were over.
But they seem so very much further away now.

the huge thing

Bagpuss, Guinness, Tess, Humphrey Horace, Henry and Matilda, Bramble and Pippin, Fanny and Not Fanny, Lucky, Professor Blamoose. Cats, a dog, gerbils, pigs, a hamster, goats, rats. I, we, mourned the passing of these pets, or their disappearance when their fate was unclear.

The first person in my close family, and my first grandparent to go, apart from Papa Ping's dad who died when Ping was only six, was Lala, his lovely mum, when I was in my early twenties, and that hit hard. I was a mess at the funeral, and even more so at the grave, as they lowered the coffin. Indescribable tears, unutterable feelings.

A girl a couple of years younger than me who travelled on the same school bus suddenly stopped getting on. I heard the story, but couldn't comprehend someone getting cancer at twelve years old.

Hosepipes pumping fumes into cars in garages, accidental farmyard accidents, bike and car crashes; these tales all swirled around school air, but it was never anyone I knew, so no sense of it was made.

My mum's parents, my adored Granny and Grandad, left us when I was in my late twenties and early thirties respectively, and it was so sad. Again, I didn't get it, and the only, clichéd, comfort was that they had both reached eighty and beyond, but it still seemed so wrong.

I attended a packed church service for Papa Ping's second wife who tragically died far too young, and a humanist funeral for the good friend of my Auntie Whoosh; distant relations passed away, and older friends of older friends.

I watched them fall, those stars of stage and screen that I had never met but, in some cases at least, felt I knew, as they were woven so tightly into the fabric of my generation; still I didn't understand the concept of them now not existing.

I dreaded, with a passion, the first death of someone I was *really* close to.
I imagined her, or him, or them, and how it would be.
I cried in anticipation.

I mourned with all my body before it even happened.

I feared it, I pre-empted it.

I talked tearily about it, often to him.

Who would it be?

I was sure it would destroy me.

Convinced I wouldn't cope; how could I?

Inconceivable.

And in the end it was him.

The last person I expected. The death I had awaited, trembled over, wept for, felt cold inside and dissolved into unstoppable tears because of.

It was him.

In terms of blows, knocks, hammerings, this kicks everything else into orbit.

Any past grievance, petty or otherwise, is nothing but a bedraggled sweet wrapper fighting a strident north-easterly wind, a fleck of bereft cement tumbling from an old beamed ceiling, an old turd being booted further down the street by an unsuspecting passer-by.

Any hurt, or heartache, or painful event, does more than pale, it vanishes into insignificance.

Even the loss of those I lost before can't, won't, even try to compete.

When you have nothing to compare it to, little things are huge.

When there is a huge thing, there is no room for anything else of any size.

Maybe the huge thing decreases in stature, in force, in power, with time.

Maybe little things start to worm their sneaky way back in, or start gnawing away, small chunk by small chunk, at the huge thing; bored of its ubiquitous presence, of energy bowing to it constantly, they slowly diminish its strength.

I can only hope that those tiny burrowers chip away enough to minimise this pain.

Yet I pray that my perspective on everything stays true, in that I remember what is important, and what is not, and live by it.

Right now, however, although I hope for a change, my reality stays large.

The huge thing is huger than anything I could have dreamed of, even given my over-fertile imagination and propensity for exaggeration.

It bestrides my narrow world like a Colossus; it lowers its behemoth-like weight onto my fragile shoulders and refuses to leave or let anything escape. It forces me to mount its flanks and speeds off into the abyss; as I try to jump off, to roll onto soft, fresh, pliant grass and hide under dandelions, with dragonflies circling innocently and ladybirds tickling my arm, I cannot; my body is magnetised to its rabid, hurtling form, trapped for now on a journey through hell.

And back?
I hope so.

green cross code

I crossed the road today using old instincts, honed over years. I caught myself doing it, and as I reached the other side a feeling of relief swept over me. Not for having traversed safely, although that too, but for not thinking about it while doing it.

We take it for granted, knowing how to cross a road. The innate intuition for sensing the movement of approaching vehicles, the negotiating of cyclists and other pedestrians, the intelligent guesswork, the reading of indicators and the listening to the crescendo of engines; it is all something that does have to be learned as a child. I think back through the last months, as bit by bit this engrained knack resurfaced; four months ago I couldn't step off the pavement for very, very long minutes, and only then if there was no traffic within a mile. My European habit of looking the other way didn't help matters, and my regression into a confused toddler scared me. Angry roars of motors, throttles given fully, the screech of tyres or the blast of horns all conspired to keep my legs immovable as I stood, unable to act, shaken and paralysed. Three months ago I was a little quicker in pushing off from the sidewalk, two even more so, but I would still often hover on the traffic island, lingering nervously, unsure and afraid for my life. So ridiculous, but this thing did that to me; the confidence you amass, the unthinking certainty, the blasé assurance, is obliterated.

The resurfacing of accumulated judgement through experience is nothing but a good thing, in any sense.

But I'm wondering if I will have to relearn everything.

Cross the road. Go through the door.
Walk to the other side of the field. Hike up the mountains.
Scale the ladder. Climb the tree. Ascend the steps.
Go through the other doors.
Whatever is there, be there.
Do a cartwheel. Dance. Sing. Dare to dream.

Repeat.

second-hand food

16th February 2017

Actually chuckling today, a lot, at some of his ways. His quirks. Especially food ones. I should do this more, laugh...

We were always, constantly amused by each other; our sayings, our *very* repetitive sayings, our own language, and the way we pronounced so many words, never got old. The day before it happened he had laughed so hard, after we had said something that would have been incoherent nonsense to almost anyone else. "Are we going to be talking like this when we're ninety?" he asked. "Of course we are!" I replied, laughing too, unaware of what would occur the next day, unaware that he would never reach that age, unaware that all too soon we would never talk again.

Well, I'll keep chanting our sayings, and keeping our language alive, as will lots of my family members and a few friends, even if sometimes it pains me. And if I happen by some miracle to reach ninety, I'll do so even more.

I am remembering...

His refusal to eat anything that wasn't still piping hot, or finishing someone else's leftovers even if he was still hungry – 'second-hand food'.

Being pescatarian, he ate fish, but nothing with 'tentacles', and he would always, *always* mime tentacles.

His asking for extra spice on every single pizza he ordered in my presence, and never getting it; chili oil was always brought out as a poor alternative. Cue a rant about "I do my job, why can't they do theirs?"

The refrain "hot tea, hot tea, hot tea is good for me" at least seven times a day.

His insistence upon any chocolate item being put in the freezer, so it tasted 'better'.

His need to always have HP sauce, Branston pickle and Marmite to hand any given time; could he have been more English?

His washing up of everything except the cutlery; never the cutlery.

Calling vegetables he didn't like 'moss'.

His over-careful cutting out of the insides of tomatoes.

His exuberantly concocted special mash, his fine onion soup.

His almost passing out after most meals, sometimes even getting up from the table and lying on the floor, having eaten so fast and so much.

Saying "boo'ah" for butter with a proud glottal stop, in a non-specific northern accent that was supposed to be Mancunian.

His inability to converse whatsoever while eating, in case the meal got cold.

His new-found love of 'posh ladies' – crisps in a bowl, not out of the packet.
The packet always being opened from the bottom, where all the flavour resided, rather than the top.
(Note, for those not in the know – crisps are 'itchy ladies', for reasons fairly difficult to remember.)

His horror of the existence of tea towels – 'germs'.

His swearing that he had only put in a couple of chilis, as we cried hot tears.

Only buying a bottle of red wine if the word 'oak' was on the label.

Having breakfast in various proper London 'caffs', ordering two slices of toast, one with beans on top, and one with egg on top, and never, ever getting what he had asked for. Cue a rant, etc.

His declaration at the end of the meal – "that was the *best* thing I've ever eaten!"

and always

15th February 2017

Somewhere on a far-off island you smile.

From across the land to where it spoons the sky
you will watch the world turning.

Before sunrise,
after you have visited me and others in dream,
you will hover,
waiting for the dawn you usually missed in your fifty-three years,
and revel in its beauty.

After midnight,
before you drift away from the notes
still scenting the air
in haunts you once frequented,
you will remember.

And always, always, I will remember.

don't mention the war

14th February 2017

I'm not for a second saying that I would be, or have been, any different. In fact I know for sure I have reacted in this very same way. There is something in all of us that responds in this fashion, in Western society at least. Not for a miniscule moment am I criticising, because I understand the sentiments behind it, and the engrained, unconfrontational manner in which we deal with it. It's just an observation. Not until you are in it, truly in it, do you see it, do you find it so strange, and feel so keenly that these patterns are maybe not the right way to go about it.

I'm talking about not mentioning death, not talking about the person who has gone, not being able to bring up the subject. The skirting around that avoids having to get to the heart of it. Especially for English people, perhaps, although I couldn't say for sure, the fear that they will upset you is greater than the need to ask, and genuinely want to know, warts and all, how you are. Of course, of course, of course they care. Of course they love you (or at least like you, depending on who it is), and all they want is for you not to have to go through this. All they want is to take it away. All they want is for you to be better. And I love that, and hold it close (and want it too...). But the magic wand does not exist, and I personally feel that by opening up more, by chatting about the one we miss, and his or her life, and his or her ways, and what we shared, and by remembering and telling stories, but by also not being afraid to get inside the real feelings and emotions that are flying around, the healing will happen faster.

You have to cry, you have to grieve, you have to go through it. I believe that if you don't, and you file it away and lock away the tears, you are only saving them up for another time, when you are not ready for them, and they have multiplied, or grown into a hard, bitter, dark feeling inside you, and might stand a chance of destroying you.

Many days, sometimes weeks, have gone by without his name touching the air around me. I am forced to shoehorn him into the conversation, often awkwardly, with no discernible link, out of desperation for all of this to be acknowledged. It feels false, self-conscious. If he was alive, he would be talked about as a matter of course. But now everyone is tiptoeing softly around him, and around me, and is frightened to rock my already fragile boat. As I said, I would be the same, I'm sure.

Perhaps by not discussing it, people think they are distracting your mind, and relieving you for a moment of the otherwise constant pain. And they are, they are.

Perhaps they are so scared of tears, of emotions that they can't control or help, that they prefer not to risk a deluge.

Perhaps the 'press on' habit of getting on with things, of there being a shelf life to grief, is too unquestioned by too many.

Perhaps some people feel they have talked about it enough, and that is also probably true, but in my case maybe they have talked a lot with others, but not so much to me.

I reiterate: I understand, I get it. But it's just such a puzzling place to be in right now.

There reaches a point when you burst inside, are incredulous that all aspects of life are on the table, save this one. You cannot believe that the world is unchanged; for you it *is* changed, irrevocably so, but that is just you. For others it is a temporary change on the whole; if the fabric of their existence is still in place, then they are capable of putting things in boxes and moving on. Of course they will open the boxes from time to time, and feel, and grieve, and acknowledge. But those lids probably stay down when ordered to; my box, and my lid, have not yet been constructed, and when they finally are, I doubt they will obey so easily.

piece number seven, or melody number 75,000,000,000

13th February 2017

Blocked.

I've written one part of piece number seven, cascading piano using the first chords from piece number one, and a reinvention of a theme from number five combined with another from another. But that's it. As the rare sun streams through the window onto Papa Ping's piano, I feel content at least to be next to this beautiful beast I have played for *cough* years. But I'm still blocked, and keep cascading down the notes while my fingers, mind, and whatever other parts of you aid in creativity, search wildly for inspiration.

The idea for this final piece on the album is to reprise all the other themes. Number six has yet to be birthed, so this could prove tricky. The others all have two or three leitmotifs within them that could be reharmonised, and given a different key, tempo or time signature. In theory, then, most of the work has already been done; so why is this proving so hard? I think the problem is that there are too many possibilities; I want to choose the best way of revisiting each melody and I have no idea what the best way is. All very subjective, obviously. Those brand new, to me anyway, ideas, that landed upon or in me in a flash of inspiration, become something to work *with* rather than receive or create, and it should just be a matter of arranging the pieces into new patterns. I love patterns. I love the endless jigsaw of music, or art. But I also feel pressure to treat each jigsaw piece well, and not force it into the wrong pattern just for the sake of it. I feel hopeful that it will become clear, or at least less cloudy, but for now I'll just twiddle around on the keys and admire the sun-kissed colour of the Bechstein's wood.

One theme in particular, from piece number two, I'm pretty fond of, and want to give a few outings to; I can hear it modulating, endlessly, using different instrumentation or a changed style each time. It is a ten bar phrase, and the last bar leads by default to a different key from the one it begins in, bringing in the new tonality effortlessly. I feel as though I have stolen it, though; it came to me without too much toil, indeed it just appeared, and it felt so familiar and right that it made me suspect that I had plucked it from a memory of someone else's work.

Again, pondering where ideas come from. Being momentarily blocked gives you time to pontificate, and wonder how the thing you are failing to do gets done. Of course there are many methods, if you vaguely know what you are doing musically, to unblock and at least set in motion a possibility of a new idea: choose a few notes at random and give each one at least five chord friends, then pick one of the five for each and see what you have: take something else you have written and play it backwards, in a different rhythm: play in your least favourite key to get yourself out of your comfort zone and spark something new: leave your instrument or studio and go and listen to another piece of music, come back and try to copy something about it, and you will find you bring your own spin to it that can then be worked into something more your own. All these tools and many more can free the blocked composing mind; I suppose it is just a romantic hang-up, wanting the bolt from the blue and the whirlwind of inspiration each time, when in actual fact sometimes you just need to graft.

Back to the idea of repetition, of fake originality, of pilfering others' work by accident. It doesn't take much to convince yourself that whatever you come up with will already have been done, because surely there are only so many notes, and combinations of notes. Or so you imagine, until you actually do the maths. Apparently, and this was not calculated by me, if you write a two-note melody, keeping the notes to within 1 octave, there are 25 possibilities. For a three-note tune, 469. Four notes, 7,825. Five, 122,461. Ten notes – wait for it – around 75 *billion*.

No wonder we sometimes freeze, panicked at how many choices we have! Seventy-five billion, and that is only if your melody stays within one octave, and has only ten notes; neither does it take into account all the possibilities of rhythm, harmony and musical structure or style. If one wanted to look at that with the glass half empty, it could negate the thrill of having created something original, because now, armed with that statistical knowledge, it seems impossible that you *could* ever repeat something that has been done before.

But instead of seeing it as half empty, instead of feeling that being original is too simple because of the infinite number of mathematical probabilities available to us, let's call the glass half full, and understand that the combination of notes was a choice, and it was *your* choice. An informed choice. With luck, an inspired choice. Something that only you could have made. That all the things that go to make up you, your essence, your experiences, your feelings, have created this thing, this something. That you unblocked your fear of being unoriginal, not because of maths but because simply, it came out of you, and it was new to you. And hopefully you like it, this one idea out of the seventy-five billion, and are happy with it, and that should be enough. And if you're very lucky and someone else does too, you've done something right.

control

I control the dust.

Any speck of filth, fleck of grime, crack in perfection, is wiped, obliterated, erased and hidden away from memory. In one of the dustiest parts of the world, containing unimaginably omnipresent tiny critters, and winds bringing Saharan sand that covers everything in its path, I must be queen, and rule my queendom. Clothes are fastidiously folded, bins are regularly emptied. Every item has its home. Insects and spiders are taken outside and placed carefully in a sheltered area away from the apartment. I regulate what goes in and out of my body.

I need order. I need a routine. I need to not use anything unnecessarily. I will become a character from a Murakami novel. Toru from The Wind-up Bird Chronicle. Aomame from 1Q84. I must create the quiet, methodical feeling that comes out through his pages, even though his worlds twist in unexpected ways; a solitary routine, everything in its place at a certain pace and at a certain time. Neatness, organisation. Precise cooking of healthy food. Endless cleaning. A fitness regime. Jazz. Perhaps a cat. Calm. A white, airy space.

I must control the dust.

I wrote this almost a year ago; an exaggerated account of my need to control my environment, and therefore my life, but wrote no more than this; I didn't know where the story was going. I had just moved to Las Negras, a stunning, strange part of the world. Instead of the large rented house I had lived in before, I felt I needed to downsize to a studio flat, with all my possessions in one room, and found the perfect place without even trying. How lucky, I thought. I was thrilled to be there, living near the sea for the first time. I was starting over again in a new world, but with a lifeline of great friends only a couple of hours away, the time it took to drive to my old home in Órgiva, and of course the regular visits from F. I was struck by the beauty around me, I felt calm, and I was writing a lot. I had no work, but was sure it would turn out fine. I spent happy hours wandering around on my own, exploring, and wondering what new connections might be made, or what new inspirations might grab hold of me.

I had spent five months living out of a suitcase, between different places in Spain and England, and nearly a month out of the five living in my car. I had given up that rented house that I had lived in for five years, and the last night there, on the 30th September 2015, was tinged with both excitement and sadness, as I wondered where I might end up, and what life might bring.

I needed control, and felt it more strongly than ever before in my life, possibly because of the previous nomadic five months. And yet since that time I lost control of everything. I lost it exactly one year after I had left my place in Órgiva, on the 30th September 2016.

My long-term love has gone. My life as I knew it has changed, irrevocably, forever. I know, more than anything else I know, that I have *no* control. No control over what happens from now on, to me, to anyone. How arrogant to think for a second that I did. How easy, and stupid, it is to assume that *you* are the one calling the shots in your own life.

So where do you go from here, this place that is undeniably uncontrollable? Surrender to being tossed around in the breeze, on a good day, the storm on a bad? Give up entirely on plans, on anchorage, on future dreams? Let go of holding onto assumptions, to those close to you, to 'next time'; accept that this minute could be the last one you live?

No, and yes.

Yes, let yourself be directed by life's breeze, because really you have no choice. No, in that if you have a decision to make, make it, and make it a good one.

No, because to give up on dreams and plans and 'next times' would be sad, and restrictive; just don't *presume* they will happen in the way you think, if at all. As long as you are aware of that, you should be free to scheme and dream, if it is part of what makes you you. Yes, therefore, to letting go of assumptions.

No, never ever let go of those close to you, even if the scared part of you wants to shield yourself from the potential of more loss, more death and might be tempted to close the door and not feel too much for anyone, in case. No, no, no. They are what save you, they are what it is all about.

Yes, accept that this moment could be your last. Perspective is queen, not you.

san valentino

In a few days it will be Valentine's Day. Not something I ever really paid attention to. Enforced showing of love isn't really my thing; I prefer to declare it out of Hallmark's reach. He was in agreement, so we ignored it. Although, just after midnight, when it was officially the 14th, he would call or send a message, asking me to be his 'veeleenteen'. It was said ironically, yet at the same time underlyingly not; neither of us wanted to be cheesy and buy into the 'normal' world and its commercially romantic ways, but we told the other we loved them every day. As so many people do, I'm not saying that was unusual. But we didn't travel the same conventional path that some do, in so many ways, and we railed against what was seen as the done thing. Our sweetness, our own version of cheese, was unaffected by the world around us.

This year, though, this day is paining me. Every shop window, supermarket aisle or TV advert is sticking the knife in further. Big blow-up hearts explode in my face, gangs of gigantic teddy bears leer and laugh at my retreating, running form, roses stick their thorns into my naked desolation, swathes of cheap chocolate melt around me and turn to mud that sucks me into blackness. Couples holding hands make me cry inside or out, and secretly watching people kissing, out of the corner of my eye, feels like spectating on a sport I've never played. That part of me has been erased, for now, and any pieces left untouched by the eraser have been shut down, by me. My mind can't go there, my brain short circuits if I think too much about it. My body is just an alien, a clump of flesh, a stranger's body, a thing that functions but doesn't feel. I carry it around, sometimes looking at it as if from afar, and half-remembering how someone used to love it, until the gates clank determinedly, angrily shut, and I turn back into an inanimate object.

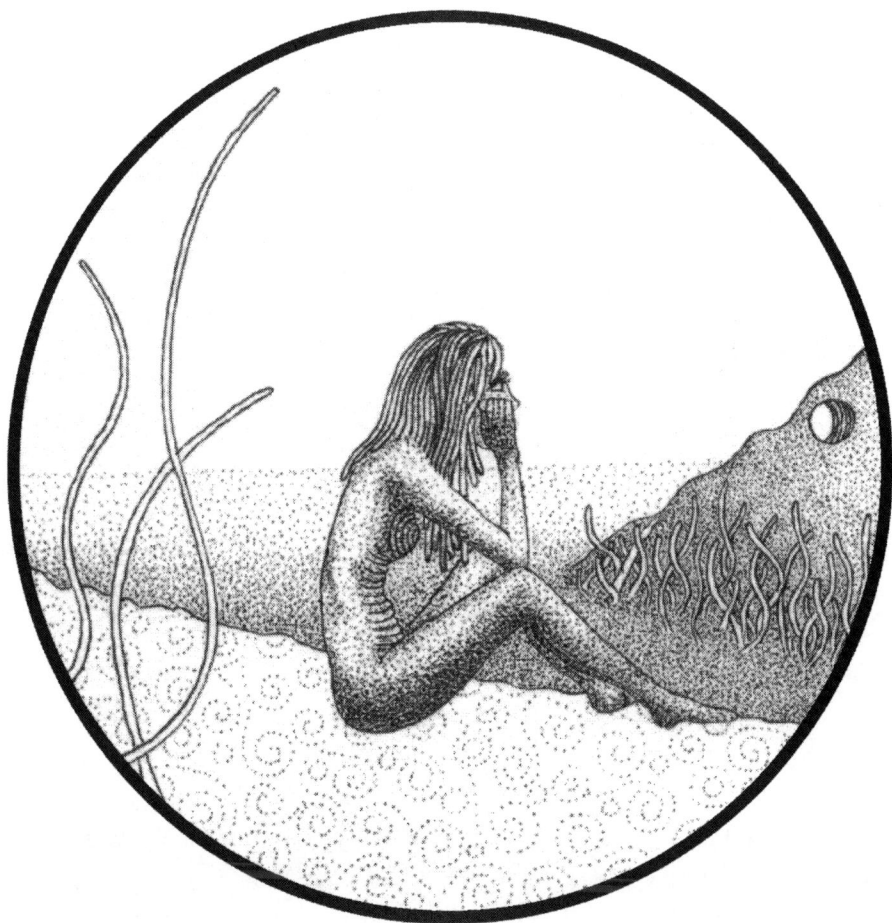

four-letter word

If I could ban one word in the English language, it would be this one. This go-to, reality-obscuring, detail-skimming default mechanism, installed in most of us Brits as soon as we can comprehend and interact, should have to leave our vocabulary's shores. Its limp, inadequate sound mushily exits my mouth all too often, and is making me mad. It seems to have a mind of its own, and *will* be heard, *will* override any truth that might be slower off the mark in the race to reply. Before the real emotions can be expounded upon, there it is. 'Fine'.

Today I don't feel fine. Not at all. Not for a second. But I said, to three different people who asked how I was, that I was fine.

I know it's a polite sidestep; it's a way of not burdening others with your own woes, a way to make them feel comfortable. Not everyone needs to know or even wants to know how you are. Sometimes you don't particularly want to go into details. Sometimes it's just easier to say 'fine' than "Actually I feel the worst I've ever felt in my entire life. I'm in the darkest place I have ever known. I am sadder than I thought possible. I want to scream, howl, punch. And you?"

It is somehow tied up with how we all react to bad news, to death, to someone who has gone through something we don't know how to ask about. You and your own engrained responses are just as much a part of this strange dance of denial we frequently perform between ourselves. And *to* ourselves. Does saying something make it partially true, momentarily true? If you say you are fine, and act as if you are fine, are you slightly more fine than you were just before they asked how it was going? Possibly. I don't know. But no doubt I'll keep saying it more often than not, to test the theory, unless it really is made illegal to utter this particular four-letter word.

Whatever words you use, I am struck today by how utterly changeable my moods are, and how the mood you think will match the moment doesn't seem to want to show itself. I can talk normally, even occasionally in detail about what happened, and be dry-eyed, stony, numb, or, dare I say it, 'fine'. Other people talking to me are sometimes more emotional than me, apologetic for being the one in bits when "it should be you who's crying, not me!" As if there is only space and tears for one person at a time to weep. Maybe that's true in this story, now we're further down the line. Because I can leave them, turn the corner, see a spider's web glisten in the sunlight on a drainpipe, and lose it entirely. I can be shopping, wandering down a supermarket aisle, absolutely unable to make a decision on what to buy, and crumple in the chocolate section, crumble next to the frozen vegetables. I can hear the schmaltziest, most laughably bad song in the world, and feel my face get wetter with every note. I can see an older couple walking along together, and dissolve. It strikes at any time, in any place, this crying game; the more inopportune moment the better, it seems. On the occasions it is expected, it has often sidled off for a crafty fag.

We all have this, I suppose. This ability to continue, to converse, to appear alright, to even *be* alright for a while. And I suppose each while gets longer. Well, I know it does. And you harden to every single sight and sound that used to split you open, and only get affected by some of them. And then only by a few of them. And you have more and more conversations where you are not constantly questioning your bizarrely controlled composure, and when your calmness is genuine.

And maybe, after more days than you can imagine, you really will be fine.

letting go

9th February 2017

I know that somehow, at some point, I will have to try to do what I was incapable of doing before – let go. Let him go.

From this position, one hundred and thirty-three days after he let go of this life, or, more truthfully, this life let go of him, it seems an impossible task. But one day, I suppose, a necessary step.

Letting go – I tried to in the past, during those many years together. Despite the profound, unarguable love we shared, things did not *always* sit right with me, and my mind strived for it to be what I dreamed it being. From time to time that mind reasoned that if we didn't tick this box, or that, if this was left unsaid or undone, if these things were not shared, if those things never changed, then logically perhaps we shouldn't carry on. On a few occasions that reasoning overtook all other emotions, and I could imagine ending it. I *did* end it: for a day, a week, once for two months, but I always went back. The imperfections never outweighed that innate oneness we had; the frustrations never pushed me into finishing it for good.

And now it has finished – for bad, as good is absolutely not the right word. My choice has been taken away. It is over.

And he has left me wanting more.

Much more.

He has left me with a permanent question mark and unanswerable thoughts.

He has left me hanging by gossamer thread over these love-smashed cliffs, wanting to climb back up and into his arms, but knowing I will dangle here for months and years, until I find the courage to cut the cord, fall into new hope, and let go.

the ostrich approach

8th February 2017

I finally did it. And it didn't feel as depressing as I thought it would.

I always preferred the ostrich approach. It'll never happen to me. It only happens to other people. Or, it will happen, but it'll happen much later, and I'll deal it with it then. Nearer the time. When I'm older. Like mortgages, or insurance, this was another grown-up straight-world thing that I wasn't going to bother with. More in a terrified way than a rebellious one; nevertheless the idea of planning for my demise, timely or otherwise, was firmly buried alongside my head in the sand.

Oh, but then it did happen to 'other people'; it happened to him. He at least had something in place, being, because of having kids, a little more in the grown-up world than me, much as he tried not to be. But for so many people, there is no 'nearer the time'. They don't have the chance to ponder the possibilities as they get older. The ostrich well and truly screws up.

And it really hit home, after witnessing at close hand the potential logistical nightmare, that I have swerved the idea so completely that if it happens to me other people will be left to clear up the mess I left behind. I own nothing of huge value, but it's not really about that; it's about choices, about what you would prefer to happen, if, or rather, when. It's about making it easy for the others who are already having to deal with something they never thought they'd have to deal with. About them being able to access your bank accounts, having all the contact numbers of your friends who should be told, about them having your pin numbers and passwords and codes, so that there is no unfinished business that is impossible to sort out. So that the things that will, inevitably, need to be paid for, can be paid for out of *your* money, so others aren't put in a position where they have to suddenly find thousands of euros, or pounds. Especially if it happens abroad; even if *you* live there, how can you expect your family or friends who don't to plough through red tape in another tongue, another land, on top of everything else?

I realised soon after it happened that I had no clue what anyone I know (apart from him, I did know that), would want to happen. Even with those closest to me, I wasn't sure if they would choose cremation or burial, a pretty basic part of the whole process. Of course you don't talk about it; I could no more bring myself to imagine losing them than I could imagine dying myself, and so the questions are never asked, the subject is never brought up. You can make an educated guess, obviously, but now I really feel it's a mistake, all this swerving. It can potentially cause upset, or disagreements between family and/or friends of the one who has gone, if things are not spelt out. What about organ donation, for example? Maybe they would have wanted that, but didn't have a card on them, and never mentioned it. What about the type of service? You could say they're gone, so what does it matter, but I think it *is* important, only in the sense that those who are left behind feel that it is 'what they would have wanted', and not some false compromise.

These are obviously not instructions to anyone else, this is just a personal realisation I had; that these things *do* happen, and, for me anyway, I feel strongly that I just want it all sorted out, there in black and white. So I did it. Printed, witnessed, signed. I feel relieved, not sad. It was good to clarify a few things, and make sure there were no loose ends that might cause unnecessary fraying of emotions, should I shuffle off sooner than expected. And I felt just a tiny bit grown-up, and a little less ostrich-like.

one out of five

7th February 2017

Clutching empty air,
my arm outstretched trying to
find him next to me.

This is unusual;
we don't sleep apart, we stay
connected all night.

We spoon, every
hour or so changing from one
side to the other.

We spoon so well, it
is my favourite feeling
in the entire world.

Both ways are perfect;
clasped in his firm grasp I am
protected, warmed, loved.

But I prefer to
be the spooner rather than
the spoonee; it makes

me puddle, awash
with something I can't even
find the right word for.

I can smell him; he
must be there, but on the edge
of the bed, hiding.

Maybe he fell down
the side, as I have fallen
many times, taking

the duvet with me,
and making him wake and laugh,
or sometimes harrumph.

I roll further in
towards the other side of
the sheets, still searching.

He must be under
the bed, sheltering from a
storm inside his head,

forgetting I am
here, ready to stroke him out
of any nightmares.

Ah, I feel something.
His smell is stronger, filling
my nose with relief.

But he's very soft;
has he melted in the night,
lost his form, his bones?

I touch the shape of
what I think should be him and
then I remember.

It's just a pile of
his clothes, covered in his smell,
without him in them.

creation, dissolution

6th February 2017

Bringing something to life... the creation of a new world, peopled by two.

Imagining it, being unable to sleep for it, being drawn to it, floored by it, daydreaming about it, wanting it, believing in it, suggesting it, trying it, testing it, acknowledging it, loving it, being excited by it, nurturing it, hurting it, deconstructing it, reconstructing it, breaking it, mending it, doubting it, being convinced of it, comparing it, sharing it, overestimating it, undervaluing it, mistrusting it, discussing it, flirting with it, torturing it, being scared of being in it, being scared to be without it, needing it, needing to be free of it, romanticising it, criticising it, getting too involved in it, grabbing it, throwing it, running from it, running back to it, crying over it, smiling over it, being warmed by its strength, worried by the power of it, accepting it, fighting it, rolling with it, rocking the foundations of it, smoothing it, being at peace in it, being at ease with it, loving it all over and over again.

Forming habits, setting things in stone, enjoying the familiarity of the stone, the heat of the evening sun on the stone, feeling content with the stone, then wanting to take a hammer to it and see how much it will shatter.

Fearing rejection, fearing changes, fearing being the needier one, fearing the loss of the independent you, fearing that you will be exchanged, fearing that it will not be enough, then saturating yourself with it so entirely you shock yourself and those around you.

These are the luxuries you have within the parameters of an ongoing romance, of a long-term liaison, of a well-travelled path deeply trodden alongside someone else... these are the fluctuations, the Yin and Yang, the human frailties and disparate needs, the ebbs and flows, the natural changes and the perceived control you both have over what comes next... these are what you probably take for granted.

You imagine that if it is ever to be the end of this story, either you or the other, or, far more rarely, both, will have decided, declared it over, drawn a line under it.

And then an end comes sooner, and more abruptly, and more horrifyingly, than you ever dreamed possible. The fluctuations just fluctuated irreparably in the wrong direction. All is ruptured, all is torn. And the luxury of choice is swept away. I chose. He chose. We chose.

And now what? I choose life, yes. Trainspotting style. Beyond that, I can't see.

risings and settings

One hundred and twenty-nine risings and settings of the sun.

Four waxings and wanings of the moon.

One whole autumn, a segment of winter.

You missed this spinning of the earth.

I missed you spinning with me.

freezing feet

Papa Ping told me that he had heard it was not a good idea to make any big decisions for at least six months after something like this. To give yourself time to think with a little more clarity; to not hurl yourself into another major life change too soon after having experienced one. Over a month ago, not even three months after it happened, and despite still being very much cocooned in my family's various nests, I started ruminating on what to do with myself, once I felt strong enough to fly alone. Where to go? And I felt, with the bits of my soul less in tatters than the rest, that I should go to live in France. Paris or a southern city. I pondered, spoke to people, read up on places, and in my whirling haze decided upon Toulouse, somewhere I have never even visited. My logic is always a curious creature, but here I was saying emphatically that I would move there, rent a place, start again; I was so sure that it would be the best thing to do. I had ruled out the capital because of price and its size, and because I knew the 1920s Paris in my mind was not the reality of 2017; to embark upon an existence in such a huge city, going there with nothing, seemed crazy even in my craziness. Marseille is by the sea, Bordeaux also a little too close for comfort. Montpellier was a possibility; I'd been there a couple of times to do gigs, and liked it a lot. But I felt I wanted to be in a bigger place. I suppose it was about losing yourself, attempting to run from what you can never run from, and being absorbed into a large, anonymous environment where you can try to rewrite your story.

So, Toulouse it was, with a Montpellier back-up. I half-planned to do a recce with Papa Ping; we looked at dates, airports, prices. I spent a lot of weeks in France in my head, but it was an opaque France, a vague France, one I couldn't quite grasp, see clearly, or imagine, other than in a very general sense. The reality, and logistics of it, escaped me.

It's still something I would like to do one day. I've wanted to live there, or in French-speaking Switzerland, for quite a while, and I've missed city life in the last few years in many ways. The half-and-half idea has been and probably will one day again be a goal; half the time spent in a French city, the other half somewhere epically beautiful and hot, probably Spain. I have to accept my financial limitations, but at the same time have always had the hopeful dreamhead of most artists; that anything could happen, and anything, if you really set your sights on it, is possible. On va voir.

But before that possible future, before the half-and-half dream potentially unfolds, or whatever else this world has in store for me, I find my frightened stomach falling fast and running, running. What was I thinking? Setting off with all my worldlies, having somehow rented a place to live from afar, landing in an unknown city where I know absolutely no one, harnessing the energy and positivity needed to launch yourself into a new space, hitting the ground running and hustling for bands, gigs, galleries, students, anything, everything; searching for new friends, walking the streets alone, sitting in cafes and bars and music venues watching the world turn without knowing how to join in. Old me, writing this, still feels the excitement of that, and yearns for it, somewhere inside. But new me, or at least temporary me, is too scared. I can't do it. I have feet so cold they are freezing. I don't want to be so alone. I need people around me, close to me, once I leave the sanctuary of family and friends here in England, and there is only one place in the world where that could be.

I'm going to move back to Órgiva, the quirky little town nestled underneath Sierra Nevada, in the Granada province, where I lived for five years. Someone in my family had already suggested it, but at that time I rejected the idea because it seemed like going backwards. Now it seems the only way forwards. Because I might flail, fail, break, slump, crack, but I can do so knowing I have a network of great friends I adore that will make sure I don't lose it completely. Who have been there for me throughout all of this despite the distance and will continue to be; who will pick me up if I fall too hard and keep the circle of love going; who knew him, and knew us, and miss him too. I find it almost impossible to look forward to anything these days, but this idea is warming up my feet.

water signs

I might not be the first one to notice this, or think of it. And I know I am prone, always, but especially now, to reading into things. To giving importance and meaning to the probably random, significance to the coincidence.

But I can't help being struck by his album cover. The front image is of a guitar he was very proud to have, one that was rescued from the submerged Gibson guitar factory after the New Orleans flood. He bought it, took it to his favourite luthier in west London, and made it playable again. He loved guitars (or anything really, buildings, cars, antiques, places), with a story, with some kind of history. With such a journey behind this instrument, coupled with its stunning, original look (even I, who never quite shared his excitement for custom body finishes, vintage headstocks or locking wing nuts, thought it was a beauty), it felt really special to him. Consequently this waterlogged guitar was chosen for the album photo, and with his great friend and photographer J, water droplets were added to the image. So, a drowned guitar, in water.

Another photo inside the CD shows him on a sofa with a picture of water behind him, which I hadn't even really noticed until today.

And a couple of months before it happened, I took out his CD to play it, and it was drenched, completely soaked. It had been one of many in a CD rack in my flat, and none of the other discs above or below it were wet. I couldn't understand it. Yes, there was a plant perched on top of the rack, so no doubt a bit of water spilled onto it somehow. But onto none of the others. None of them.

And when I was numbly going about trying to pack some things in cases to come back to England with Biglittlebro in October, I wanted to take his CD. I couldn't find it anywhere. Gone, like him.

You can't tell me that all that's not a little strange.

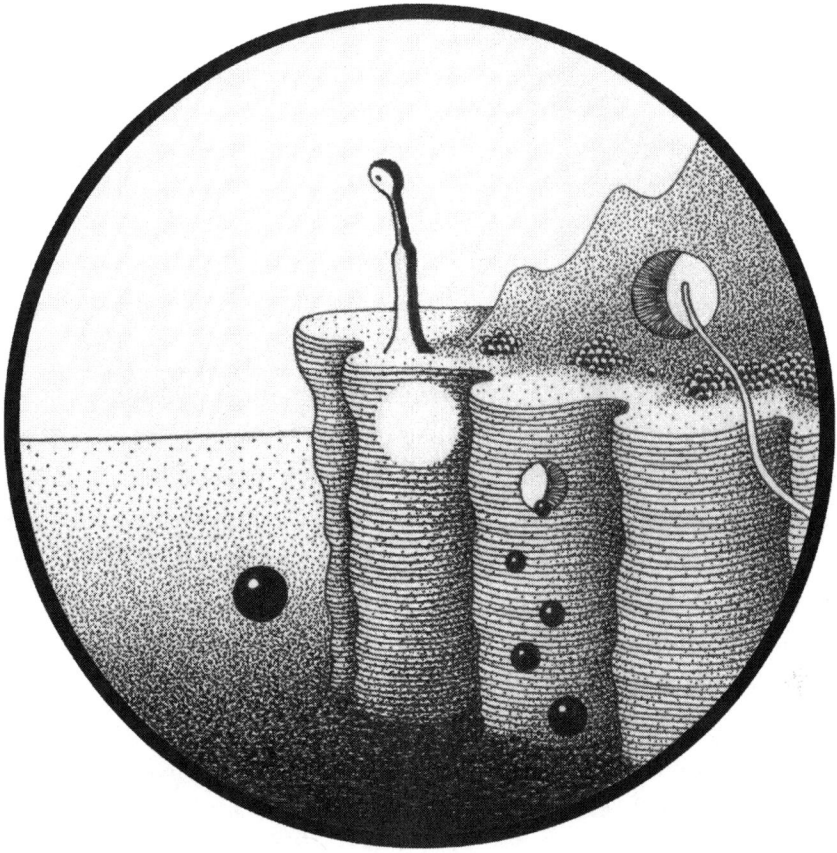

Also this – an image I have drawn many times, in various pieces of work. I never thought that maybe I was drawing a future me; a sad, lonely figure contemplating the sea and what it did.

Yes, I'm reading into it all. Trying to make sense of it, therefore constantly clutching at 'signs', odd occurrences, and noticing things that almost certainly have no profound meaning. But how can I not? When there is no sense to be made, we still search for it.

Water is everywhere, and is portrayed so often in so many styles, to provoke such a variety of emotions; it is there to stir, to calm, to sell you stuff, to obscure, to hint at other worlds and suggest magical qualities, to depict courage or fear, to transport you to a moment of serenity, to simply be beautiful in a painting or a photo. I can never escape it; I suppose I just have to try to make my peace with it, drop by painful drop.

the comfort of strangers

Speaking about it all to a stranger, the objective unknown ears of a therapist, is a shift of gear. You usually can't help but vet yourself whilst speaking to someone you know well; you are wary of exhausting them with every weary nuance, every crumb of pain, every shred of anguish, ad infinitum. You are very aware of their approaches to things, their views, their sensibilities, and their desire above all for you to feel better, and you tailor your words to fit them. Even with the closest people to you, no matter how often they implore you to be honest, or how many times they say that they are there for you to listen, to help if they can, whenever, wherever, you frequently hold back. You don't want to bore; the endless not-so-merry-go-round in your head gets dull if it leaves your skull, or so you believe. You know you already repeat yourself enough, and in the moments where you have a small amount of control over what exits your mouth you would rather spare them the monotony, and talk about them, and their lives, rather than copy paste copy paste copy paste your angst.

I know for sure they would say that many people talk incessantly about the most inane things, over and over again, and that your situation deserves at least as much airtime. But self-consciousness is bedded in deeply, and you try to change channel.

Ironically, with those that want to talk about it, about him, and are totally open to doing so, this is how I often behave. When people are doing the swerving themselves, I get anxious or upset that it is being stepped around, and want to change back the channel to my broadcast again.

For whatever reasons and despite knowing I have many outlets for my grief, talking to someone who is trained in such matters, and knows nothing about my relationship before she starts to ask questions, is a release. J, my 'almost' stranger (I met her once before, briefly), has met me for a drink and a talk. She has angles on things that others perhaps do not; her questions probe in different ways, with different results. She is just chatting, it's not a formal counselling session, and her generosity with her time and energy is incredible, and moving. I drink Guinness, she has coffee, and we talk for hours. She is far from the impassive, opinionless idea of a 'shrink'; instead she, with real warmth, listens and comments, suggests and reacts, in the most natural way. I feel like we could be friends, and in other circumstances perhaps we would be. She seems to get it all, and more, and I come away feeling better, calmer, and at least momentarily lighter, after her wise words and caring approach. I should do this again sometime, with this stranger who now is not.

portraits

Papa Ping had asked me to draw a portrait of the two of us. He has quite the collection of my work on his walls: his parents, siblings, children, grandchildren, late wife, stepdaughters, one of his dogs, himself.

I had already done one of Biglittlebro and E, and Ping wanted a similar one of us to hang in his kitchen stroke gallery.

I hadn't got around to it; my list of 'stuff to do' is hefty at the best of times, and I'd had a busy summer of gigs with four different bands, creating an installation for an art space in Almería city, and settling into a new home. Then I had a run, or so I thought, of visitors, family and friends coming out to stay with or near me in September and October. It was going to be an autumn project. The autumn that never came, not in the usual sense. Sure, it was there, it happened, it autumned. I just didn't notice it. I couldn't call it autumn any more than I could call life 'life', or me 'me'. Everything had changed. Everything *has* changed...

I was also searching for the right photo to draw it from, and couldn't find the 'perfect' one of both of us together that would work when translated into lines and dots. So, it was going to be a composite of two photos; I have done this often before, but it involves a lot of jiggery pokery trying to get the angles and shadows right to make it look natural, as if you really were there together in that captured moment.

I suppose it doesn't really matter in the end that I haven't drawn us together, given how many thousands of photos of us exist, and how many millions of memories, but I can't put into words how gutted I am that I didn't get around to doing it. I know I could still do it; I could do it right now. But it hurts too much.

a normal abnormal day

31st January 2017

It's the end of the month.
The end of January 2017. That makes four months.
Feels like four days. Four weeks. Four years. Four seconds.
Four lifetimes.

I walked my new habitual walk, as fast as I could, as rain threatened and a cold breeze blew. Down from Papa Ping's house, past the castle, across the narrow stone bridge and alongside the river. I tried not to look at the water much, as usual, but each time I dare myself to look a little longer, and chant something inside my head. There is always the flashback, but I look up at the trees, and stare too hard at the buds, willing them to open in front of me, and stomp my feet too hard on the wintry ground.

Back in the house, I sat on the piano stool, and examined my hands.

I borrowed a sax from a friend of Papa Ping; I had to teach someone online. I haven't played for four months. I brought back my mouthpiece from Spain, reluctantly, rejecting the idea of ever playing it, or anything, again. I stuck it on this borrowed instrument today, and blew. It worked. It was more or less the same as it ever was. I have a strange love-hate relationship with the sax; in the right setting it can feel so good to play, I can express through it, it feels part of me. But the right setting contains multiple variables, so doesn't occur very often. In the wrong setting it's just a weird duck quacking. At the moment I am feeble, as well, and it's a really physical instrument. It helps to feel strong, to be powerful, and I'm not. But it quacked, and that will have to do.

I sat at the piano again, which I'm not too feeble to deal with, and tried to play one of my own pieces. It didn't work.

I went out for soup in a café at lunchtime and bumped into a friend from school. She asked if I was with anybody – we haven't been in touch since sixth form, and know almost nothing about each other's lives. Cue one of those moments where you hear a voice slowly uttering "umm", then fast, too fast, saying it was a long story, but... and the story is unfolding and spilling out from this voice, calmly, too calmly... and you wonder who is speaking, who it is that has decided to tell this tale, in detail, too much detail... and you watch the expression on your old friend's face as what she thought would be a light-hearted anecdote of romantic calamity or a humorously complicated affair turns into something she doesn't know how to react to, and you think your face is normal, too normal, but maybe it isn't, and maybe it is frightening her, to see not only how the years have creased me but how those comparatively innocent times we shared have changed into this, this thing, this reality.

Home again and drained, I went into the living room where the piano sits, waiting impatiently for me, and went out again.

I stared out of the kitchen window for a long while, looking at the shivering woods at the end of the garden, hunting for squirrels with tear-filled eyes. I was listening to the pianist James Rhodes playing Chaconne in D minor by Bach, arranged by Busoni. I, on Papa Ping's recommendation, read his memoirs, and was so drawn into his story I wanted to hear every piece he mentions; this one in particular, which represents a pivotal moment in his life, is incredible and you feel his story with each note. There are bars that wrench out every drop of ache, that squeeze each memory so tightly they disappear into nothingness, that pull your head inside out.

I sit at the piano again, inspired, and this time manage a few bars without mistakes.

push and pull

I push and pull against who and what I am,
torn and split and wrenched between a memory of myself,
and this emotional wraith.
On quiet days I simply move from place to place,
functioning,
occasionally whispering to myself in spiked phrases
in an attempt to stir a thought or two
that don't include him.
On quiet days
I just want to empty out the overflowing
unstoppable
river of white noise.
On louder days each shop window reflects the internal noise
as I stare at my passing figure
and try to recognise something in the movement,
only to be reminded of someone else.
On louder days
everything hurts
and the glass shatters at my feet.

dislocation

29th January 2017

I was with a group of people, friends, but I'm not sure who. We were talking about him, then all looked up. Somewhere, up very high, almost as if he was on a balcony but nothing quite that tangible, we saw F. Not him, a shadow of him, but we all knew who it was. He moved across, from left to right. He lifted an arm, and waved at us. His hand was dislocated, longer and at a strange angle; he disappeared from sight, and I woke up.

So far I have never dislocated a wrist, or broken a bone, torn a tendon, twisted an ankle, or fractured a femur. It's not that I have not had any medical problems, but they have always been inwards, nothing to do with limbs and movement. They have felt part of me, for good or bad. My motion has never been restricted or completely curtailed; my body parts have remained attached as always. The idea of dislocation, where a part of you has detached from the rest, and floats apart from its normal position, less a part of you than before in a sense, is how I feel now. It's how I feel in terms of my connection to my old life.

It is geographically factual, as I am dislocated, temporarily living here in England, away from what has become my home country, Spain. Away from my musical and artistic 'career'; away from close friends, from all my things, from the landscapes I breathed for many years.

It is emotionally true, as the love I had with someone has been cut away; an invisible but tenacious bond has been loosened so much that I am floating freely, adrift (as is he, but in a different realm). I am dislocated from his touch, his voice, his presence, his entirety. I am dislocated from our story, wandering in high grasses searching for familiar footprints.

It is mentally accurate, as memory and fear eat up my stability, and horrors tip up the already slightly precarious balance of my mind. I am dislocated from logic, from a way out of my churning, troubled brain; poisonous, stifling leaves have grown over the exit sign, hiding it from view. I fear I will not find it, even though you all say that I will.

sketch book

I just came across a sketch book from quite a few years ago – I think when I was living in Barcelona – that Biglittlebro had thrown into my suitcases along with some other art materials when I left Spain. These text drawings seem to resonate with me now.

'there's nothing in this slippery moment to use as a foothold'

‘heavy, empty, trapped’

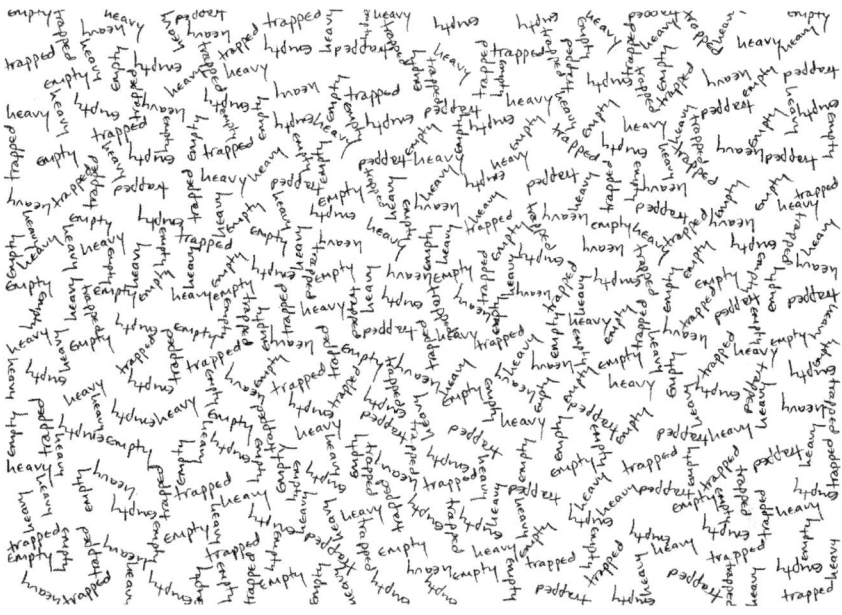

‘breathe, find breath’

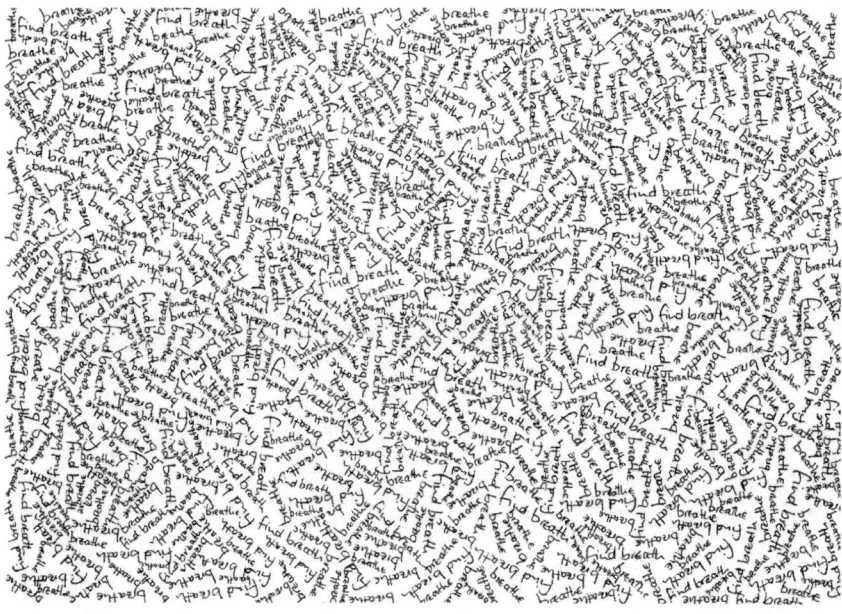

'inhale, exhale'

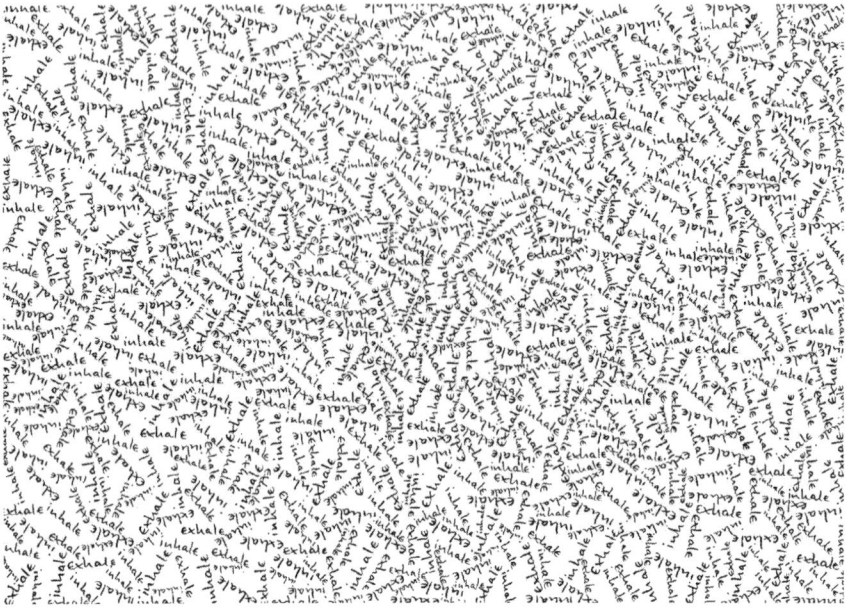

'change, find stillness'

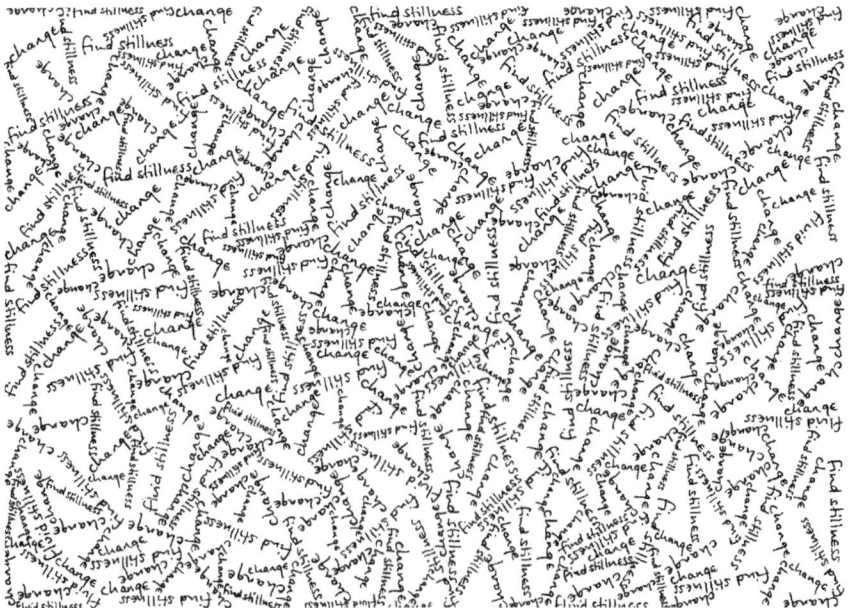

and this, unfinished, one

your tides will flow
wash me away
drown my mind
watch as i disintegrate
watch as i disintegrate
wash me away
watch as i disintegrate
drown my mind my tides will ebb
wash me away
your tides will flow
wash me away
drown my mind
your tides will flow
my final thought swept to sea
your tides will flow
watch as i disintegrate
wash me away
your tides will flow
wash me away
your tides will flow
drown my mind
wash me away
watch as i disintegrate
your tides will flow
drown my mind
darkest waters clothe me
watch as i disintegrate
drown my mind
wash me away
wash me away

here, and there

Every place is a place that had him in it; this is a strange, torturing fact. I can see him here, and there, in these rooms, these streets. The vision is almost strong enough to convince me he's real. I have such a sense of him being there; I see clothes, posture, expressions, fragments of different moods. I feel touch, smell his scent, hear his voice, his laugh. The whole of him, while there is nothing.

I dare to step inside The Golden Lion, a pub in Papa Ping's town we frequented in December the winter before, while we were staying up there. Its roaring fire and ancient beams, patterned carpets and local characters (Crossword Man, Soup Lady, Dog Guy), drew us in from the cold, and it briefly became our habitual cosy refuge in that chilly English month. The half of Guinness helped my recurring anaemia; the local ale helped his everything. We always sat at the table closest to the flames, at my insistence, and people-watched in and among talking ourselves.

We wondered if certain people came and felt more at home there than in their actual home; we imagined them as lonely beings, whose daily pleasure was coming to this bar for a pint or three, chewing the weather to death, deciphering cryptic clues, and belonging. We might have been wrong, but it still got us thinking about when we would reach their age; would we have a favourite haunt, a familiar sanctuary, would we embrace the world of crosswords? I could imagine him, elderly, finally allowing the grey to do its grey thing, big-bearded, still handsome, probably with a golden Labrador or similar, becoming more of an ale connoisseur as time rolled on. Enjoying the habit, the simplicity of good things. Saying, "I used to play a bit," if the subject of music or guitars came up, and the other locals smiling, knowing how amazing he was, before the arthritis kicked in, and appreciating his self-deprecation.

So after many peers over many weeks and months through the window, and many turnings away, unable to deal with confronting this place once inhabited by him, by us, I stepped inside. All was as it had been a year or so earlier. The same girl at the bar, who we had chatted to about Barcelona. There was

Crossword Man in his usual chair; in came Dog Guy, his animal in tow. But no Soup Lady; she was a less regular regular, but I hoped she was still around. I sat at the same table that we had always sat at, this time facing an empty chair. I drank a half of Guinness (my anaemia had returned, unsurprisingly), and felt the fire at my back. Snippets of our conversations flitted through the air and flooded my head; I saw his face, felt his mood, his hand on my knee. He was a strong person, a powerful being in a way; you knew it when he was around. And the memory of him, in that place, one year on, suddenly snapped me in two.

I didn't order a second half.

when only friends will do

I have spent a few months cautiously navigating Hollywood's seas, trying to escape my own head without having to confront its waters. Literally; it has been surprising how difficult it is to find a single film that doesn't contain an ocean or beach scene, stormy seas or fishing on lakes, river dramas or boat adventures. I feel confident that a movie set in New York will keep me safely on shore, and then there is a moment on the banks of the Hudson, or someone diving into the water with the skyline in the background. Everywhere is suddenly by the sea, even London, Paris, Berlin. The geography of the world has changed, or is it just mine? Perhaps there is a contractual obligation for each film to include a beach at some point. I understand; its backdrop perfectly represents so many emotions that we all feel, and can underpin countless dramatic clichés, but I have come unstuck so often as dread uncoils itself from within my sofa-bound frame as I realise where the characters are heading.

My nephew Hispeed has been amazing; on the occasions when we decided to watch something together, he vetted the trailer, fast-forwarded through the entire movie to check for anything that might send me out of the room, even phoned friends who had seen this particular film to ask them if there were any dodgy sea moments. The sweet care he showed for me made me feel so protected; the fact that someone who is still a kid himself can be so mature makes me hopeful for the future.

Without his guidance, I have swerved away from films, and my default viewing matter in these last few days has become that little-known American series Friends. Despite having seen all of the episodes at least twice, it's somehow one of those shows that can always warm you, always distract you, always make you laugh. It's not high art, but it is written so well that you can guarantee that you will feel better after seeing it, not worse. I'll get back to films, as I love losing myself in another world for a couple of hours, and will no doubt continue to run them by Hispeed first whenever I can, but this week only Chandler Bing will do.

each and every

25th Janu

That force you had, that opinion so clear.
That humour you hurled when stupid strayed near.
That smile your eyes transmitted to the room.
That file you downloaded from the womb.

That laugh that lit your face from within.
That charm, that sneeze, that scowl, that grin.
That look that spoke so transparently.
That wit you possessed inherently.

That time you chose left instead of right.
That sleepy kiss, that angry bite.
That word of yours no one else understood.
That thing you did that only you could.

That love you gave and needed back.
That day your jealousy painted us black.
That year you squandered ignoring dreams.
That week you decided what everything means.

Each and every, each and every,
fragment of you, moment of you,
feeling of you, memory of you,
is swirling, whirling around the world,
turning, churning, as you become blurred.
Each and every, each and every
minute without you
carves me into even smaller pieces.

temporary elation

24th January 2017

We were in a far-off land. Someone had booked us into a deluxe hotel, and we were standing outside the back of it. We walked slowly towards the edge, across fresh, glowing grass, and saw the most incredible view below us. Huge sweeps and swathes of multicoloured hills, a patchwork pattern softly undulating its deep magentas, tawny browns and vivid oranges from left to right. Beyond that, gigantic mountain ranges, higher than any either of us had ever seen. We looked behind us, over the top of the hotel roof, and saw more peaks, some of them snow-clad. We held hands tightly, smiling at our luck.

I had the sensation that I had lost him for a while, although the reason was unclear, and that now we were together again it would be forever. There would be no breaking it, no ending it, nothing to stand in our way. This was it. We felt both elated and yet somehow sad. Elated to be here, joined again, and know that whatever had happened and cleaved us apart was over. Sad that we had missed all those hours, weeks, months of our story, and had mourned the other; the residue of this sadness felt as if it would rest with us until the end.

the absence of colour

I am not in any way, shape or form, religious, and stay well away from any doctrines or organisations of any kind that dictate how I or we should live our lives. I never understood, although I absolutely respect their right to do so, women who wear the black of mourning for years and sometimes for the rest of their lives, upon the death of their spouse; I suppose I saw it as simply following man-made rules, which goes against my grain.

But now I find myself more comfortable wearing black. It's not something I thought about and obviously not something that my family or culture would impose. But I realised the other day that almost all the clothes I am wearing for the last three months or so have been black. I find I don't want to wear colours. They don't seem right, and again there is no morality behind this, no particular train of thought, but I am simply staying away from them. Is this a primal thing, then? A strange, basic instinct? Or has black become so engrained in even our non-religious lives as representing sadness, death, despair that I automatically veer towards it as a second skin during this period?

I don't know the answer, but I do know that for now to be clad head to foot in black corresponds to something inside me, and feels appropriate, however bizarre that it is to say.

the body substance

22nd January 2017

Rock gently from your pelvis. Move in tiny circles in one direction, widening the circle each time. Make the loop as wide as you can. Push forwards as you reach before you, lean as far backwards as you can without losing your balance. Keep breathing regularly. After a few minutes, gradually decrease the movement and bring it back to centre. Start again, but in the opposite direction, increasing the circle, decreasing.

This is the first physical activity apart from walking that I have taken part in for almost four months. It feels good to move, to stretch, to unfold, to disturb the sleep of my joints, wake up my sockets, to be aware of my body as my body, rather than just lugging it around, unfeeling flesh draped heavily over exhausted bones.

Apart from peeling myself out of bed and pouring myself back in again, drifting between rooms, trying to stomp outside for at least half an hour each day to de-cobweb and empty my head, I haven't used my body. I haven't thought about it, haven't really looked at it, haven't noticed its presence except for in the moments I hypochondriacally think it is failing me (which, to be fair, are many).

It's strange now, as the Kundalini yoga teacher breathes out forcefully, with us following suit, bending and extending, twisting, turning, elongating, for me to climb into forgotten postures, feel my atrophied muscles snap to attention under my untouched skin, rediscover a part of me that had been swept aside. This body is mine, this flesh is mine, and it needs to be entwined once more with my mind, my soul. The rediscovery of yoga brings me a little closer to myself as a whole again.

this has created

21st January 2017

A screaming chasm,
a dream phantasm,
cold desolation, shaking desperation,
punching depression, a death obsession,
heightened fears,
a lake's worth of tears,
illogical phobias, feeling lonelier,
a constant unease,
a life on its knees,
grey hairs, anxiousness,
weight loss, neediness,
eyesight failure,
erratic behaviour,
and a hole where he should still live

but also

longer moments with those I never normally see enough of,
unexpected bonds with unexpected people,
a nearly finished album of music,
reconnections with disconnected friends,
art as sanctuary,
new takes on old stories,
beautiful messages that reach out to me and start the healing,
a perspective that surely can never be forgotten,
awareness that I am not really alone,
cyber hugs,
cat kisses,
fierce embraces,
and a circle of love.

I can't say the word

20th January 2017

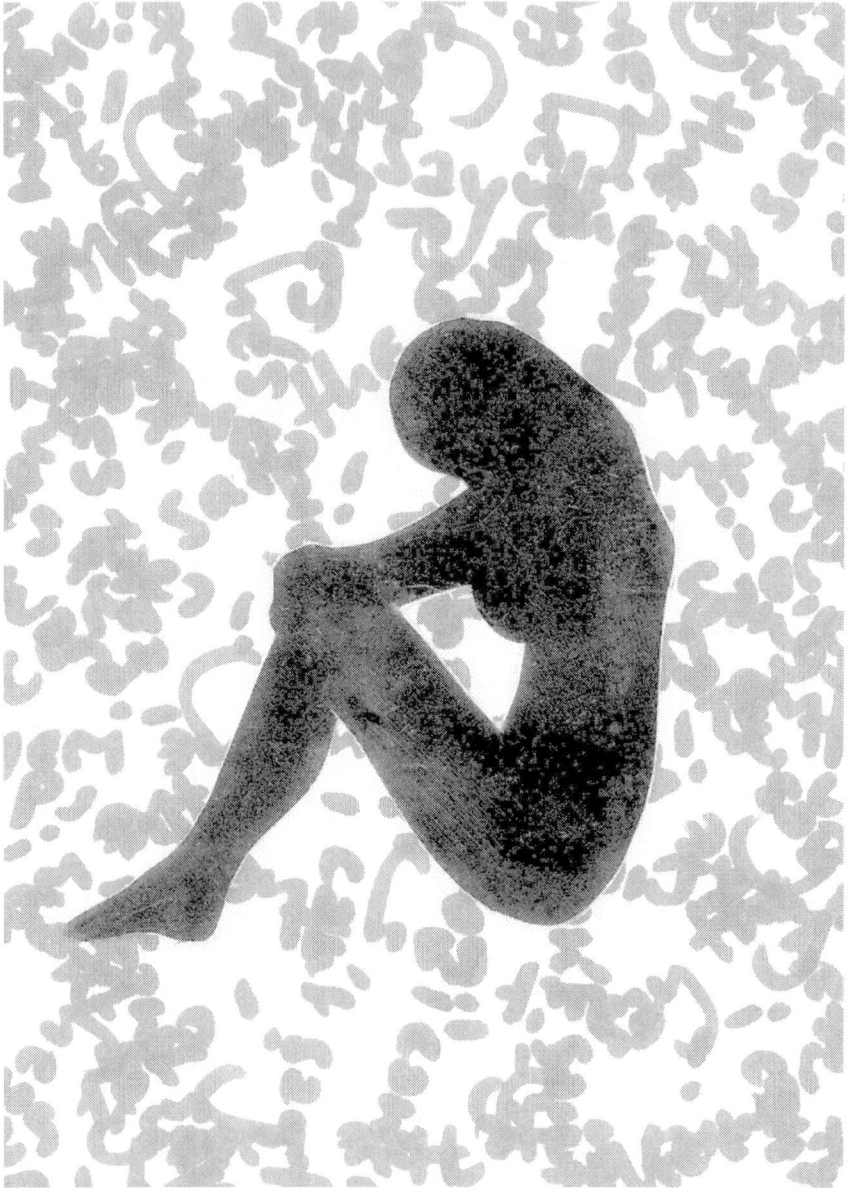

imprinted

If we were scarred by every touch, stamped by each contact with another,

if a brush against flesh, a graze along skin, changed the colour of that place,

if the most touched parts retained a depth of hue more profound than the most ignored,

if each person who had collided with us in whatever sense left a different colour,

how would our landscape look?

How would our bodies be?

His trail would have saturated me, his pigmentation transformed me.

A renovated room, an embellished entity.

Marked forever.

Imprinted.

As I am.

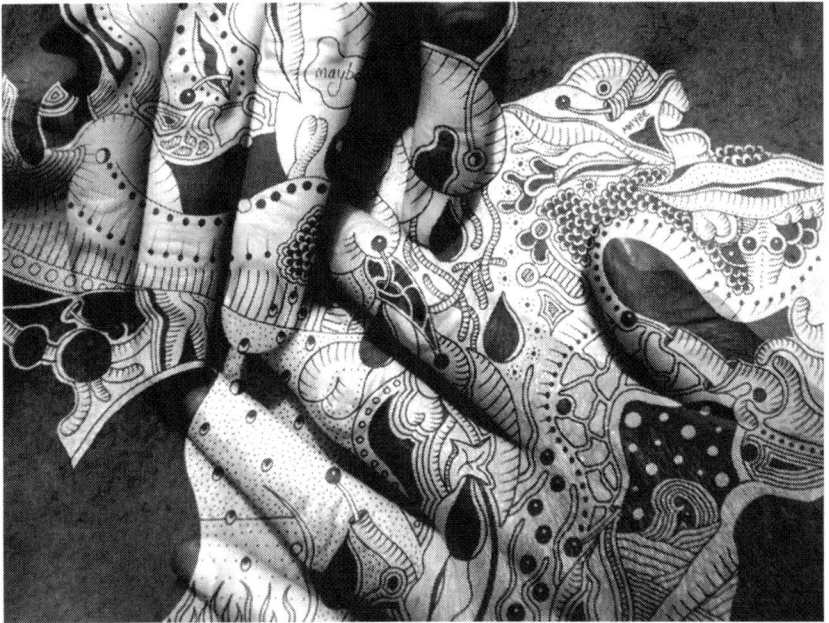

au revoir

I say au revoir to M, my best friend from my life in Spain, as he pulls away in a taxi bound for Victoria bus station, en route to Paris. He came over to England a couple of weeks ago in early January to visit me and my family, and do some recording together, and has saved my soul.

Someone from another life in this one; the strangeness of that, along with the amazing person that he is, has made my days lighter, easier, almost normal. I needed this: to switch off the angry grind of my grief, be able to dry out my drenched, forgotten happiness and let it flap around my head for a short while. The circuits of my brain, programmed for three and a half months to encompass only misery, trauma and at best numbness, have been redirected through a hazy recollection of when the world was mostly okay, to a state where I am able to think that perhaps it still could be.

I know the high is temporary; I feel I might crash later on, as his cab turns the corner onto the Old Oak Road and disappears. But the knowledge that this state is possible, is achievable, and might well come again, coupled with the recent, positive memory I now have, is worth any crash that may lie ahead.

locked-in syndrome

17th January 2017

Locked into a brain that throws sharp, pointed stones at your logic, and rakes furiously through the leaves of your calm, scattering them far and wide and out of sight.

Locked into a freezing basement, where the cold steel doors slam shut and the sinister strip lighting blinks on and off, and your own head straps you to a chair and tortures you.

Locked into fear, stuck inside anxiety. Repetition, repetition, repetition of what might go wrong. Pre-emptive panic, the foretelling of flight not fight.

You can't get through this. You won't get through this. You'll lose it, you won't be able to breathe; how can there be enough air, how can humans survive down here? We are not supposed to be here, buried under dozens, hundreds of metres of earth and pipes and rats and airlessness. Our place is above the surface, with oxygen and winds and space and rain. Our feet should feel the soil; our journeys should be shorter and more meaningful. We should all own seven cubic metres of personal air, to carry around with us and avoid this sweaty, unpleasant contact with strangers who breathe too much.

The doors won't open at my stop. The carriages will hesitate between stations; the air will stop circulating, we will be too hot to survive. We will be trapped, claustrophobically freaking out, forever.

I can't get through this. I won't get through this.

It's just the Central line. And a tiny bit of the Northern. It's only forty-five minutes. I am insane.

The doors slide apart effortlessly as we reach Camden tube station. We step out of the petrified bubble that has housed me for less than an hour. I cry, I laugh. We walk to Camden Lock, out in the beautiful open air, not locked in.

poem for lost things

I am travelling by bus from Manchester to London with M. The journey is too hot for January; the minutes drag as I wish it over, like all journeys nowadays. Where has my wandering spirit wandered off to? I just want to arrive, not to go. I know, 'life is the journey, not the destination'. I wholeheartedly agree. But in this case, in the case of public transport, I don't.

At least this travel is in French, which always adds a drop of gloss to the matt of ordinary things, a sheen to my slump. We alight at Victoria, weary and in need of liquid refreshment. The streets seem unfamiliar; I lose my compass confidence, my navigatory knowhow. I used this station countless times in my twenties, the National Express snailing me up to my old lands a few times a year, but I don't recognise it. I'm supposed to be the local, the tour guide, and I am lost.

Brutishly loud; brimming, teeming with everything and everyone and everywhere. Calm-crushing babble, ear-dissolving sirens, peace-piercing roars, cries and beeps and shouts and phone tones and crashes and sneezes and engines and bells and screeches and nostril-engulfing odours of diesel and dirt and coffee and cumin and sweat and soup and bleach and brake fluid and life.

This London almost scares me. This London I adored, embraced, dreamed of then dreamed within. This London I skipped around, gigged around; this London I moved around endlessly, from room to room, flat to flat, area to area. This home. This home is alien to me, as I am to it, and as we enter a cafe and order a herbal tea (odd in itself), it feels right that the waiter thinks I'm French, and chats away about his home country. I am alien; I am not a Londoner, not even English. How has this happened? I don't mind it at all, in fact I quite like it, but as we leave to try to find a bus to take us on to East Acton, it is slightly unnerving to play the tourist like this. We circle, and cross lanes, and tread pavements, asking bus drivers and pedestrians, and even when we find the right chariot, I don't understand how to pay: the driver won't accept my proffered farthings, and I feel a hundred and three as I ask the elderly lady in the purple quilted cap what to do and what to swipe. I suppose I haven't lived here for nine years, but I may as well be in Beijing, in Beirut, in Budapest, for all the street smart I have right now.

Lost things.

Lost knowledge. Lost courage.

Lost footprints in much-walked soil.

I am quite lost.

Where are the landmarks in my existence? Where is this brand new compass, forced upon me like an unwanted Christmas gift, pointing? The notches in the bark, the red string tied around the trunks, the criss-crossed branches have all disappeared; my path through this ancient, overflowing forest is unmarked, my trail blurred, my route back impossible to find.

Pulled from under me, the rug of my everything ripples in the sluggish brown air before my tired eyes, and somersaults tauntingly back and forth. I watch it hurl itself cloudwards, casting a fleeting glance back at me as it rounds the roofs and goes in search of some other gullible soul to deceive. I never truly believed its comfortable weave and soft woollen stitching was there to stay, but I never truly believed it wasn't, either. I thought I'd be the one to chuck it out on recycling day.

I left my city nearly a decade ago, and now it leaves me standing, confused.

I suppose I left him here too, in a sense, although we never left each other, could never leave each other alone. Now he has left me. Standing, confused.

solo

15th January 2017

I relax into the sofa at Biglittlebro's studio, safe with him at the helm. M is doing some extra takes of his guitar solos from yesterday's recording session with a live band; he seems more relaxed than he was yesterday, and he plays like a demon, amazing as ever, but I know he's not happy, is never completely happy, with what he does.

Improvising is a strange beast. Pulling something out of the bag under these kind of circumstances, with the red light on and onlookers looking and your own personal pressures, unnerves me at the best of times. I don't know about anyone else, but I always dream that some magic will happen, some miracle, that transforms me into a different player; some switch will be switched that renders me capable of playing better than I ever have before; I can imagine playing a fountain of a solo, cascading notes, with passion and force and beauty. Record is pressed and more often than not I seem to only produce a dribble, a murky puddle, a stagnant pond filled with my overused phrases and go-to licks. I haven't ever suddenly gained ten years of technique overnight; I haven't surprised myself, only bored. It's hard to conjure up the fire; I know I'm going to have to try, after M has done his bit, but I feel so uninteresting and exhausted I can't imagine my fingers doing much burning up and down the keyboard.

Interesting, how we change when watched. I feel I play better alone, my solo solos more inspiring. It could be a simple case of perception, and for some the pressure of an audience or the thought that something is going to be set in stone in a recording might up their game. But I don't feel it does mine, and when surrounded only by me I am relaxed, which I suppose is the key.

Interesting, looking in on myself from afar, how I change when watched, in all ways. Someone else said that when grieving you have a sense of observing yourself interacting with others. When I am alone, which is rare as I have chosen the route of clinging to others during this time rather than battling it solo, whatever I am is real; when I'm not, I feel as though I'm in a badly acted, depressing theatre production that I never wanted to be in, and certainly not in this role. Nothing is real, and you wonder if the 'audience' are as unsure of reality as you are. Everything feels self-conscious, playing a dramatic part you didn't rehearse; you are hyper-aware of others watching you, and you are not sure if you are acting in the right way. If there is a right way (which obviously there isn't, but that doesn't change this strange dislocated perspective that engulfs you and makes you doubt even your doubt), no one has told you. You are feeling your way through a process you are not, can never be, prepared for, much like someone handing you a highly complicated chord sheet for the first time and telling you that your improvisation on it is being recorded and everyone you have ever known will listen to the outcome.

I improvise, and my soul's solo wheels uncertainly around the auditorium that is my world.

our future

Dear F,

I write of nothing but the past, our past, your past. But what of our future? Just as we were potentially nearing the point where countries might have collided, airspaces might have aligned, timings could have been right, and dreams could have coincided, this happened.

Were those years that now, in retrospect, and in a certain frame of mind, seem in limbo, as if waiting for something to push us one way or another, wasted? A waste of time, of longing, of wonderings, of frustration? Did those years get tired of the wait, of our inability to decide or jointly change, and make the decision for us?

Or was it all simply never meant to happen in the conventional way for us, and in fact those years were not wasted, and rather were the best use of our time and our love? Did we innately know that, despite our habitual doubts during time apart, that this suited our personalities, our lifestyles, our relationship? Was to be in our bubble, in the end, the only way we could be?

Did you think about it as much as I did along the way? Now you've stopped thinking, and I have to wonder for both of us. What would have become of us? And suddenly now I remember, like a dart through my crippled heart and head that you used to say that all the time: 'what will become of us?'

And now we know.

three atoms

13th January 2017

Some racing left, some escaping right,
others fleeing out to sea,
diving under rocks,
skimming sand and shells,
streaking away from the scene of the crime
before the police arrive.

Some washed up on the stony shore,
lying there bewildered
to see such a commotion
and such sadness on land,
waiting for the next day
to be sent skywards
in the late summer sun.

Over the following hours,
days, months,
and for up to four thousand years,
they are forcefully separated from each other
and sent north,
south and east,
across to Algeria,
up to France, down to Morocco,
on and on,
on and on.

Their memory of what they did
is erased over time;

just another contact
with something
in the wrong place at the wrong moment,
and the playful exuberance
and innocence
with which they killed
is recycled
endlessly
over endless miles
and centuries.

Where are they now,
the water molecules that
downed him, submerged him?
In one wave,
in forceful formation,
in an effortless surge,
they took him away.

Where are they now,
these trillions of three atoms
that joined together to break us apart?

never

He'll never read this...

never hear me wonder out loud about what I will write today...

never know his story, our story, is being shared...

never know for how long I'll miss him...

james dean

James Dean died on the same date as him.
Sixty-one years earlier.
Live fast, die young, etc.

F didn't live so fast, except in his car. There, yes, he was fast.
The year he didn't get a speeding fine deserved champagne.
His recurring nightmare was that he would die in a car crash.
He dreamed it so many times, and recounted it so many times;
even I thought that would be the way it went.
I bet he never dreamed in a million years
that it would be the sea that got him.
It would surely be the open road.

But in other ways he wasn't fast.
He was a lounger, a long sleeper.
He napped like a cat.
He was a cup of tea and daytime tv browser, albeit slightly ironically.
A snoozer, a happy-to-be-home-watching-a-film-with-wine night-timer.
A party hater, except for smaller gatherings with good friends.
Not one for clubs, for wild times, for rock 'n' roll clichés.
Not a manic dreamer like me, not a rabid hustler.
Not running around, chasing his tail.
Not fretting about the lack of time available to do everything.
Not scratching an itch that never goes away.
Not like me at all.
He took it quite easy, really.
Waited for things to come to him.
If they didn't, he would take it badly.
He would stress.
But he still wouldn't sprint to catch them.

However, dying young, like James Dean, yes. Too young.

Not old enough to think it might really happen to him, not yet.

Not old enough to acknowledge that time could run out.

That he might have missed the boat on some things,

or even that he could still jump on board if he acted quickly.

That he was fallible. That life was fragile.

No chance to age (dis)gracefully,

no time to become the old-timer with all the stories.

True, he will never age the way he feared.

His eyebrows never went completely grey,

despite talking about the looming possibility for forever.

He kept his hair, his figure.

He managed to keep it all at bay way after most others his age.

He was still beautiful.

He knew it, and fought ever harder to cling on to that.

He had to think about having to reinvent himself,

if he wasn't the pretty, moody, enigmatic one anymore.

I watched him battle this, year after year.

Adjust the coordinates, move the goal posts.

I told him he was lucky, I told him it didn't matter anyway.

But he still feared it, the loss of who he had always been.

And then what...?

Pointless worrying. Like most worrying.

Like all worrying.

Something will happen if it will happen.

Worrying about it happening won't make it occur, or stop it from occurring.

It is the thunderbolts that strike out of nowhere that will floor you.

I wish I could have convinced him of that.

I wish he could have worried less, and enjoyed more.

top threes

Blue, silver, white.
Dolphin, snow leopard, arctic fox.
Jeff Beck, Michael Landau, Steve Lukather.
Red wine, gin and tonic, real ale.
California, Scandinavia, France.
Toto, Journey, The Beatles.
Cadbury's fudge, dark orange chocolate, Curly Wurly.
Titanic (!), The Green Mile, Gladiator.
Valley Arts, vintage Strats, Tylers.
Salt and vinegar, Thai sweet chilli, Lay's campesina.
Breaking Bad, Dexter, Six Feet Under.
Steve Perry, Karen Carpenter, Michael McDonald.
Potatoes, tomatoes, garlic.
Rome, Los Angeles, Barcelona.
Michelangelo, Dali, Leonardo da Vinci.
Green Wing, Fast Show, Alan Partridge.
Classic Saab, Porsche, Mustang.
Indian, Thai, Italian.
Spielberg, Clint Eastwood, Ridley Scott.

What maketh the man? Top threes.

Always open to and usually amused by my insistent playing of this game, the answers varied through the years (and I'm not completely sure of the car category, as I glazed when that subject came up – his car friends would know better), but, however annoying it was to be forced into impossibly choosing, I liked the insights it could bring... and however well I knew him, his answers still sometimes surprised me.

My top three of the worst things that have happened to me in my life: losing him, losing him, losing him.

holes

Why do I draw holes in everything?

My mountains always have circular apertures; my bodies too, in unexpected places. Secret universes contain white nothingnesses (which could also be viewed as entities: stars and moons, the polar opposites of nothing). The earth's surface is strewn with sinkholes, waiting; globular matter surrounding a void floats or lies in piles. Trees have spheroid fissures; chess boards have spaces out of which emerges growth of some kind.

Are holes flaws, or are they strengths?

Are they the cracks that allow us to see through the perceived normality into hopeful realms, or do they point to the incompleteness, the fallibility, the melancholy of all things?

Every hole is surrounded by something, and every something has a hole. One does not exist without the other.

Losing someone creates a hole. This is a deficit, a negative, a bad space. Can it ever be turned around? Can the losses we bear one day become fertile ground, able to be seeded and planted with unforeseen positives? Can utter angst at the devastating ripping of our lives' fabric be alchemised into other emotions? Determination, perhaps, to survive, do more than just survive: gratefulness that you and many others are still here and that there are things to be done: acceptance of all our inevitable ends, and so, ultimately, a peacefulness?

Right now, I don't think so. I cannot think so. But I have read enough, and heard enough, and seen enough of the elasticity of human suffering to allow for the possibility.

the day before

It was such a great day.
It sparkled, like the sun on the sea below us.
It was filled, without sounding too cheesy,
with so much love between the two of us, and between friends.
As last days on this earth go, it certainly wasn't the worst.
I suppose going out with a happy bang is preferable to so many other ways.

An invitation for an aperitif with relatives of my lovely landlord. We drove down the hill from my place with S and G, and spent a couple of hours with an adorable couple of people, who seemed happy to show us around their place, and enjoy time with us. We hadn't understood what aperitif meant at 11.30am, and thought it would be a coffee, and if we were lucky a biscuit or two. But it became apparent that we had miscalculated, as cava was brought out, and platters of crackers bearing various kinds of meat. Three out of the four of us being vegetarian meant a lot of apologies, and a lot of food for the one carnivore. And a lot of food slipped surreptitiously to the two expectant dogs, that actually belonged to my landlord and lady, under the table. I remember him, defying the wishes of our hosts, feeding them constantly. I nudged him with my knee, and tried to stop him plying them with titbits, feeling embarrassed, albeit amused, when he was rumbled and told off gently. But he was obstinate, immovable, in such things, and couldn't see the harm in treating the animals to yet more food. He adored those dogs, especially Romeo, a big black Lab who liked to shout at strangers as they approached his territory but soon cuddled up. Well, he adored all dogs, all cats, all animals, and would lie on any bit of dirty ground just to play with them.

A lazy afternoon, a late lunch, the four of us watching the two enormous geckos who balanced precariously on a bush next to the terrace for long minutes, sunning ourselves, chatting endlessly. Intense moments between us, both sad at him leaving in two days, and planning for the next time together.

An evening with other friends, J and J, who were spending a couple of days in Las Negras, finally finding the time to visit and relax in Cabo de Gata, the area I wouldn't stop talking about. They came up to the apartment S and G were renting for the week, which is attached to my landlords' epic house on the hill, bearing liquid gifts and good vibes. We spent many hours together, on this, his last night. We drank gin and tonics, cava, wine. He insisted on cooking up a fine spicy slop with his legendary mash, and force feeding it to our guests who weren't hungry but couldn't say no to his proffered plateful. And it was so good. We covered religion, music, art, the royal family and many other topics in a mixture of Spanish and English, with me translating much of it as fast as I could. We laughed, a lot.

We also, and this is haunting, talked about films, and for some reason a lot seemed to be horror at sea movies. As mentioned before, I like a top three game, and was forcing them to play it, and, as also mentioned, Titanic was his first choice. As always, I scoffed at it, having not really enjoyed it, and feeling it wasn't nearly as good as the hype made out, but he stuck to his guns, saying it was a brilliant film. We moved on to others, the one where day-trippers on a yacht all dive off the side, only to realise that they had forgotten to put the ladder down the side of the very high boat, and that there was no way back up. The one where a party go out scuba diving and two who weren't signed in at the beginning get left behind. Etc.

He wanted me to tell J and J about his spiritual side, his seeing of ghosts, his guides, and his knowing that there was something else, something we would probably never understand. He rarely opened up like that, rarely made himself vulnerable to people he hardly knew, but him doing so is a testament to how well we all bonded that night despite language barriers, and how comfortable he felt with them.

After this, I can't help always thinking about my last night. Worrying that it could be this one. This one, when I'm in a dark, sad place, and not at all enjoying life. Or that one, when boring things are frustrating me and making me petulant. Or the other one, when someone you love is deeply unhappy and you feed off their blues. I agree with the sentiment of living each day as if it were your last, but in theory it is too tiring. To endlessly be conscious of our ever-decreasing days is too depressing. Suffice to say that although I will *never* take anything for granted again, and *never* imagine that something might not go horribly wrong, and *never* be complacent about my own life and that of others around me, I don't want my every waking moment to be consumed by thoughts of my last day, or night. So I had better stop thinking.

soaked soul

7th January 2017

A soaked soul, burned.
Diminished by flame, dried to dust.
Flesh reduced to flecks of DNA, mere particles,
unrecognisable cells.
If they were thrown into the indifferent air,
which ones would restrum the universe,
as his long guitar fingers used to do?
Which ones would lie lazily, as he often did,
content to do nothing much?
Which ones would reluctantly explore,
be drawn down into rabbit holes,
be blown along unfamiliar pathways,
be pulled upwards into treetops?
Which ones would be carried on random winds,
to sting the eye of a stranger,
to cause another to rethink?

A soaked soul, burned.
How could this have ever happened to him, my F?

I stand, naked, on a cliff top, with my back to the drop below. The melancholic breeze whispers in serpents and song, as pines on distant hills watch and wave. I grip the silvery blue urn, unable to decipher its meaning; whose is this, what am I supposed to do with it?

He calls to me, passing on the back of a swooping gull, saying "remember. Remember everything. You were the one, you were my puddle".
I shout back, soundlessly, "and now what do I do?"

the definition of ausencia

I remember clearly, despite the crushing fog that covered me in those first days and weeks, saying to G that, "this will be what defines me." I saw ahead, my future as the-one-that-had-*that*-happen-to-her etched upon me from head to toe and from whisper to whisper. I saw this experience as defining me in the minds of others and altering forever how they treated me; I saw my loss defining how I saw myself, and how I saw my place in the world.

It is early January, and I still feel that I am defined in this way, and will continue to be, in my mind at least. I can't get past the absence of him, of him in my world. The certainty that he, who occupied most of my adult life, would remain a part of it has been shot to pieces. Each piece twitches and sobs; some limp away from me saying, "I told you so, I told you not to trust in anything, ever". Some circle me, hissing, telling me that I will never be happy again. Others have vanished, leaving sweet notes in trees and messages in the damp earth, saying, "but at least you had what many do not", or "as long as you remember him, he is there", or "you will be okay, you have to trust in that; he would want you to be okay".

I could run, hide. Immerse myself in strange lands, where no one knows my story. Reinvent everything, paint myself in bright colours, wear a mask. Cave-dwell, detach from all I know.

But why would I want to turn my back on the circle of those who surround me, in their different ways and from different distances, with support? It is precisely *because* they know my story that they surround me, that they watch over me carefully. And yes, they may define me as the one that needs protection and care for now, but I don't really feel that those who truly know me will define me like that for much longer. They see future stories; they believe, for some reason, in my inner strength (that to me is utterly invisible or even non-existent). They see the absence of him, and some feel it keenly themselves, but they are not defined by it, and so they project me into a new life where I am not defined by it either.

Absence. Ausencia, in Spanish. I was part of an art exhibition in Barcelona called 'Ausencia' seven or eight years ago. All the works were black and white, and touched on the theme of absence; I related to it, and might have even come up with the concept if memory serves. My work for the last ten years has been almost exclusively in black and white, so that part was easy. But now I wonder if I wasn't also referencing my own ausencia, the gap in my day to day life where he wasn't. Our homes were far from each other, and our life dreams never managed to match up or catch up; we lived constantly with absence and with the loss of the other until the next time.

It was a choice; on the face of it, it was *my* choice, leaving London for Spanish climes, and risking losing him in the process. To me it was a choice to experience a new country, a new lifestyle, to move, to learn, to grow, and the adventure was never meant to exclude him, quite the opposite. I had itchy feet, and wanted to live (and study) in a foreign city, and he didn't, and couldn't, and it was as simple as that at first. But as time went on, and as years swung by, and we were still together, and his kids were older, it became clear that it was his choice as well; he chose not to let me go from his life, but he also chose not to join me in my world abroad, when he could have. I was happy in Spain; he wasn't that happy in England, and said so. On the face of it in the past few years, it was more his choice than mine.

I just wish we had had less ausencia now that that is all we have. But I can't start doubting our decisions along the way; I shouldn't question why or how we lived like that now, and have regrets; I shouldn't overanalyse whose choice it was to do this or that. It was how it was. It was a whirl, it changed and was changed, it was reassessed frequently, it was cried over, it frustrated us, it was stopped, it was started again; it was a whirl. A lot of years, whirling. But at its core, and the reason, the only reason, why it didn't fracture and break, was how we felt about each other. How deep that love ran.

Sometimes I try to conjure up the feeling; the feeling I had when we held each other, nuzzled, talked in our own language, laughed, held hands, spooned. I nearly capture it, but even its essence, from a far-off place, makes me hurt too much, and I back off from its memory. Maybe I'll get closer to it one day, and be able to feel it again without dissolving, and remember, and know that it existed. Maybe the presence of that feeling, and not the absence of him, will define me.

where so much is forgotten

Today I play, for fun.

A normal thing, normally.

But a forgotten thing in these days where so much is forgotten.

And too much is remembered, too often.

I play Papa Ping's piano as M, having just arrived in England last night from Paris, plays the guitar.

I sing; I try to remember the lyrics.

We practise our songs that we are going to record in a few days in Manchester at Biglittlebro's studio.

Papa Ping listens next door in the kitchen, and tells us afterwards how much he had enjoyed it, how upbeat it was, how exciting.

In the last two months I have been seated at the piano so much, but it has been soul-searching, note-searching, trying to conjure up something that might do him justice, that could convey all I want to say.

And, obviously, it hasn't been very upbeat.

But this is good.

A rediscovery.

A slipping back, surprisingly effortlessly, into what I did before 30th September 2016.

And what a good feeling it was.

To know it was possible.

burrowing outwards

4th January 2017

The turn of the year a few days ago sent me spiralling down into tunnels of saddened, sodden earth. I could feel the weak winter sun at my back, getting slowly smaller, as grief overwhelmed me anew and I sank. People often say grief comes in waves, then stumble over the end of the sentence, apologising for using that word. But it *is* like that. Something like this, like this loss, like this devastation, comes and goes, strengthens and diminishes. You can try to build a fort out of sand against it, and it will hold out for a while, but it will soon be swept away.

I try to hide these moments inside, if I am staying with a parent or two; I don't want to make their helplessness in the face of this thing that happened to their daughter, and their feelings of powerlessness to take it away, kiss it better, sit me on their knee and sing me a soothing song, any worse. Although they do all, in their own very individual ways, often manage to plaster my grazed shin and calm my tears and distract my mind, I want them to feel I'm getting better, and not upset them further.

So, as now, staying with Papa Ping, I save my spiralling for my bedroom, or my walks. I know I *could* cry in front of him if I wanted to, I know he would be happy to talk and try to help if I started the conversation. But some instinct tells me to play down my down, to strive towards a stable state, an equilibrium that doesn't involve too many dramatic lows.

And sometimes that pays off, sometimes it works; after some secret tunnelling, I find myself moving towards the gentle glow of light again. The oppressive earth that had housed me is left behind, for a while at least. I stand, and shake off its remnants. I drink a coffee with Papa Ping, and we laugh about something or other. The sun shines through the trees at the end of his garden. We look forward to driving to the train station and picking up my friend M, arriving later today, knowing that a different energy is often a true healer. The day passes in a calm way, and the evening brings M, dinner and wine, and, sure enough, the energy in the air and in me is changed. I have burrowed outwards.

misery's varnish

3rd January 2017

Staring at the TV screen,
another universe dancing,
colours I don't recognise, emotions I can't feel glancing
off me, memory cracks, and through the sliver I
glimpse me in those same colours, and shiver
to see this face, my place in the world seeming
fine and right,
more day than night,
and then it slams shut,
my being whirls heavily,
matter breaks my mind, and it really doesn't matter that I
live down this hole, nobody's going to be able to pull me out,
I'd shout if my voice hadn't
frozen in my throat,
I float below this pointless existence,
offering no resistance to the serpents crushing my life,
no rush to save myself with the knife I find in my
hand and slice their grip and cut their overwhelming hold,
my hand's too old,
my grief too cold to fight and
so their blackness shudders on through me.

Huddled in my omnipresent
duvet this descent is daily,
hourly, fractured minutes pass as my
glowering demons shower me with memories,
reasons to be are flailing,
suffocated by these bruising tears that no one hears,
each droplet spears my
locked-up heart and smears its stains
throughout each part of that life through the sliver,

that nearly-forgotten person,
that giver and taker of happy,
that lover of all with wings that flapped,
her robe is lying discarded,
tarnished with misery's varnish and
I can only, tiredly, wonder at
why it all unravelled
and how to sew it back up again.

last words

2nd January 2017

You know when you try desperately to get a dream back? Try to re-enter the world you were in only seconds before, but can't grasp it, can't find your way inside it again?

That's how it is trying to remember the last, short conversation we had, whilst walking down from the car and onto the beach. I know it was something I brought up, and that I wanted to talk about it more with him later, but I simply cannot find it. I just want to know what it was we said, but it is as slippery as those dream fragments that run through my fingers as I grab the morning air.

I'll start walking

1st January 2017

Every day he stayed with me at my place in Las Negras, we would make at least one trip down the hill, either to the village, or further afield, exploring other parts of the natural park, or travelling to wherever I was playing that night. Every time, as I went to turn the car around, he would say, "I'll start walking," and set off down the road. I used to dawdle, taking my time, so he would have to saunter further. It was quite an uncommon sight, him walking. Usually any suggestion of going somewhere on foot rather than driving would be met with an arched eyebrow, and a declaration that walking was rubbish, that that's what cars were for. It always amazed me how he managed to stay slim, given his immense laziness in that department...

He never made it to the bottom of the hill, which had become his goal, although he got quite close once. I always caught up with him before then. Looking out for him as I drove around the curves, seeing him lolloping along, arms swinging jauntily, hair blowing in the breeze, never failed to make me smile.

It's the first day of this new year, 2017. Who knows how many more years I'll have on this planet? Who knows how many more times he would have walked down the hill if he hadn't run into the sea that day? Who knows if he would have ever made it to the bottom before I picked him up?

Keep walking, my non-walker, and I'll catch up with you one day.

(insert word of choice) new year

31st December 2016

I thought Prince was bad enough. And David Bowie.

And too many others.

It's not just from my point of view; it seemed to be the general consensus that 2016 was a terrible year for losing people.

Every time there was a celebrity death, he would text me, writing "deeeeeeaaaads", and I would have to try to guess who it could be.

Little did I think...

Now, when I hear of the passing of yet another, I wait for his text, then cry as I realise he'll never know that they died.

2016. Worst year ever. Subjectively speaking.

Here's to putting it behind me, slowly, gently, cautiously, painfully, however it happens.

Here's to new horizons, as the old ones have been pulverised, shattered, blasted out of existence by his departure, leaving only a flat, stark, barren landscape and a trail of dust in the sky.

Here's to an attempt to move forward, and grab whatever life I have left fiercely, passionately, and not let this destroy the rest of my days.

Here's to trying, at least.

Happy New Year.

in any order

Falling towards a new year.
Stumbling through jagged days.
Tripping over the darkest thoughts.
Falling apart.
Pulling the pieces back together again, in any order.

Slipping on death's ice.
Sliding away from self.
Toppling towers of certainty.
Falling apart.
Pulling the pieces back together again, in any order.

Limping down aching boulevards.
Wilting in my desolate garden.
Missing him too much.
Falling apart.
Pulling the pieces back together again, in any order.

(re)connections

I saw him far away, approaching, running towards me.
Almost in slow motion.
I was so happy to see him;
now we could reconnect,
touch again.
I couldn't wait for him to reach me.
He ran straight past, without looking at me.

And I woke up, drenched in reality.

Later on today I went to visit great friends of his with S and G,
for a post-Christmas drink.
Sitting on the sofa, still not understanding anything, I listened.
I vaguely interacted. I tried to connect.
I drifted off, as is usual these days.
My eyes were drawn to the sideboard.
There he was.
In photo form.
Wearing *exactly* the same outfit as he wore in my dream that morning.

statistically speaking

28th December 2016

372,000 annually worldwide.
Jeff Buckley.
Around 400 in the UK every year.
Natalie Wood.
Around 10 every day in the USA.
Brian Jones.
5000 migrants in the Mediterranean in 2016.
Whitney Houston.
Over 400 in Spain every year.
Percy Shelley.
437 in Spain in 2016.
Virginia Woolf.
Eighty-three in Spain in July 2016.
Alan Kurdî.
Eleven in Andalucía in August 2016.
Ophelia.
One in Las Negras in September 2016.

spiralling

This staircase leads nowhere. Nowhere I want to be, anyway; just an endless, torturous spiralling hell I cannot escape. I climb, using every last remembrance of former strength, round and round, higher and higher, over and over again; each time I hope to see you there at the top, looking down at me, smiling, holding out a warm hand, but I find myself at the bottom once more, cold and exhausted.

An Escher nightmare, an impossible dream. You are never there.

what if?

26th December 2016

What if he had come to see me another time,
instead of that week -
maybe a bit later in the year
when swimming in the sea would not have been so appealing?

What if we had never gone to the sea that day,
but had stayed in the apartment garden,
maybe just dipping an occasional toe into the swimming pool?

What if we had gone to the sea that day,
but he had swum in the other direction
and avoided that wave,
and had come out of the water,
slightly shaken but wearing a relieved grin,
saying, "That was a bit scary, the waves were stronger than they looked"?

What if S had managed to resuscitate him,
like in the movies,
and he had coughed and spluttered,
throwing up endless water,
and just been a little weak for the next few days?

What if the lifeguards who had been there all summer long,
a couple of hundred metres from where it happened,
had not finished the season two weeks earlier?

What if the ambulance helicopter had happened to be in the area
and had not got there too late?

What if this was all a dream,
and he was sitting next to me now,
and I was not writing this?

as we were

It was a difficult decision. Christmas often is. No matter how hard I try to swerve the relentless behemoth that it has become, commercially and emotionally, it is not easy to not care what you do on that 'special' day. Even if you ignore it, you do so self-consciously.

I decided that to be where I was the year before, with Biglittlebro and his family, would be too painful. Much as I wanted, and want, to be near them, the gap where F was on his last December 25th would be too apparent. And I didn't want to cast a dark cloud over what should be a happy moment, knowing I couldn't force merriment. The one before was, he said, his best Christmas ever, and he had already asked Biglittlebro if we could do it all over again. How could I stand it, going through the day noticing every phrase he didn't utter, playing every game he didn't play, hearing every laugh he didn't laugh, eating every mouthful of Christmas dinner he didn't devour, feeling every kiss and squeeze he didn't give me?

There were other, lovely offers, from family and friends, to spend the day with them. But in the end I followed my gut, my heart and my head, and they all told me the same thing: that I had to be with the people I was with when it happened. I think for all three of us it seemed important. Not necessarily to dwell on it, or even talk about it, but to acknowledge it, be there for each other, in our circle. So I travelled down to London to be with S and G. S's mum was also supposed to be there, but at the last moment was too ill to join us, so it really did end up with just us three. As much as I missed seeing her fantastic mum, somehow it was meant to be. And it was the right decision. It was relaxed, easy, and I didn't have to compare it to any other Christmas past. We *did* talk about him, we *did* go over things, we *did* cry. Because we, and only we, were there, it is our shared experience for all time. Bound together in something so terrible it seems unbelievable. We were as we were. Circle of three.

But it was fun too. They made me, and make me, feel better, and utterly supported. Plus there were cats.

missing

Signed, sealed and delivered to G, the piece of art I have been working on for the last two months. 'Missing' has been my therapy, as much as the piano compositions, but in a different way. With the music all my emotions are at the surface, and I feel every note and chord with open wounds. With this drawing I was somehow able to cut off, lose myself in my parallel world that has served me well throughout my life. I never knew where it was headed, but like the album I'm writing, it was for him, and for me. And now it is for G, and it is wonderful to pass it on to someone who might love it as much as I have loved doing it.

23rd December 2016

D B A A D

Cheeecliuut for leeeunch.

Five notes, three words in our language.

One little ditty, repeated every day we saw each other (and ate chocolate after lunch, in case our code doesn't translate so easily).

One phrase that never failed to make us smile.

One group of notes that are now set in musical stone, forming the theme for piece number three.

The original 'song' was such a happy one.

This one is in a minor key, because how could it not be?

And I cry each time I pick out the melody on the piano, wondering how happy can turn to sad so easily.

the final touch

Surrounding swarming, teeming life with still, solemn blackness,
darkness always hovering on the peripheries of springtime,
hemmed in by twilight,
the shadows close in...
but I am protected from them, by my circle.

anti antidepressants

aconite

valerian

rescue remedy

ignatia

nytol herbal

sweet chestnut

ashwagandha

chamomile tea

zopicione

water violet

bromazipam

agrimony

boots sleepeaze

sleepy teas

valium

lavender

arsenicum album

fennel tea

star of Bethlehem

Some of the items on my shopping list...

A few of these things were only taken in the first week or two, when sleep and everything else was impossible.

The rest are ongoing experiments in the quest, nearly three months on, to escape sleepless nights, and to somehow live through trauma-filled days and calm my stricken mind and help my broken heart.

The doctor suggested antidepressants, twice, when I went to ask him for something just to help me sleep. He said the sleeping pills he was loathe to prescribe me – and that I didn't end up taking the second time, they were just a back-up – were more addictive than antidepressants, and that I should consider the latter. I was shocked at how easily they could have been given to me, and determined to fight this, if that is the right phrase, myself. I don't want to numb the pain, disguise the truth; I don't believe it's the way forward. However hideous it is, I am clear that it is something I have to live through, day by day, and that I must feel each and every emotion as they hit, raw and wounding and debilitating and crushing and destructive as their pureness might be. If I don't, if I cloud these feelings by trying to medicate them away, they will still be there, waiting to get me when the drugs stop.

Also – of course I'm depressed, as in sad, as in utterly broken! But there is a clear and precise reason for that, and I am again surprised that pills are seen to be a cover-all for any kind of distress, whether specific or not in its origin.

Meanwhile, I'll keep on shopping for tinctures, hoping to find something that can tip me into dreamland for some blissful hours away from the reality I must be awake for.

pride marches on

20th December 2016

As I pick through possible notes on the piano, working on piece number five, which has turned into something I'm finding hard to actually play, I, as always, think of him. Today I remember him complimenting me, telling other people that I had so much talent, how I could do this and that. It was nice having someone who was proud of me.

We shared a deep, deep respect for each other and our artistically-orientated endeavours. We moved in different ways; he concentrated on one thing, his guitar, and it showed. Countless, endless hours and years honing his skill, and not just that, but countless, endless hours and years studying the technical side as well, something that a lot of musicians disregard. His knowledge of effects, pickups, pedals, amps et al went towards his search for, and finding of, the perfect guitar sound to suit his playing, or a particular gig or recording; *such* a connoisseur, *such* an expert. Me, I spread myself thin, bouncing between music and art and writing and back again, so I'm an expert in nothing, just alright in many things. But he respected that I was creative in lots of different areas, although he used to sigh and say I would never ever be satisfied, that I would always have an itch to scratch, creatively and otherwise. (He was right, unfortunately. But I can't choose just one thing.)

Not easily impressed, it took a few years and a lot of tough love for him to respect my artwork. As I learned, and hopefully improved, and focused, all the criticisms he had levelled at my paintings and drawings became apparent for what they were: encouragement. And then respect. Musically he had always had that for my songwriting, my playing of various instruments, and my sight reading of sheet music. And, with the latest strand I started in earnest just over a year ago, he was my biggest fan; he couldn't wait to read my next short story, and gushed about them, even the 'spoken word' ones as he called them, that flew in a different world to the one in which his brain worked. Coming from someone who rarely read books, it could be seen as a strange compliment; after all, what would he compare my writing to? But it was so warming, even if over the top, when he used words like 'genius', and told everyone about the latest offering. He believed in me, and in that way made me feel special. The feeling that gave me, of someone having my back as I travelled precariously through this world where to be creative and keep at it despite never getting to where you imagined you might get to is a challenging journey, was such a good one. I miss, already, his reading of my as yet unwritten next story, his listening to my latest recording (which will be this piano album I am writing for him), his viewing of my next drawing (which is my therapy as I live through darkened days), and I miss what I will never hear again: his compliments, his total pride in me.

I had his back too, of course. I was there, always, to hear his tales of strivings, of successes and failures, of dreams, and to support him. I believed in him. The world isn't fair, and we know that, and I know it especially now, but I always felt it was a crime that he had never been recognised and transported onto a larger stage as a guitarist. Simply put, he was amazing.

And that pride we had in each other was not just confined to musical or artistic areas. We were proud in other ways too. Proud to walk into a place or down the street together; proud to say this is my chimp. You can never truly know, but I'm pretty sure we both felt the same. I'm still proud. Proud to have been with him and shared so much and loved for so long. Proud that we were proud of each other until the end.

I miss...

I miss waking up to you...

I miss us making our morning sound, 'MMMmmmm'...

I miss being curled around you...

I miss you curling around me, breathing softly, holding me tight...

I miss smelling your smell...

I miss gazing at you, waiting for you to wake up...

I miss feeling you there beside me...

I miss you more than I can ever explain...

another room

He is in another room.
The room next to the one I am in.
I saw him recently, but now I can't see him anymore.
I am with my friend L.
We both know he is going to die.
He knows it too.
I can picture him, there in that other room.
His hair is long; he is wearing a black leather coat.
I wonder what he is thinking about.
We are all waiting for this death that has no particular reason,
that involves no particular illness.
We are not talking.
We don't know how or when it will happen,
though we know it will be soon, probably today.
We don't know why.
We just know.

I wake up before it happens.

swinging

17th December 2016

Filling in the final dots on my drawing, 'Missing'.

I drew the swinging girl feeling just like that; swinging precariously from a branch that might snap at any moment. I cling on tightly, knowing what could floor me, hoping the tree will hold, hurtling through dense air and emptiness, aware of the beasts that hide in the undergrowth and snap at my heels, afraid to stop swinging and touch the ground where the truth lies, afraid I will never come down from this height and will rest forever suspended between horror and unreality.

Swinging between emotions, between despair and confusion and anger and sadness and madness and disbelief and neediness and loneliness and sorrow and ever so occasionally, with the help of these wonderful people who surround me, the lighter, brighter emotions: a glimpse of happiness, a smile, a laugh, a positive thought, a good memory, an inspiring possibility for the future.

I think I will be swinging for a long time. But I hope I will be able to stop one day.

tiny pieces

16th December 2016

I am so cold.

I can't get warm.

My hands are ice,
my feet,
my core,
my nose,
my cheeks,
my hair.

My skin shivers.

My insides contract.

My blood chills.

My mind is frost.

My heart has been cut into tiny pieces and each one is freezing.

yogic triggers

15th December 2016

K, Littlebigbro's partner, suggests we do yoga together. This might help my breathing, or rather, my inability to breathe properly. It is sound advice. I find myself clutching at air all too often, and have done since it happened.

I have been like this before now as well, enclosed in hot, crowded public spaces, or simply enclosed, or occasionally simply hot. A new one is the feeling that I can't swallow food, or that I have something randomly stuck in my throat that won't dislodge, and I won't be able to breathe, and that will be that. An enormous anxiety that envelops some of every day at the moment. Looking in from the logical outside, I can see that it is pretty ridiculous. I can still breathe through my nose, even if this apparent obstacle refuses to go down my throat. But it leads to panic, and the one thing that *does* dislodge is reason. Stir-crazy wheeling of thoughts, a scrambled, frightened head clutching at life believing it is over. Sweating palms, wide eyes, dizziness. I observe myself in this state and am angry that I am being like this. This is not who I want to be. But it takes over.

K and I do some gentle stretching, with me following her lead. Loosening the neck, the shoulders, we stand and move in almost unison. She then lies on the floor on her back, arms outstretched. I feel uneasy, but am not sure why. I get down, and do the same, and am immediately flung back to seeing him swimming in the water, or to be more precise, floating on his back in exactly the same position. At that point, he was fine. Nothing had happened. But what it conjures up, in a rush of intense fear, makes me have to scramble to my feet and take my body away from the memory.

It is incredible how a physical action can trigger an emotional reaction so strongly. These bodies of ours move in mysterious ways.

lost

14th December 2016

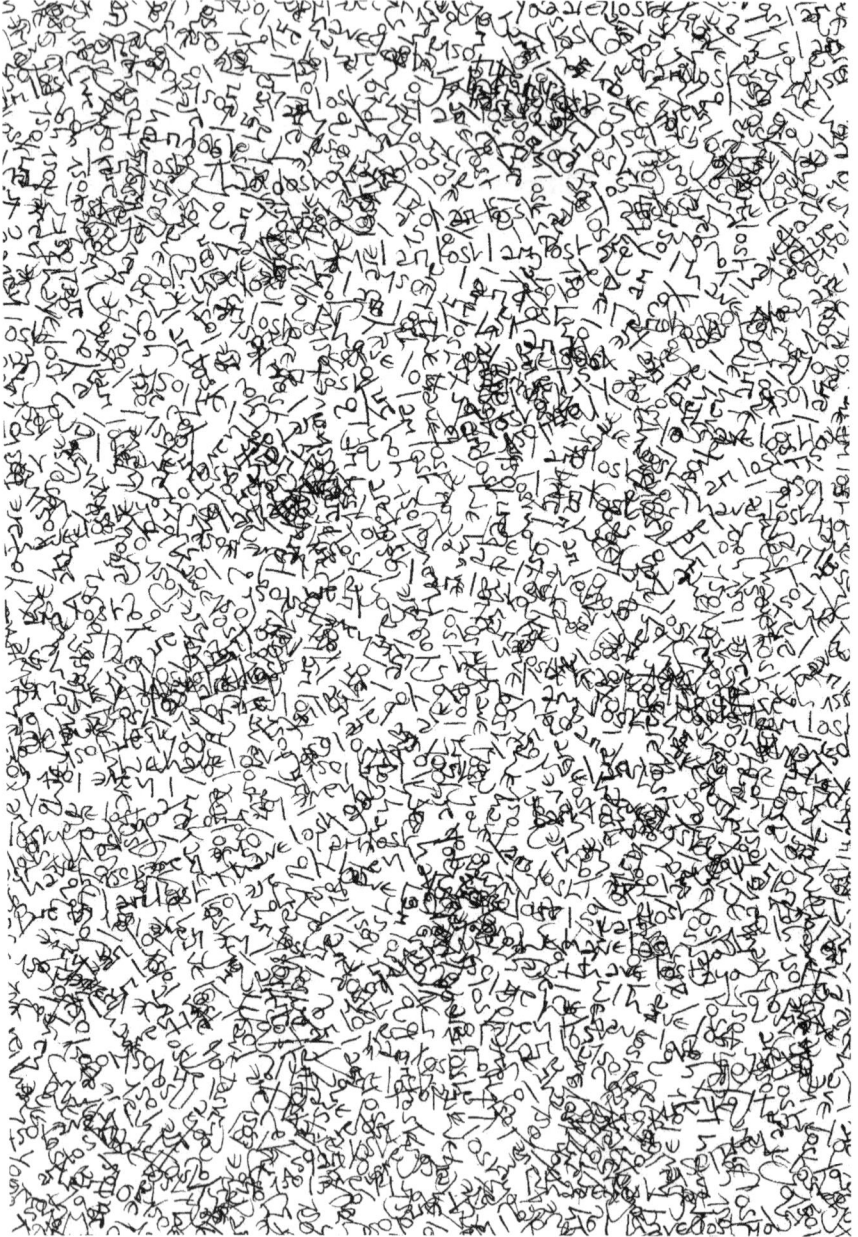

angry heart

I am angry today.
Angry that he has gone.
Angry that I have to live without him.
Angry that it was such a stupid, pointless way to go.
Angry at the waste.
Angry at the sea that took him.
Angry at that wave.
Angry at those without compassion or acknowledgement after it happened.
Angry at the ruin that is me right now.
Angry at the nightmares S, G and I will endure forever.
Angry for everyone else who also loved him.
Angry for his children and their lack of a father.
Angry at those who made parts of this even harder than they already were.
Angry at myself for not fighting that.
Angry at the hole I have to try to live around.
Angry for the loss of our love.
Angry for the sadness that pervades the air.
Angry for the things we will never experience together.
Angry that he will never kiss me again.
Angry at everything.
Angry at life.
Angry at death.

brother sandwich

12th December 2016

I wake up, thrown violently out of a dream, a world in which he still existed. I look around the small room where I nest when at Biglittlebro's house, and see F on the shelves, propped up against the wall, on my bedside table. See us together in past lands and distant moments. I turn all the photos around, hide them hastily, blinking back tears. I can't look at him anymore; I can't have normalised on a bit of paper that which is not. I can't bear to regard his face, the face I adored; I don't understand anything, but I innately know that I have to not see him for a while. Misery shudders through me, and sobs start to flow. My door is open, always, as I am afraid of being in total darkness, and leave the landing light on. Littlebigbro hears me, and rushes in. His huge hug envelops me, as Biglittlebro also arrives. How lucky to have these two amazing beings, my blood, my kin, my loves; how safe and cared for I feel, sandwiched between them. They hold me tight, and I start to calm down, and I half wish that my tears would never dry, just so that they will never leave my side.

dancing girl

Despite the state I find myself in while creating this, there is much joy in this drawing. There is darkness, there are obscure lurkings, maybe, but more than anything it points, I think, to life as it was, as it is for others, as it could be again for me: full, complicated, mysterious, overwhelming yet with possibilities of peacefulness, dense, sensual, beautiful.

I suppose I have built a bank of images I keep coming back to, since I started really getting into art about fourteen, fifteen years ago. Female figures, ladders, other worlds, doorways, trees, fronds, moons, spirals, holes in bodies and in hills, piles of entangled body parts or wormlike creatures, eyes, mountains, spawn, hair, circles, and, more recently, snakes, sinkholes, big cats and chess boards.

And the sitting girl figure, the lonely one.

So is it just a natural reflex, a learned motion, an habitual pattern that makes my pen move? Is it nothing to do with me, and how I am in this moment? If so, the power of art is even stronger than I imagined...

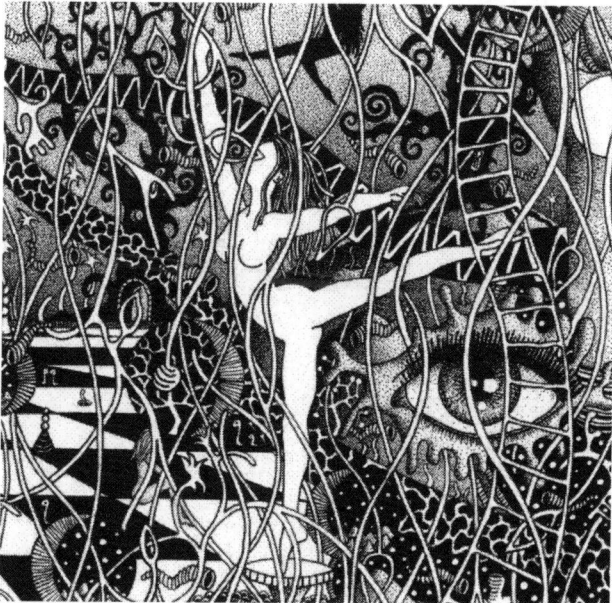

ten minutes

10th December 2016

He died.
It involved a car, a long building.
But suddenly he is back.
We get to spend his last ten minutes together again.
Just ten minutes.
It is very specific.
I am over the moon to see him.
I hold him so tightly, never wanting to let go.
But we both know what will happen.
It will involve a car, a long building.
He wants to pack a lot of things, a lot of clothes, for his journey.
I persuade him not to pack everything,
knowing what will soon transpire,
so that I will be able to hold something of his afterwards,
and inhale him.

I wake up before the ten minutes are up.

doing okay

Recommended by a family friend, who is also a counsellor but knows me and knew him too well to be able to give a formal session, I visit a female counsellor in the village where Mum and Papa Dos live. Papa Dos silently and secretly and sweetly pushes the money for the session into my hand, and escorts me up the steep hill behind their house, both of us huffing and puffing up the tiny path that winds up at an unpleasing angle given my far from hardy state. The air is wet, the views of the distant sliver of sea pushed out of sight by my resistant mind. It feels bleak up there, close to the north-east coast, and I go towards my first ever therapy session with trepidation and uncertainty.

I needn't have worried. S is a lovely, gentle woman, and the hour passes quickly as she asks questions and I babble nervously. She asks about what happened, of course; she asks what I am doing to make myself feel better. I tell her I have started writing some piano pieces that are channelling much of what I am feeling, and are my poem to him, to us. She thinks that is a positive thing to do, and encourages me to keep on with it. Timewise, she is surprised that I am even talking to her, given that it has only been just over a month since the funeral. She says it is still so early, it has happened so recently, that I am probably only just beginning to grasp it, and process it, and that it will take time, so much time. But that on the face of it, from what I have said, and how I am dealing with it, I'm doing okay.

I walk back down the hill, still pushing away the water below, feeling nothing.

I go back to M and PD's home, and pick up where I left off on my drawing, that shelters me from thinking too much, but can't help wondering what okay really means.

how can I...

How can I make the person laying there not him?
How can I force the one not breathing to breathe again?
How can I make those unseeing eyes look at me once more?
How can I make those lifeless limbs hold me tight as they used to do?
How can I erase these images?

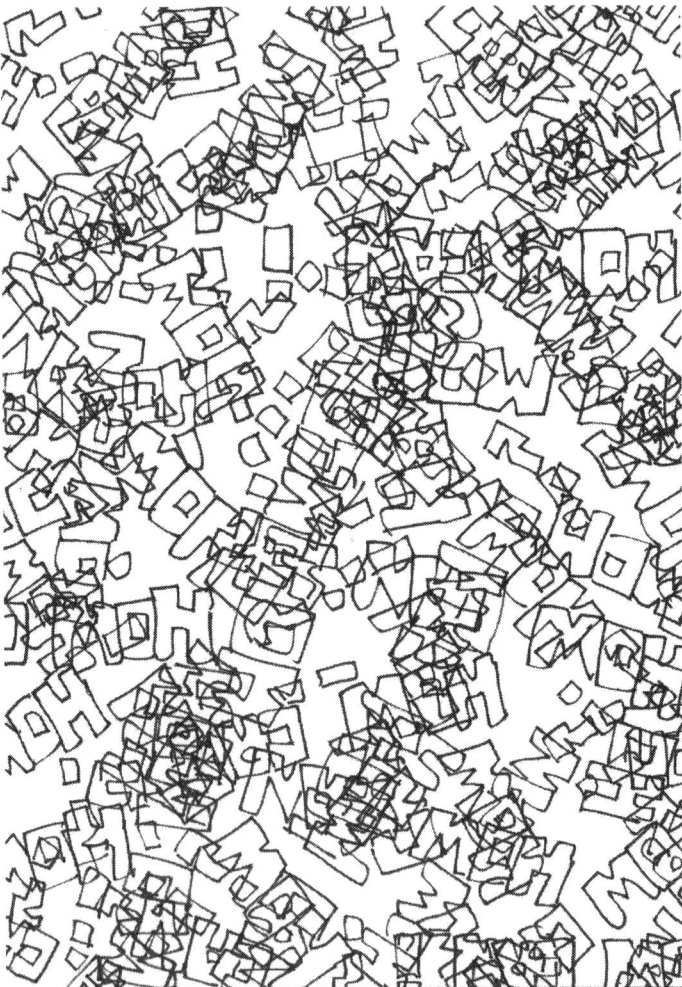

if I write

I love these moments when I have so much to say, in such an intense manner, and life is hitting me between the eyes, hard, and I need to record, to recollect, to understand, to dream, to just talk, and no one is here to listen so I have to type, and I feel more alive than at other times...

I just watched 'Interiores', a film/play about sibling rivalry, artistic angst, madness, written by Woody Allen in 1978; it made me want to write, more than anything... Why?

I haven't written anything of note, and I don't know what I have to say even though I feel composing with words could free me in a different way than with music or art.

But I'm scared to write, to really write.

I have no story that needs telling.

If I write it has to be true, to be real, to be dark, to be beautiful...

Written by me seven years ago.
Now I am writing. I have the story.
It is true. It is real. It is dark.
Beautiful?

internal ticking

6th December 2016

My internal clock has adapted to other people's alarms, other people's habits, other people's insomnias, but most of all to the tick and drip of a soul afraid to sleep, petrified to wake.

My body is trying to repair and care, but my mind will not let it, will not allow its carnal wisdom inside.

Sleep, when it comes, aided by whatever, is shallow, fraught, and drenched in fear of not making it through the night.

Waking brings fresh horror; the few, precious, split seconds of floating ignorance are shattered when the cogs start to turn and blithe dreams begin to dissipate.

I have experienced insomnia in the past, but after midnight, rather than before dawn, although it comes to the same thing in the end, only that the sleep starts and ends prematurely, or that it never deigns to arrive. But this is a whole new level.

The old days of the musician's biorhythm, putting me under in the early hours and dragging me up mid-morning, have fallen so far behind me that if I turn, I can only just make out their carefree speck kicking up dust as it rolls to the bottom of my former universe.

And it is not, in any way, a good thing. I want nothing more than to doze all day, and temporarily shut down, escape this semi-existence, this half-living, this crushed whole.

Now that days begin, in my opinion anyway, stupidly early, that means even more hours without him.

That means even more of my soaked sentience being doused and redoused in monotonous and momentous surges of loss.

That means even more wretched retchings as I imagine his last seconds and choke on seawater of my own making.

That means even more chance of playing with the switch of suffering, the fire of fermenting blackness, and the dead dolls that regard me, blank-faced and menacingly, from the back of the cave I am forced to climb into each day.

My internal ticking tocks me into the longest days and the deepest chasms.

The tick tock of life gone, of life wasted, life behind me, behind him; the tick tock of scared futures, of love running out, of nothing ever catching up with this miserable moment to tap it on the shoulder and say, "wait – it will be better."

Tick tock; it is slipping away. It *has* slipped away. Maybe I have lost what I refused to admit was my everything, and I can't ever make up for that, can't ever move past it, can only listen to the constant tick tock of 'this love will never happen again, he is gone, and you are finished'.

the part I cry on within has disintegrated

5th December 2016

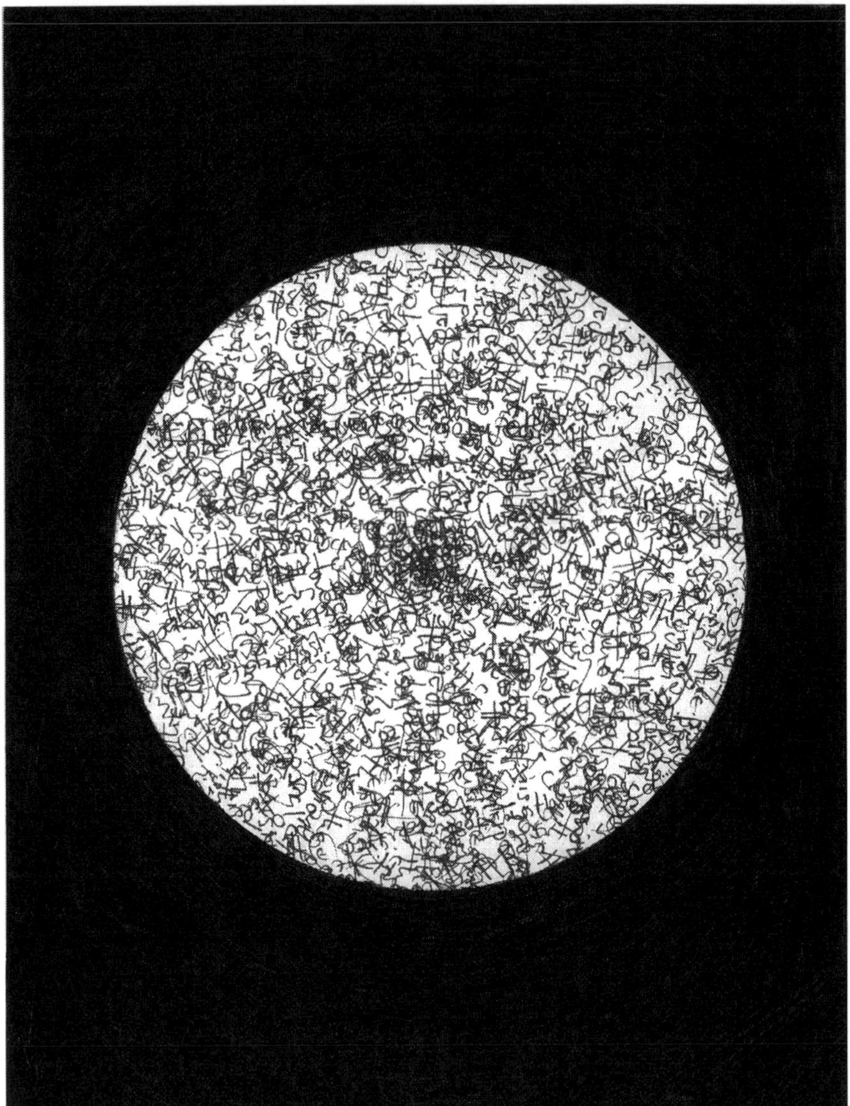

all I can do

4th December 2016

I fall into the worlds I create with a force, as if dropping from a great height, but gently, as if carried downwards on protective wings. These dreamscapes shelter me within their black and white embraces; these known shapes blur the indomitable clarity that flicks my shadow and batters my brain. I grip the fineliner, knowing it holds the key to losing myself, to melting into the innocent membrane separating this dimension from the next, to distancing my memory from this moment.

I am holing up for a week at Mum and Papa Dos's house. They are struggling, I think, with the husk of the daughter they knew, the empty shell that sits, drawing, for hour after silent hour. They try various methods to rebirth the creature I was: playing music as I work, talking of other things, offering their habitual hospitality and love and support – in short, trying to make me feel better. I feel bad as they shuffle around my barely mortal, coiled snake skin, but cannot summon the energy to be as I used to be.

To get through the day, to manage not to choke on fumes of forlorn thoughts, to suffocate on stifling sorrow, or to break completely as has my heart: this is all I can do.

I don't know if you know it

My F.

I am clouding you in poetry (possibly your least favourite art form), illuminating you in random, personal memories, covering you in streams of consciousness, explaining us in musical phrases and strokes of the pen and alliteration.

I am hunting for our essence and our depth and our click and our meaning and our vibe, and without you here I only have myself to consult.

I am reaching out with destroyed neurones and pulverised emotions to touch us, to find us again, to bring you back to me, to shout about you to others, to celebrate what we had, to serenade the sadness now we have not.

I phrase you like this, I rhyme you like that.

It is real, it is not real.

It is my reality now, and perhaps what I write was also yours before, perhaps not.

I feel you as memory, not as spirit beside me.

I feel you as all the things we were, as all the things we could have been.

I feel you, I ache, I yearn, I weep, and I don't know if you know it.

radio silence

2nd December 2016

He was never much of a talker.

But now his silence is deafening.

the black jumper

1st December 2016

His sister has, though it pains her so much,
been looking through his things for me,
to find a couple of items that she could send.
I clothe myself in the black jumper that has just arrived,
the only thing I had asked for.
I touch it, stroke it.
I hold the cuffs in my fists, I pull down on them desperately.
I will never let go.
I inhale him, I feel him.
I sense him.
I am hurled back to the thousands of times he wore it.
Two months after he disappeared,
within these dark weave I am with him again.
I imagine I will wear it every day, every night, to keep him close.

He always said I smelled right.
I always said he did too.
That natural, animal attraction,
an odour that was perfect,
that sense of fitting together.
We had that.
Now I have it alone, for as long as his smell lasts in this black jumper,
fitted dejectedly around me, and then it will disappear forever.

when we

30th November 2016

Today I am being bombarded with memories; small moments that prick, ancient histories that punch.

When we lay in the bed in S's flat and he told me he loved me for the first time...

When we scaled the three hundred steps in the Sagrada Familia cathedral in Barcelona and I got jelly-legged vertigo at the top...

When he presented me with a painting of us spooning, with the words 'you're the one' written on the back...

When we drank cocktails in the revolving restaurant in Times Square and he talked about his brother...

When we gave each other looks that excluded the rest of the world, when we didn't need to speak to know what the other wanted to say...

When we gazed up at the late night sky from the terrace, waiting for the shooting stars that I always seemed to miss...

When we sat, curled up together, binge-watching boxsets of series and devouring films...

When we teamed up as partners for one of the many holiday games with Biglittlebro and his family, and were proud of each other's knowledge, proud to be together...

When we walked down the street together and he reached for my hand...

When we went food shopping together, both petulant at having to do it, both nevertheless amused by the other's hatred of it...

When we lounged on hot Spanish evenings and my niece Mrs Cole asked question after crazy question about the universe, and between his answers and my brother's, her mind was blown, and our sides were aching with laughter...

When we...

When we...

When we...

check the gas

29th November 2016

Check I have my keys, phone, purse.
Check the cooker in case a gas ring has been left on,
knowing no one has cooked on it since last night.
Check the back door is locked.
Check where the cats are, especially Stanley.
Where's Stanley?
Search downstairs, search upstairs. On the bed, of course.
Come downstairs.
Check the gas fire isn't on.
It hasn't been on all day, why would it be?
Check the cooker again.
Check the back door again.
Check I have my keys, phone, purse again.
Reach the front door.
Go back upstairs to check Stanley is still there, was really there.
Come downstairs.
Breathe out heavily, despise myself.
Open the door.
Check Stanley hasn't suddenly materialised at my feet, ready to escape.
Leave.
Shut the door quickly and double lock it.
Pause.
Unlock the door, go back inside, close it behind me.
Check the cooker again.
Walk back to the front door.
Open the door, checking Stanley is nowhere to be seen.
Shut the door quickly and double lock it.
Make myself, force myself to walk.
Leave the house behind.
Go and do whatever it was I had to do in the outside world.

One day as he left the house he heard a voice whisper 'check the gas'.
He went back inside and the gas cooker was on.
The whisper saved him.

Another time it hissed 'check the tyres'.
There was a nail lying on the drive, just where he would have driven over it.
The whisper saved him.

I always wanted a whispering voice that could save me.
I check, and I check, and I check.
Why won't he whisper to me and tell me it's okay?

And where was his whispering saviour that day?
Why didn't it warn him not to go in the sea?
It could have saved him.
It could have saved him.

my move

These chessboards have started appearing in my work. I guess I am about two thirds of the way through this drawing, and as it unfolds before me, unpremeditated, this particular image, completed today, somehow sums up both the art and my life.

Behind the girl is darkness. Before her lie all the possible moves she could make. Escape routes in the form of ladders leading who knows where. Portholes into other realms. Exuberant life forms weaving in front of my eyes, hinting at new growth.

It's not a game where there will be a winner or a loser, this existence. At this moment I feel like a loser, as in I have lost. But in times to come I can make my move. Choose the square to land on, plot the journey after that. Be aware, wary of counterattacks, and the probability of taking an ill-advised route. Have a goal, but be ready to change it.

It's how we all live, isn't it? Imagining we are in control, that we will make it to the other side intact, setting out with purpose and confidence. Making decisions based on other people as well as our own desires, ambitions and needs. Doubting the path we have taken at times; coming across obstacles that block our way and doing our best to jump over them. It's no different for me, only that the odds seem stacked against me right now. Only that the game of life has dealt me a vicious hand. My obstacle, my losing him, is the biggest hurdle I have ever had to leap over; I'm not convinced that I have the strength to do it. But I'm hoping my fiercely competitive streak will prevail at some point, and that I will make my move one day.

secret page

This is my secret page. This is where I am hiding all that I will not write, deep inside the blank paper. All that we shared that I cannot share, all that we did and felt and spoke of in our sealed bubble when no one was watching or listening. Beneath the smooth surface of this secret page live countless moments. We live here.

taking for granted

26th November 2016

We never took 'us' for granted. How could we, given the distance we lived apart, and the lack of domestic routine we had together? I'm glad of it. Never got too bored of each other, and never assumed anything. Never got stale. Never went the way of so many couples who stay together through habit, misplaced loyalty, fear, and grow to detest the very air the other breathes. Always grateful for the time we had together, the bubble time, the us time. Always surprised that we were still together, despite the odds.

It's hard to find any positives within this situation. But that is one.

Of course, I would have liked the chance to take him for granted. I would have liked the chance to get bored of him. I would have liked the chance to take for granted the fact that I could always talk to him, and that he would always be there. I would have liked the chance to watch the attraction wear away, the passion fade, the love change or evaporate, and to have the choice, if that happened, to walk away. But that chance has been taken away from me, and all I can do is try to be happy for our 'thing' that never became stagnant, for the absence of ennui, and the fact that we loved each other as much as ever up until the last moment.

blockage

25th November 2016

Something is stopping
me from imagining his
last moments on earth.

Some immense, metal,
black door slams down in my brain,
won't let me go there.

Blessed prevention;
whatever or whoever
constructed the door

has done the right thing;
it won't help anything to
try to reconstruct

what he might have thought
or felt, if anything, as
it happened so fast.

This blockage, this gate,
this filtering out, this blind
covering that window,

this haze, this cloudy
state that overtakes my mind;
I truly thank it.

papas

Papa Ping phones me every single day, and keeps trying if he doesn't get through.

Papa Dos sends me an email every single day, with thoughts, encouragements, stories.

Both papas are there for me, every single day.

They both know what it is to lose someone.

They are both doing what they can to get me through this, check on me, distract me, reassure me that I am not alone, care for me, show their love.

Best papas ever.

shower power

23rd November 2016

Taking a shower still fills me with dread.

The correlation between a morning douche and what happened is tenuous to say the least, but my mind works overtime to attach fear and panic onto all everyday routines and especially this one. (Obviously when it comes to abnormal, out-of-comfort-zone actions it has a field day.)

I take my phone with me into the bathroom without fail. If there is no one else in the house, which still sends palpitations hurtling through my heart, I need to be able to get hold of someone in case something happens. What, exactly, would that be? The old fear I have of being trapped in the toilet? But I don't lock the door. Slipping in the shower? Falling down the loo? I am ridiculous, repeatedly so, painfully so. Nevertheless, the phone stays.

There is another reason. Distraction. The mere proximity to water, albeit innocuous household water, sends my head spinning, and I see him lying there, lifeless. Every time. Every time I am in the bathroom. Every time the terror creeps and rises until I cannot breathe. I need distraction. Music playing while I brush my teeth or wash my face. For the (excuse the details) few minutes I might be sitting down, I scroll through, searching for a video clip, something inane to take my thoughts away from that beach, from him on it. It almost works. I have perfected a superspeed showering technique, so as not to touch water for too long. And I breathe a sigh of relief each time I am out of it.

The power it holds over me, the cold grip of its banal normality, is something I have to work on. Or maybe it will simply lessen with time, and one day those bathroom visits might not send me flying into hell.

winged freedom

A ladder into the mouth of winged freedom.
Suspended above a life that crowds,
that swarms.
It is all too complex, too confusing, too impossible to navigate.
Oh to fly free, high above it all.
Escape.
Drift aimlessly.
Soar purposefully.
Leave this moment behind.

undone

21st November 2016

Sky pressing in, ground too liquid to hold me,
I am wedged between the two, soaked and crushed,
my breathing shallow, unsure.
Maybe I will crawl out from this claustrophobic void in a while.
For now, nothing in my mind stays for long.

Bursts or drops of acrid clarity,
something close to remembered normality,
last as long as the next swell of incoherent tears
or greyness doused in furious fears,
and the in between is just in between…

The need to turn off the world for a moment is real.
I want to rock in the corner of a white room,
dressed in white,
be fed clear soup
and feel nothing.

handholding

20th November 2016

Interlocking, our
skin brushing, as the air is
swept aside roughly

to make space for our
hands, gripping tightly onto
the other's, breathing

that fleshly sigh, that
bodily understanding
as palpable as

ever it was, the
relief in our fingers and
palms as powerful

as the first time, when
the encountering of this
primal sensation,

the feel that felt right,
pushed away the rest of the
world and its demons.

This, the simplest of
manoeuvres, the most basic
of humanity's

expressions; why did
it feel so good with him? What
made it so perfect?

Now I curse myself
for taking it for granted,
this hand of his that

pulled me to him, that
stretched across metres and moods
and pavements and sheets

and told me I was
part of him, that we belonged,
that this touch was the

sign that signalled the
very essence of us, the
inexplicable

joining of two lives,
that made sense even as it
did not; that through

this connection we
were entwined and that we should
never forget it.

slinky muldoon and sing ping

19th November 2016

He whispered them. He knew them.

He connected with them far more easily, and willingly, than (almost all) humans.

He was never angrier than when one of them had been mistreated, never calmer than when one was under his hands.

Shy creatures approached him, finding their nerve; over-excitable beings were soothed.

He spoke their language, and it never failed to fascinate me.

A couple of months before I knew I was going to move out of my rented place in Órgiva, in the middle of summer over a year ago, a cat started coming around. Incredibly timid, strangely beautiful, too slim, she skulked on my terrace, daring to come a little closer each day. I watched her, admired her, but was aware of the many, many strays that bounced around the roofs at the backs of the houses, and didn't think much about it.

Once he arrived, though, he melted, as I knew he would, and began enticing her across the threshold with treats. We couldn't get near her at first, but I remember the long hours he spent lying on the floor near the food he had left, watching, waiting, and his triumphant beam when she finally ate out of his hand melted *me*.

We called her Slinky Muldoon. During those long, hot weeks she started to nestle in one of the chairs, let us stroke her, and I began to get too attached.

One morning she had company. A little tabby male, obviously hers, crept behind her, not as nervous as she had been, more easily caressed. Pretty soon two chairs were occupied during siesta time, as we gazed at them and smiled. His name was Sing Ping.

My wall I had put up, for no apparent reason except the curtailing of freedom, between me and having pets was being demolished stone by stone, even as I knew I would leave soon, and it was possibly the worst thing that I could do. But his happiness persuaded me; his insistence on letting them be with us whenever we were at home brushed those fears away. Us, Slinky Muldoon and Sing Ping. For the first time we had made a family, however temporary.

When he left in September, back to England for work commitments and his 'normal' life, there I was, not responsible for these animals, not exactly, as they were wild cats, but feeling so, and counting down the days to the end of the month when I would have to say goodbye. I couldn't take them with me, despite how often he (half-)jokingly said I should; I didn't even know where I was headed. Extricating myself from their presence was one of the hardest things I have ever had to do (until now), and was made much worse by the knowledge that I could have prevented the slow slide into falling in love with them; it was, or had been, avoidable pain.

I still think of them often, wondering if they managed to melt someone else in the neighbourhood and install themselves in another home nearby, and if their new names would suit them as much.

I always, laughingly, told him it was his fault. And it was, really. He could never resist an animal; he could never stop himself from coaxing or helping them. I went along with him, knowing it would potentially break my heart, our hearts. How could I not? The time spent with him and them has engraved itself on the banks of my brain as one of 'those' moments; a time of contentment, a warm togetherness, a pure sharing. I can say that no matter what, it was worth the sadness I felt after I packed up and left them behind.

I don't need to write the next sentence.

fading away

18th November 2016

Sometimes I can't remember his face.

The more I try, the more it floats hazily further from me.

How can that be possible?

That face I knew so well, and had looked at, touched, kissed, stroked so many hundreds of thousands of times, is disappearing.

I can remember all its components. His eyes, hazelnut with flecks of green and orange, that he called his 'peanut eyes'. His immaculately groomed eyebrows. His strong, perfect nose. His lips, the bottom one fuller than the top. His teeth, the top ones Hollywood straight, the bottom ones slightly crooked but usually hidden except during his biggest smiles. His Clapton chin and the various forms of topiary he sported upon it through the years, my favourite being the full 'bob' beard. His one frown line between his eyebrows, and the amazing lack of any on his forehead. His little ears, the right one with two silver hoop earrings. His freckles that occasionally showed their cute faces.

All the parts of the puzzle are there.

But I can't seem to fit them together, and make it work or make the pieces into the whole face.

Before photos what happened?

Did people completely lose the images of their loved ones? Apart from those rich enough to have had portraits commissioned, I imagine so. Did they fade, like he is already doing, but completely, without the mountain of paper or screen triggers we have access to now?

Digital images, hanging in dust-kissed frames, line my computer's corridors. Real photos are suspended in albums, calling out to be opened. All he was should cover the walls of my mind's memory, and yet he is being papered over by time.

He is fading away and I don't know how to bring him back.

onto another world

Is he through there?
I gaze endlessly through the window, onto another world.
Serpents slide by me, lilies beckon.
Vines surge, tendrils hang over my head.
I am being watched, but I watch with unparalleled intensity.
I could turn around; climb the flimsy ladder, away from here.
Leave this moment.
Stop looking.
Stop searching.
But the deep night sky holds me in its infinite expanse.
I imagine he is around, in this strange darkness.
Floating, flying, his essence observing me at the window.
Trying to send me messages, trying to console me.
I pretend I can sense him.
For a minute it soothes me.
Then coldness overwhelms me, inside and out, and I go back to bed.

fight it

16th November 2016

You have to fight it every day, K says to me.
Fight the panic.
And it *is* a fight.
Try to breathe properly.
Breathe yogically.
In through the nose for three counts, out through the mouth for four.
Try to be calm.
Try to be logical.
Nothing is happening right now.
Nothing is harming you right now.
It is all in your mind.
Only you can control it.
But control it you can.
Control it you must.

Break it down.
Break it down into small pieces.
What exactly are you panicking about?

Is this PTSD?
Am I still in fight or flight mode?
How long will this last?
For how long will I panic over nothing?
The worst has happened.
What could be worse?

Fight it.
Come on.

a tentative try

15th November 2016

It has been over six weeks. My world has tunnelled inwards, caved in, imploded; life before seems a curious chimera. I have my nests, my guardians. But occasionally I am thinking about after. After this period of burying myself in their arms and lives, at some point I will have to move on, regain something of what was me.

I have an idea that might introduce me back into the still-turning world outside of me. Dipping a tiny toe into something I used to do. I was working a few hours a week, teaching for an online music school. Piano, clarinet, sax, songwriting, music theory, with students all over the world. The couple that run this school, R and P, have been so kind; I didn't know them very well before, but they have become good friends, and were so supportive when it happened. They got other teachers to cover my lessons, and told me to take as long as I needed. The circle grows again, unexpectedly.

I put my thought to them, that maybe I could try with just one student, see if I am capable of normal speech, of reaching back into mists of time and grabbing hold of my enthusiasm for music, sharing it with others again. They thought it was a great idea, and that it was also good to take it slowly. I might not be able to hack it, who knows.

But I did it. The student, Y, is a lovely young woman from Saudi Arabia, and although I had thought I wouldn't go into why I had been away, I found myself answering her question truthfully. Even then, despite her reaction, despite her sympathy and concern, I somehow kept it together. The words are starting to come out by themselves now; it is beginning to become an often-told story that almost doesn't belong to me anymore. Just vowels and consonants. Just sounds.

I am aware that, being self-employed, and in the field of music and art, I am living through this loss in a different way to many, practically speaking. Some people would not have the choice or the chance to not work for weeks and months on end, for fear of losing their jobs. The bills would still need paying; the rent or mortgage would not disappear. Others have children to look after and be strong for, or are carers in other ways. To be able to just be, to be given this time to rediscover my way, is down to my incomparable family, friends old and new, and their endless generosity.

my littlebigbro

We sit watching the first three Harry Potter movies. I have steered clear of them since they first took over the world, being a bit anti things that are overhyped and omnipresent. But he thinks it's time; the perfect kind of thing to hole up and watch, and distract my head. And he's right, after all my protests for endless years. Cosy sofa moments that we have never shared before, having never lived anywhere near the other, and so only meeting up for holiday times in various places.

The reason for all this shared time is the worst. But I'm still happy we have it.

He works doing a graphic design commission for a needy Christian singer, trying not to boil over with frustration at someone else's inept instructions; I sit quietly at the kitchen table drawing, comforted beyond measure to know he's there behind me. I feel safe.

He cooks fabulous meals for us; feasts, no less. He has inherited, like Biglittlebro, and unlike me, Mum's culinary skills, and I'm happy to sample his wares. We chill together, mainly stay at home; it feels peaceful, and healing.

We go for a walk around the water park in Chorlton. The last time I was here, a few weeks ago with Biglittlebro and E, I was very wobbly, and the water element made me freak out, become terror-stricken, descend into airless panic and gulp for oxygen. I wasn't ready. I'm still not comfortable being close to a lake, or passing by the river rapids, but it is less traumatic. And we walk and walk, and talk and talk, and it's so nice to do. And we walk and walk some more, and then get lost. I don't know this area well at all, and he has maybe forgotten it; either way we find ourselves miles from where we thought we were. I feel frightened, even though we are near civilisation, and not in some wilderness, but he, as always, soothes me with his logic and presence. I haven't done so much exercise for a long time; I think we end up walking for about three hours. By the time we make it back I am dropping, and the only thing for it is a piggyback. I feel nine again.

While Biglittlebro and E are away, Littlebigbro has taken so much time out from his normal life in Portugal to babysit me; it's amazing and heart-warming beyond belief. Between him and his girlfriend K they are the comfort blanket I need, the safety net when I, all too frequently, fall; they're the calming ointment, the practical advice-givers, the huge hug whenever it's needed. Circle of love. Thank you forever.

it's not possible

13th November 2016

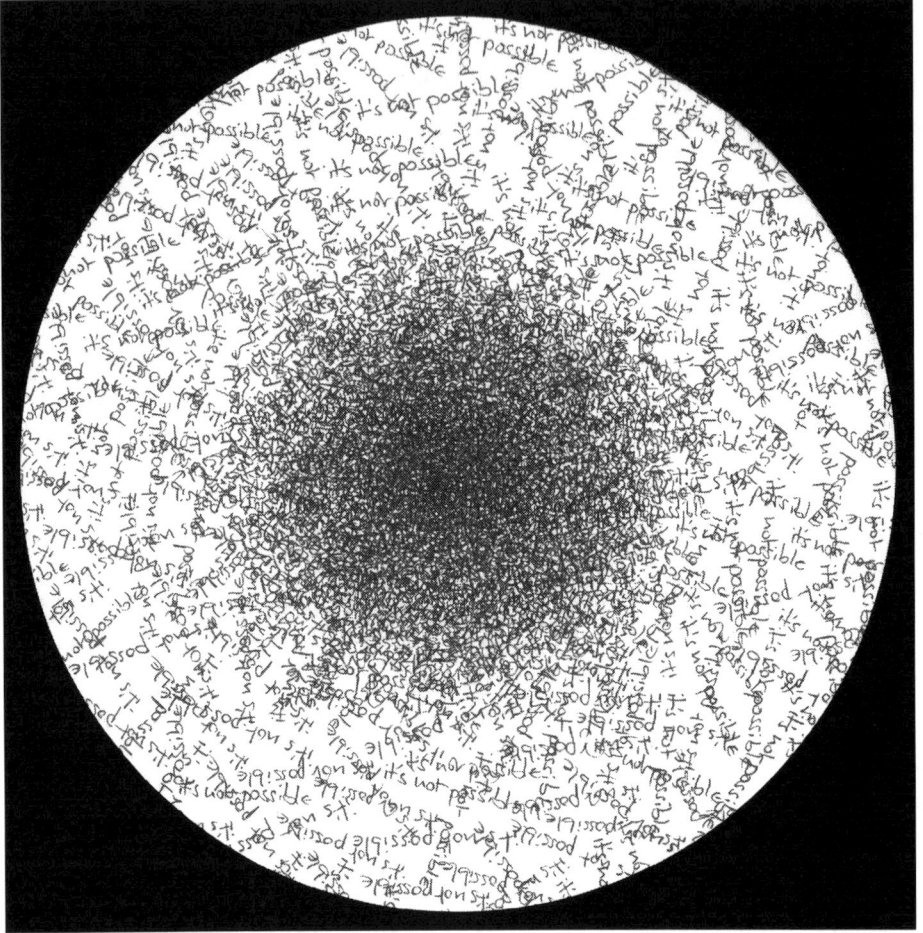

land of the unbrave

12th November 2016

I set my alarm (not that I ever need to these days, having been jolted out of my normal patterns into minimal, tortured sleep, and in recent weeks into slightly more dreamtime but annoyingly early awakenings), to be sure to be up to see Biglittlebro and E off. They are going to America to visit her family for a couple of weeks, a trip that was supposed to happen earlier but was postponed...

I join them downstairs for breakfast and chat and watch them hurtling around, checking they have everything. Littlebigbro and K are poised to drive them to the airport, and they are all about to leave, when the ground suddenly opens up and drops me into a chasm, gasping for air; inside my mind gathering, swarming clouds make my balance faulty, my vision dim. My palms start to sweat, my hands shake. I keep quiet at first, but know I am starting to rock, and go pale; hello panic attack. I tell them I can't swallow, that something is stuck in my throat. Nothing is, as usual. And I really didn't want to act like this just before they leave. I don't know why it's happening. But then I do. I imagine it is partly because I'll be left alone in the house, and I'm scared to be alone right now. And partly because Biglittlebro has been at my side from almost the first day after it happened, steadfastly holding me up, holding me tight, holding me together as it all fell apart. And now he's leaving for two whole weeks and I can't bear it.

They assess the situation, the four of them, these four rocks of mine, and K decides to stay with me and make sure I'm okay, and not alone. I try to get it together, so that I'm not a complete mess as the others drive away, and she makes me calming tea and holds my hand. Biglittlebro promises he will phone often, and send messages, and that he will still be there for me, if not in person.

It works, and K's caring presence smooths me back into almost normality. But I am left shaken by how little it takes to throw me, how precariously I sit astride life, and how afraid I am of the monsters below who thrash and snarl at me, waiting for me to fall.

rainbows in my life again

I received a package today.

A beautiful crystal inside, with a note from Papa Dos:

'so you can have rainbows in your life again'.

One of those small happinesses he is teaching me to hunt.

dreams and canoes and chance

10th November 2016

In my tiny attic room, with the skylight that swung outwards to reveal the fields and river below, the disused quarry on the hill opposite, and the sunsets I loved to gaze at, I spent my teenage years dreaming. Dreaming of many things. But during one, strange period, and I can't remember my age at the time, I had a recurring dream that caused me to wake, shaking and scared, full of utter dread and despair. It was recurring in the sense that the same thing happened, but not in the sense of who it happened to.

For consecutive nights I dreamed that different members of my family drowned. Each time it was so vivid, so real. Not just the event, but the aftermath. The feeling of doom, horror, survivor's guilt, anguish. I never managed to pinpoint what had triggered them. Perhaps it was simply something in a book I read, or a film I watched. But those dreams stayed with me for years.

When I was seventeen I nearly drowned. I was part of a sixth form outdoor activity class, trying out abseiling, rock climbing, orienteering, and then canoeing. I had missed the class where the safety instructions for this were taught, and no one had thought to fill me in. On the day we drove to a village a few miles away, then walked down to the river, it had been raining hard for days. The Tees was swollen, turbulent, but our teacher insisted it would be fine. The water was churningly brown, probably freezing, and I was a little nervous, but clearly not enough to give up the idea and stay on shore.

I climbed inside, the instructor who hadn't instructed fastened on the spray deck, and I pushed off, wobbling into the fast-flowing current. For some reason, the others had all gone ahead, and my only real thought was to try to catch up with them. But it was soon clear that I was powerless, as the boat, despite my best attempts to control it, steered its own course. I hit a particularly large swell, and the canoe turned over. And yes, the water was freezing.

It was at that moment I realised, whilst upside down, my head brushing branches trailing under the water and rocks on the riverbed, that I didn't know how to get out of the spray deck, which was trapping me inside. It felt like a long time in those rapids, thinking I wouldn't make it, but it was probably no more than half a minute in reality. I held my breath, and using every ounce of force managed to wrench off the canvas; holding on to the canoe I surfaced, petrified, panting, beyond relieved, only to bang my head multiple times on other branches that lined the river.

I was lucky. Just a few scrapes and a fear of canoes that lasted until about two years ago, when I had a paddle around a flat sea, very close to the shore, in a friend's kayak, and more or less overcame my phobia. Not for long...

In the following years, *both* my brothers also had close calls in canoes. What does it mean? It could have been any one of us, caught in an innocent moment of recreation, then swept under by Nature's force. Did we survive for any particular reason? Why didn't he?

I suppose it is one of those things that happen more easily than you think. Certainly, since I lost him in this way, I have heard more stories of other similar incidents than I thought possible. You just don't really believe it can happen. Until it does. You just don't really believe you will lose someone. Until you do.

sevens and threes

9th November 2016

Fifteen white cups on the highest shelf. I group them in threes.
Eight glass jars of powders: cinnamon, nutmeg, chocolate and more.
I take one away.
Make the numbers right.
Make the numbers right and he will come back.

Count the tiles. Count the blue tiles.
Fourteen from the wall to the door. Seven, seven. Good.
Eighteen across the room. Seven, seven, three, and take one away.
Make the numbers right.
Make the numbers right and he will come back.

Eleven round tables. Seven, three, and take one away.
Thirty-five wooden chairs. Five groups, yes.
Six people in the coffee shop. And me. Seven. Don't count the girl serving.
Make the numbers right.
Make the numbers right and he will come back.

Bring back the one glass jar, the extra tile, the last round table, and the girl.
Three, and take one away.

Add all the numbers together. One hundred and eight.
108. 8 minus 1. Okay.

Make the numbers right.
Make the numbers right and he will come back.

a letter to you

Dear F,

I am searching for you. I am listening, watching for signs. SD and E both think they have sensed you, that you reached out to them, in dream, in music, in birds. Am I deaf, am I blind? Are you trying, only to be met with an impervious wall? I want nothing more than to get some kind of message from you. Is it because I'm not really sure I believe it possible, is that why you can't get through? Should I believe? I want to. I'm trying; I'm straining with the effort of being open to it. If you search, you will find, I thought. Maybe I have to stop searching, stop trying, and it will come.

Today I was speaking to E and Biglittlebro, and the air thickened. That's the only way I can describe it. It was still, it was heavy, and it made me stop speaking for a moment. I told them what I was feeling; it passed. I tried to stop it drifting away, tried to keep the feeling, whatever it was, even though it slightly unnerved me. That has been the only time something could have been you. Was it?

Although now I am remembering something I had blocked out. Upon arriving at our sanctuary, the holiday cottage belonging to my friends L and C, five days after it happened, L unlocked the door and showed us in, shutting the door behind her. After a short while we went out into the garden, and sat, numb, weighted down with impossible truths. Some time passed. The air was still, completely still. As if the world had momentarily stopped. We went back into the house, and found a large white feather in the corridor. The door had been closed all the time, and as I say there was no wind. Some believe feathers are a sign from a deceased loved one. Was it you?

That's all, though. And given how intertwined we were, there should be more. If you were able to 'get through', surely you would have done it a thousand times. A hundred feathers, a hundred dreams, a hundred thickenings of the air around me, a hundred musical signs, a hundred whispers in my ear, a hundred objects moved, a hundred flickers in the fire flames, a hundred birds surrounding me, a hundred clues in books and films, a hundred messages written in the sky and the raindrops that will not stop falling.

Do you think I would be scared? Is that why you are not showing yourself? Will you ever? Or is it all just wishful thinking in the end?

Can you read this? Can you hear my thoughts? Why have you still not returned to me? That's enough now; it's not funny. You can come back, laugh at the cruel joke you have played, tell me it was a test of my love, that you were never really gone.

I am desperate for us. Desperate to hear your voice, to see you walk in through the door. You know me so well; you know if I will get through this or not. If that is the only message you send, let it be that one: that I will not stay collapsed and broken forever. I don't need a message to say you love me; that I know. That I am sure of. But I am not so sure that I can survive. The last week tore me into too many pieces; the loss of you is too much.

I will keep writing. I love you. Please, please send me a message.

crash and burn

Papa Ping drives B and I to the train station. It feels strange to leave him; it's been an emotionally draining whirl of a week, to say the least, and I wouldn't mind staying still and quiet for a while. But I'm escorting B back down to Manchester and on to the airport, as she has to go back to Barcelona today. I still can't believe she came all this way to be with us all for our weekend events, for me, for him. What an amazing being.

As we stand there, looking up at the neon departure board, I realise I can't actually decipher it. I've noticed this a few times recently; things I could easily read a month ago are blurred nonsense. Can something like this actually make you lose your eyesight?

Hoping it's a temporary glitch, I think I see the word 'delay'. Sure enough, there's a huge problem, which would be fine if B didn't have a plane to catch. She looks very worried, although she tries to be cool. I smile and tell her it's a sign; she should stay.

We wait, and ask official-looking people, and wait. I feel the usual creeping tendrils of trepidation rising inside me, and the open station platform seems to have become closed in. Is it the lack of control I or we have over everything, even catching a train, that sets it in motion? When we finally get onto an alternative train, I have the customary feeling of claustrophobia, and certainty that there will not be enough air. I bemoan, for the umpteenth time, the lack of windows that you can actually open in trains these days, and the fact that you are at the mercy of a system, for both the air con and the doors in between carriages, and let's not even mention the toilet locks, that could fail at any time.

We share a beer, and B does a great job in calming me little by little. We talk much more about her than me, which, as well as answering questions and telling me things I really want to know about her life in my old friend Barcelona, has the added benefit of distraction. With a couple of changes, and another can, we surprisingly make it to the airport in plenty of time. It's so hard to say goodbye; she lingers outside with me longer than she should given the huge transient population of this particular airport, and we have no idea when we'll meet again. I'll miss her enormously.

After she eventually leaves, in a sad flurry, I 'brave' a tram which is mercifully fairly empty, and arrive back at Biglittlebro and E's house. There is no one home; they are both at work until about six, and I console my emptiness with their two adorable cats.

Last week was the second most intense week of my life, the first being the week it happened. I don't know how to act. I don't know what to do. All my, and our, energy has been leading up to last week, to two events a few days apart and worlds apart in terms of feelings and love, but nevertheless basically the same thing; saying goodbye. I can feel my mind, my body, maybe even my soul, untensing, bottoming out, unravelling at a dangerous speed. I know I am going to crash and burn. It's all been too much, simply too much to bear. I fear I might fall beneath the world's surface, never to be seen again, but then my Biglittlebro walks through the door, and gathers me up in his protective arms. We are both beyond exhaustion, both have nothing left. Both spent from the last month of sheer hell. But the key word is 'both'. What we have been through, we have been through together; yes, we have felt it in different ways, as obviously the relationships we had with him were different, but we were together. And without him I might really have fallen down lower than anyone could find me.

betula pendula

I wake after only a couple of hours' sleep, spaced out, head throbbing, nauseous. From the bathroom window, just as it is starting to get light, I am amazed to see snow starting to fall. Lots of it; big, thick flakes that soon cover the courtyard at the back of the hotel where we are staying, and the branches of the trees all around. It is magical, eerie, soothing, and I watch for a very long time. I find out later that DM was also transfixed by the snowflakes, watching from the next room to mine, and Papa Dos too, in a hotel a few miles up the road. The three of us, joined without knowing it, all thinking of him as the white meandered from the dawn sky.

As it starts to ease off, I get dressed and make my way gingerly downstairs, and walk into the function room where we had all gathered the night before.

The candle for his 'shrine', which consisted of a framed photo of the two of us together, a beautiful box containing his necklace and earrings, and seven of his guitar plectrums, all on a purple cloth, was out, but the photo collages we had propped up everywhere still watched me as I drifted through the room. The piano, guitar, microphone and sound system were all still in place, the notes played and sung and the words spoken not so many hours earlier still lingering in the air.

We are going to plant a tree for him today. Just the weather for it. And someone, I don't remember who but I think it was Littlebigbro, as he has been the force behind today's event, had the idea to give us all biodegradable paper, so we could write something and bury it underneath the tree. I take the paper out of my bag, find a pen, and stand by the window, looking up at the sky, still shedding its powdery skin. No words come; how could they? What could I possibly say that could fit on one sheet of paper? It should be an entire book or nothing at all. It should be exquisite poetry. It should say everything I want to say to him, which is impossible. As the flakes continue to spill, my tears start too, and I cry harder and longer than ever in my life. It is a different kind of crying; a release maybe, or a realisation, finally, that he has gone. In any case it doesn't stop, for hours, as I stand, so very alone without him, in that empty room. And as the tears flow, so do words and the pen fills the page with, in the end, a simple message. Because it *is* simple. A simple truth.

We manage to gather ourselves together after breakfast, too early after the night we all had, but we are all still more or less standing. The elegant snow has turned to miserable sleet, and a wind has got up; we exchange looks as we set off in various vehicles to drive the few miles to the village where the tree planters are meeting us. A sodden rendezvous and a sodden trudge across two fields and down a hill. Not many of us are equipped for this, and are soon drenched and freezing. The grass is treacherously slippery, and we cling to it and each other holding our breaths, willing ourselves not to fall.

At the bottom, across from a large, fine oak, is the wooden protective frame, ready for its sapling. Tree number 18, which doesn't please me, unless I subtract the 1 from the 8 to get the requisite 7. (Like Littlebigbro, numbers are important to me; they have to add up to something to do with seven or three, and odd numbers make me warmer than even ones. It's an illness.) And then I remember; it's his birth date! The eighteenth of June. Meant to be.

No one really knows what to do; there isn't a tried and tested protocol for this, not that we would have wanted to follow rules. The only idea put forward before we got here was Biglittlebro's, to play the accordion, or guitar, as the tree went in; rain, however, clearly stopped play. Littlebigbro steps up, and suggests a moment of silence. We all form a soggy semi-circle, arms round each other, and water falls in many directions.

The notes to him are placed in the hole; Littlebigbro and I plant the tiny silver birch, and S and G produce a bagful of daffodil bulbs which we dig in around the base of the tree. It's not a grave, and it is supposed to be a positive thing, but it's all I and we have in terms of a tangible memorial, and therefore feels as if he is there, being planted, being buried. I ache.

I'm not sure how long we stay there, but long enough to beckon in pneumonia if we're not careful, so we leave our betula pendula to fend for itself in this saturated field, and ask the oak to watch over it. We slip and slide back to the cars, and dry off in the local drinking hole, crossing fingers that the harsh winter won't snuff out the life of number eighteen.

There must be something in the human condition that causes extremes of emotions to be countered by their opposite extremes. Newton's third law, perhaps. This day, and yesterday, and last Tuesday, and this whole five weeks and two days, has and have been the worst, saddest, blackest imaginable. But as most of our tree planting group eat lunch at my childhood pub up the dale, the table I'm on dissolves into crying of a different kind. I haven't laughed that much in who knows how long. What made me crack up more than anything were the tears rolling down the cheeks of Papa Ping and B, and the perplexed looks of others who didn't understand why we were all losing it. Impossible to explain what it was, and in any case it didn't matter; it was the ridiculous, temporary relief this laughter brought that we all so very much needed.

the northern gathering

5th November 2016

So it is here.

The day of our evening for him. Not the official funeral. *Our* time for remembering, mourning, celebrating his life, whatever you want to call it.

As soon as we realised, weeks ago, how the other event was going to go, we knew we had to have our own, special, personal moment. And here it is.

Littlebigbro and K take B and I in their hired car from Manchester and deliver us to Papa Ping's. We collect DM, one of F's very best friends, from the station; they knew each other since they were about five, and stayed close all that time. I last saw DM less than a year ago, and the three of us spent many amusing hours together, as we had done often over the years; so hard to believe that will never happen again.

We make our way in the late afternoon up the dale, which is looking very peaceful as the sun drops behind the hills, the November greens gentle and warm, the river Tees snaking silver down below us. He always loved it here, and said he'd happily live in this area. He was especially keen on the idea of owning a convertible and cruising over the fells, on deserted roads winding over epic views, just us and a few sheep.

We reach the High Force Hotel around the same time as Biglittlebro and his family. Photo collages are installed, musical equipment is set up, chairs and tables moved around, food brought and laid out, rooms are investigated, other guests arrive; the preparations are a good distraction for what is churning my stomach, making me feel utterly sick, and giving me exam nerves. I feel like a self-conscious first-time actor stepping onto the stage in front of a packed audience, having no idea of my lines, or even which play it is; I don't know how to be.

I can't describe how moved I was that we were all there together, and by what everyone said, or did. Most people I had seen since it happened, but a few not, so there were those emotional first conversations to be had. Unexpected connections were made, different parts of my life became intertwined. I was sad that a couple of my best friends couldn't make it, to complete the meeting of worlds, but they were there in spirit.

I and we had compiled a playlist of his own tunes and songs he loved, to be played throughout the night, and we put on 'Unearthed' from his album just before we started the evening 'ceremony'. Too much, as always; I didn't think I would lose it so soon into the evening. I don't know when I'll be able to listen to that piece of music, or any of his recordings, again; maybe never.

People had prepared things to say, or read messages and memories sent to me by other friends of his and mine who weren't there; thoughtful, heartrending, beautiful words. Every one hit home in a different way, each person having their own recollections and individual relationships with him, and stories that revealed some of the many sides of his character and life. A few friends who hadn't written anything suddenly got up and just talked, emotionally and from the heart; it was incredibly touching. Some chose music as their way of expressing their feelings, rather than words; Papa Ping played a piece by Chopin, Mrs Cole and Hispeed sang and played two songs, Biglittlebro played his own interpretation of a song from F's album, as did I, without knowing he was going to do that.

It was all, if such a word can be used for such a tragic occasion, perfect. I felt held, cared for, protected by these people I love, as we shared our grief and memories with both tears and laughter, and an enormous pile of food. As the evening slipped into night, and the bar was drained by the hardcore element of the group, the surreal nature of the entire happening became more so the blurrier we became. Although the nucleus of ice inside my heart feels like it will never melt, the roaring fire and most of all the company of many of my favourite people in the universe temporarily thawed it.

I somehow managed to speak. I didn't think I would be able to, and I don't think anyone else did either. But I suppose I felt that this was a once-only occasion, and I wouldn't get another chance; I had so much to voice, so much to convey, so much to express, and in the weeks leading up to this night I had no idea how to condense all that into something I would be able to articulate in a few minutes. A couple of days ago, on a rainy afternoon in Chorlton, I went to a coffee shop and drank my customary, comforting hot chocolate with caramel, and wrote this, which are the words I spoke at our Northern Gathering:

There's an F-shaped hole in my heart, in my soul, in my life. But my mind is full of him. My head is bursting with him. As long as I can remember, I will remember him. As long as memories stay alive, he's still with me.

You all know him as F. But that's what he called me too. A strange mirroring, a comforting sameness, our sharing of a name had evolved over years. And now no one will ever call me by that name again.

We said goodbye so many times. So many thousands of times. We watched each other leave, over and over again, each time a little piece of us crumbling, each time a part of us aching. It was the way our life together was, living two thousand kilometres apart, counting down the days, asking each other, like kids do, how many sleeps until F-time. It was hard, it hurt, but despite it being a crazy way to live a life with someone, we could never let go of each other. So we waited, and we counted the sleeps, and when we saw each other again, the piece of us that had crumbled grew back, and the part that ached stopped aching, and we were back in our bubble. A bubble with our own language, a place where we were happy, relaxed, safe, where we laughed, shared, loved.

If we'd had the chance for a future together, who knows? The bubbles might have grown bigger, the sleeps to count become less, until all the time was F-time. I'll never know.

I can see him, walking away from me at airports, to catch a plane back to London from wherever I was, or getting into his car and driving away. I can see myself leaving him, walking into terminals, boarding trains and buses, pulling away in my car. Every single time the one left behind would wait until the other was out of sight. The other would keep turning around. Each time we would both hold our hands like this, L for I love you:

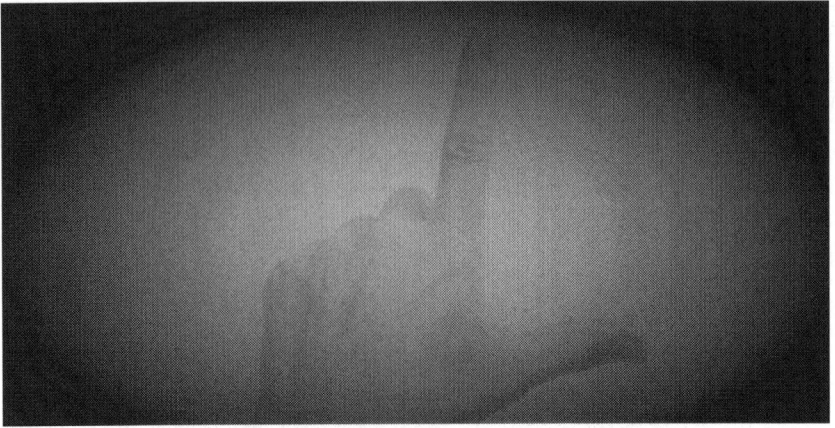

The last thing we would see, for all those goodbyes, was love.

We always thought we'd see each other soon. Get through the sleeps, find each other again, mend our pieces and stop our aches, until the next goodbye. But this time, this goodbye, there are no sleeps to count. Our bubble has flown away. All I can say is that I will hold up my L sign to him every day for the rest of my life, and will love him forever.

cutting and sticking

4th November 2016

Funny how some people can arrive into an already established group, and it's like they have belonged to it forever. B flew in from Barcelona today to join us for the Northern Gathering, and even though she had never met some of the members of my family, she became part of us immediately and effortlessly.

We normally only see each other every year or so, but I saw her a mere three months ago, when she came to visit me in Las Negras in August. She left on the same day as F was arriving, but their flight times were such that only if hers was delayed and his was early would they coincide. Incredibly, hers was delayed, and his was early. They hadn't seen each other for five or six years, but had shared many great Barcelonic moments and were very fond of each other, and this serendipitous rendezvous was such a lovely thing. And now, of course, she is reading into it, as am I. (As I am with so many things.) If her flight had taken off on time and/or his hadn't been early, they would never have got to say hello – or goodbye.

It was one of my favourite things to do for a while in my twenties: making collages. Before the heady days of Photoshop and digital trickery I would painstakingly snip around individual letters to make words for album covers or promotional posters, and cut out images from magazines to make colourful artworks. And here I am again, only this time with help, and pain. I printed hundreds of photos of him: him alone, us together, him with my family and friends, him with animals. There are a few of us, which is just as well as we are running out of time, and we are scissoring out backgrounds, and fitting shapes together, to glue to dozens of carefully cut out circles of cardboard.

We drink wine, we reminisce, we sometimes grow quiet, we mission together to finish. I love the fact that B is here with us. I love that we are all here, joined in this ache-inducing task. There is both an intense sadness and a glow of happy memories coming off the circles, a strange brew. I, and maybe we, feel an almost hypnotic drive to document all these many, many moments;

to say yes, this happened. This was real. He was there. We were there. We existed in that second as the camera clicked; we existed in the space before and after the capture. We all shared time, we occupied locations, we exchanged words, we experienced laughter and knowing glances and party games and music and views and Christmases and walks and jokes and shared birthdays and touristic sights and beauty and histories and problems and holidays and arguments and bars and concerts and hugs and tales. We got to know secrets and habits and longings and pet hates and hidden talents and personality traits and bones that got broken and illnesses that were cured and judgements and musical instruments learned for a while and phobias and favourite songs and films and first crushes and allergies and family quirks and what to say and what not to say and how to smooth and how to inspire conversation and how to make the other happy and childhood fears and lingering anxieties and least favourite smells and foods and long gone pets and how much spice was too much and youthful dreams and bitter disappointments and best TV series and unexpected morals and problems at school and what that scar was from and what was the first clear memory and the last time they got caught in a storm.

All of us sitting here, cutting and sticking, shared bits of life with him. Over years, umpteen years. We had those moments.

They existed.

erase

Today I drew a piano with missing keys. Repeated pairs of black keys, instead of the alternate two and three. It wasn't in any way a conscious thing. But it must be telling me something; I couldn't possibly forget what the instrument looks like. Why are these keys missing?

I'm only just clinging on today. Clinging on to the real, fully-keyed piano in Biglittlebro's house, desperately trying to immerse myself in composing to erase the events of two days ago. It doesn't seem possible, doesn't seem real. Getting off the piano stool, going over to the kitchen table. Trying to erase them. Clinging onto my pen, willing it to move, do something, make something. Erase them. Making yet more fennel tea. Going back to the piano, scribbling some more notes down. Erase. Back to the drawing. Erase.

It doesn't work. Maybe a walk. I decide to shuffle to the nearest park. I leave the house, after the usual triple checking of gas and locks and appliances, feeling uneasy. I walk. I try to force my mind anywhere but there. It doesn't work. I reach the park, about ten minutes away. I have the sudden certainty that the house is on fire. That it will be destroyed, their two cats killed, all their possessions gone. That it is my fault. It will all be my fault. How could they ever forgive me? How could I live with myself? I start running back, as fast as I can, which is not fast these days, I am weak. My mind shudders with what I have done. I look out for belching smoke and flames as I approach their street. There are none. I reach the house; no fire. I let myself in, and weep. And get angry at myself. An overactive imagination is good in terms of creating art and music and wordscapes, but not when you feel incapable of normal function and let a tiny doubt become a fully blown panic attack.

It's too late to put back the missing black piano keys. It's too late to erase two days ago, or what the sea did. But it's not too late to search for a cure for this madness that overtakes me when I am alone. I hope.

deluge

The constrictor knot that held me tightly throughout yesterday, and prevented me from running, is unravelling.

Whatever force inside has kept me able to (more or less) function these past few weeks, through shock and grief and fear and madness and the stress of endlessly waiting for excessively drawn-out bureaucratic procedures and devastation and heartache, is loosening its grip.

Whatever I had inside me, tensely holding everything in, waited for this moment, this 11.15am on November 2nd, exactly twenty-four hours after the service started the day before, and lets go.

It pours out of me, down my body and over my boots, onto the tarmac, gliding out of the service station and skimming around the roundabout, filtering onto the inside lane and then the hard shoulder, following the road back towards London, rolling down a small hill into a field, splashing through muddy grass, joining a tiny stream that leads to a bigger one that feeds into the Thames, and gets swept along in its current towards the estuary: but not to the sea, no, it must never touch the sea, not ever. It retreats, finding secret ways through underwater calm to the riverbank, climbs up and onto the walkway, meanders northwards through the city, finds the motorway and retraces its steps back to where I stand, clutching onto my brothers and E, and stops. Halts, just before it reaches me. I know it is there, but I turn my back on it. Walk away from it. Nestle in my family's arms and pretend it isn't watching my every move. It reminds me of how strong I wasn't, and how strong I won't be able to be. Without it I would have dissolved. Without it I will probably disintegrate, but I don't want to admit that. I want to make it on my own. I want to be able to live, learn to find strength again, without its help.

As we continue the drive back up to Manchester, I feel its heat on the back of the car. As we enter the house, and collapse onto sofas and into thought, it lingers at the front door. Have no fear, it seems to say. I wanted you to feel how it would be without me. I wanted you to want to make it on your own. But I knotted you together to keep you intact for a month, and I can do so again, if you need me to. I am a part of you. I am you.

and it all comes to this

I want to cling to Harry, S's sweet ginger cat, as my eyes slowly and fearfully open, but he is not where he was when I lost consciousness last night, curled near with one paw resting on me, as if he knew. I need his paw now. I need many paws.

We drive in convoy, S and G in one car, and Biglittlebro, Littlebigbro, E and I in the other. I don't remember eating breakfast but I suppose I probably did. We set off too early. I am afraid we might be late, and imagine how terrible it would be to miss it, and everyone goes along with my fears just to appease me. We have to cross the entire city from west to east and beyond, and the London traffic could throw anything in our path. But we arrive over an hour before it will start, so we find a nearby cafe. I spend a lot of the waiting time in the toilet, just staring into the mirror and willing myself not to crumble, not to lose it, not to run screaming. The others have tea and toast, just to do something. We are all pale, exhausted, nervous, nauseous, uncertain what to say or how to act.

I have been to very few funerals in my life. Five, I would say. One, like this, was humanist. They were all surreal. But my idea of this is beyond the darkest imaginings of an alternate, macabre Dali.

A car park... huddles of darkly-clad people... huddles I recognise, others I don't... words spoken to me I can hardly remember... the arrival of my best friends... hugs that block out the sun... a heavy moving towards the chapel... a realisation that there is a hearse parked near the door... that he must be inside... him... actually him... no... a reluctant forward motion by everyone as the time approaches... I gaze at the concrete under my feet... we near the door... a flash of colour to my right: wreaths, one in the shape of a guitar... a quick, surreptitious look again at the hearse, not understanding that the man I loved for so many years could possibly be the one it holds... my knees buckle... my family, my best friends, surround me, prop me up... a sound begins... I can't place it... and then I can... high harmonic notes played on his guitar... by his hands... his recording of the Jeff Beck track 'Where Were You'... they have made me cry before but are now the most haunting notes I have ever heard in my life... I turn, make to run; I can't do this. How can anyone do this...? I am grasped by someone, by many, and whispered to, and ushered along... my legs are going to collapse... we are near the end of the line, the chapel is almost full, and there are not enough seats for us all to sit together... there are three; I am between my wonderful brothers, who take a hand each, lean against me, hold me firmly, look deep into my eyes, assure me I can do it, give me water, tell me to breathe, they are there...

Quiet... a collective intake of breaths... then steps... the steps of four bearers... passing us to our right, they carry him down the aisle... I sense it, rather than feel it; I can't look... can't acknowledge it... I know, because I was told, that the coffin is covered in Marvel comic images, organised by his two oldest best friends, the 'Friends for Life' he wrote an album track for... I hear words, and look up... the funeral celebrant talks... about him, about some of his life... stories... but not our story... I am not a part of this... I detach, and think of someone telling me how, at their brother's funeral, they looked up and a ray of light suddenly streamed into the church, telling her that he was there, that it was alright... I see no ray of light, though I stare long and hard, and look back down at the floor, chanting to myself inside my head... I breathe in through my nose for three counts and out through my mouth for four... I grip my brothers' hands... I stare at our entwined fingers, at the bottle of water, sometimes at their faces, occasionally looking to my sides, occasionally wondering if this is all a dream... Let it be...

His friends for life give a speech and sing a song... other music is played but I don't remember what... more words are uttered... it passes more quickly than I expect... it is over... people start to file out, past the Marvel coffin, past the photo his sister took of him earlier in the year that she has framed and placed there, out into the world beyond this Hades... his mother stands up and announces cheerfully that she has seen him many times, and he was smiling, and that he told her, "I beat you to it, Mum!"... I want nothing more than to see him... to see him smile again...

I can't move for a long time... we are maybe the last to leave the chapel... I am shaking, crying... but still breathing... somebody talks, perhaps even I do... we walk past where he lies... I look the other way, then at the last moment swivel my head, take it all in in less than a second, refuse to let my mind wander too far, block it from imagining what he looks like right now, and what is about to happen to him... that flesh and blood lover of mine... there is no possible way that he will be set on fire, turned to dust... none of this is real...

Random conversations... a diverse collection of lovely people from my life... others I have never met, some of whom reach out to me... I linger, not really knowing why, by the back doors of the building, until it is time to regroup at the wake, in a golf club nearby... my tight group and I migrate to the only space left, a corner of the room by the coffee, and stay there... I am fed, although I cannot eat, and watered, although someone has turned the water into wine... I am kissed and hugged, loved and protected... I watch through glazed eyes how different people behave and interact... but I am not there... L says she wants to know what is going on in my head; where have I gone to in there? I can't answer... I appear to be calm, until after an hour or two I don't... unnerving sounds escape me, that I realise are me weeping, but in a way like never before, in a way I don't recognise... I sink to the ground, and my circle sinks with me... it feels better down there... more in keeping with the emotions flying through the putrid air in this soulless place... more real... if only I could tunnel lower, sink beneath all of this, soar out the other side into a world that hasn't shattered...

The afternoon blurs... I make it through but only just... we are, again, almost the last to leave; I thought I would be the first... the air outside hits me in all of its ferocious reality, and I feel like I will be sick... I sob... I gag... I am in the earth, kneeling in the grass... I am ever so gently pulled up, and settled into the car, where I continue to make those alien sounds almost all the way back, until Biglittlebro, sitting at my side, manages to reach me in the far-off place I have fallen into, his hand and voice finally making it through to my brain... he slowly mollifies me, quietens the screaming of my heart, holds me close...

The evening passes somehow, without me quite noticing it... is he watching us all, as we sit around, eating, sharing stories, breathing endless sighs of relief that it is over, that turn into laughter because they have to...? Can he see me...? Will he ever visit me, as he did his mum...? Will I hear his voice...? Will I see his smile...? Or, as I suspect, is that truly, utterly, the end?

where the streets are paved with memories

I can't swallow this pill. It is only Valerian, a herbal sedative designed to calm. But the idea of not being able to swallow it, and consequently fatally choking on it, is having quite the opposite effect of calm. How will I get through the journey? How will I survive tomorrow?

We are soon to leave for London, to stay with S and G for two nights. I am armed with homeopathic tinctures and black clothes.

Take it with jam, Biglittlebro suggests. He has the same problem with swallowing pills as I do, and that's the only way he can get them down.

To London. My first time in the sprawling city since the last century when F has not been within its borders. The first time I won't see him there. The first time he is not waiting for me. The first time without having our bubble. I will be near to him tomorrow, for an hour or so. But it is not him, not anymore.

"I can't!" My throat has constricted at the mere thought. In full panic mode, practical logic has flown, and good advice will not be heard. I will have to rely on the brandy hidden inside the rescue remedy to slow down my ruined, racing heart.

London. Its air is hung with infinite stories, its sky laden with the residue of moments we shared. The streets are paved with our memories, the ring roads jammed with half-forgotten recollections. Time has accumulated, time will retain. Time stores details in microscopic jars, time locks and unlocks to suit itself.

We leave; I clutch the hand of E during much of the journey. The hours pass. It is a bittersweet rendezvous once we alight in Acton; the last time I saw S and G was in Las Negras, almost a month earlier. The last time I was here, in this flat, F was too.

Time warps, time shifts like uncertain sand. Time belongs to no one, time can be stolen. Time is whatever it wants to be, and we are powerless.

shock and awe

30th October 2016

I am in shock at the elements,
the water that executed and the fire that will erase.

I am in awe at the swiftness at which lives can be taken,
existences extinguished, survivors broken.

I am in shock at how quickly the transition from him being here,
and not, took effect.

I am in awe at the power of nature,
the nature we revere but do not fear enough.

I am in shock that somewhere I felt so peaceful in
could destroy someone I love.

I am in awe of the intense horror in beauty and normality.

I am in shock, now and forever, that he has gone.

pickle

We had nicknames for everyone. That is in addition to the nicknames I already had for certain people, which he would start using too. Almost no one was allowed their given name. It wasn't a planned exercise, just a natural evolving.

My Mama Dos during my entire second decade is at my side. He called her Pickle (a derivation of her Finnish name), which didn't really suit her, but made me laugh.

I instinctively, when the hauntings come, try to find another image to replace them with. Something restful, quiet, slow, and nothing containing any memories of him. People tell me to think of the happy times with him, focus on them, use them to snuff out the demons, but it doesn't work. It makes me feel worse. It makes the gap between him being alive and not being alive even more torturous. I need new images, fresh instances to fly to. And now I have one; over a week ago Pickle was in Manchester, staying nearby, and spending a lot of time with me. We went for coffee and cake, we sat and talked, we shared comfortable silences, or as comfortable as I could be wearing my new suit of grief and agony, and we walked, slowly. We took long minutes to cross the road, both of us intuitively looking the wrong way, European style, for oncoming traffic, and me hesitating forever as I tried to gauge distances and pluck up the courage to move; we smiled at ourselves.

One stroll we took together is my go-to salvation right now. There was something in that hour with her, even as she talked of other, sad things in her life, even as we both shed tears, that draped a much-needed veil of softness, of hushed calm, over my turbulence. The day was bright, the colours vivid. The statuesque, bare trees, beautiful in their nakedness, bowed over us as we took the drying pathways around and through the park, stepping into forlorn gardens that only hinted at future flowerings, weaving around squirrels, small dogs and late-falling leaves. For brief minutes I felt something approximating pleasure, something close to contentment. It lessened the angst to be there with someone who reaches back into long-ago years, into childhood domains, into scattered memories and caring certainties; she knew me then, and she knows me now.

Her wisdom pacifies, and as horrors bite, I will search through the turmoil that is my head for that walk, that sunlight, those unclothed trees, and her spirit.

Last August he and I, along with Biglittlebro and family, went on holiday to Finland. Pickle had booked us a lovely wooden chalet by one of the ubiquitous lakes, where we swam, went boating, had saunas, read, played games, cooked feasts and enjoyed the tranquillity and beauty of that gorgeous country.

I see him, I see him everywhere, but some images flash more than others; some whisper to me more frequently. I suppose it is because Pickle is here in England with us now that I see him so often, peacefully rowing a boat on Lake Saimaa. I wonder what he was thinking about. I hope it was something good. He rowed off by himself a few times; he explored the other side of the lake with Mrs Cole and Hispeed; he took a ride with E. We only went out together once (I was not and am not so comfortable in boats), and were lucky enough to see a seal, which made his day, or possibly year. But the sight of him alone, drifting slowly on the water, manoeuvring around the tiny island we had claimed as our own, the trees and sky enveloping him, somehow stills something within me; yes, it was him and water, but the serenity of the moment soothes me if I concentrate on it hard enough.

We all sit around Papa Ping's kitchen table. All of us, save one. Comparative situations punch hardest. Remember, remember…

When we all, including him, walked through the woods below Papa Ping's house in the Easter air a couple of years ago.

When I was so happy he got to meet Pickle, after talking about her for countless years, and even happier when they hit it off. He, unlike the rest of us, never played the polite small talk game; he was either quiet or to the point, and stood on no kind of ceremony. She appreciated his straight talking, being more like that herself. In Helsinki last year, as we sat in a stylishly low-key coffee house by the port, I watched her amusement at the questions we tiptoed around and he dared to ask, at his comedic bluntness, and their reciprocative warmth.

When we all played, around the same table, games involving inventing, play-acting, and memory. When we laughed together, discovered past gems about each other, toasted the fact that we were there, and that although time had rolled on too quickly, the times we had shared were still very present. Memory. Family. Past. Powerful patterns, emotional ties, habitual phrases. All these bind.

Last summer, as Pickle walked with us to the train station the afternoon we left Finland for our various destinations (London, Malaga, Manchester), it was hard to say goodbye. It had been such a fantastic holiday, and so great to see her again. She told us she would miss us all. We said we would miss her too. He said to her "miss me most".

She never saw him again.

are you still there?

28th October 2016

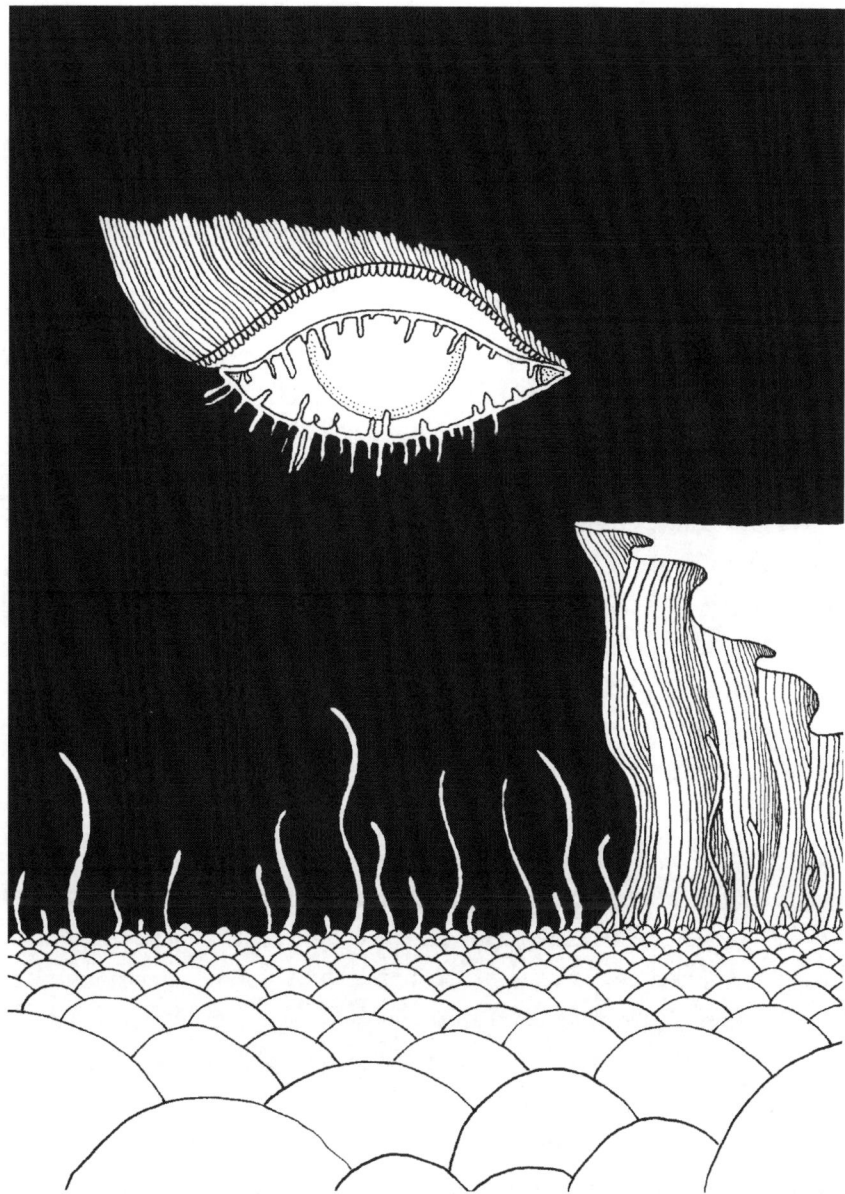

if I don't write it it will be gone

27th October 2016

All the billions of people that live and have ever lived have or had dense lives. However short the life, each second contains the essence of them and their experiences. (Almost) all have myriads of memories, pivotal moments, preferences, dislikes, genetic traits and learned behaviours, reactions and actions, passions and infatuations, brushes with birth and death, accidents, break-ups, intense feelings and passive boredom, acquired facts and skills: and all will be forgotten, sooner or later. Does it matter? Who cares? Who gives a damn how you felt when that person said that to you that day? How unusually small you were aged eleven, what the backs of your knees smell like, what you say to yourself when you wake up, how you could have been that but you are this, that loud noises make you angry, that you were drawing trees when you should have been studying for your maths exam? Who cares that you cringe if you see a slug, that you idolised and copied that person in your teens, that you think you are allergic to wheat but eat toast anyway, that you regret that night, but pretend otherwise? Who will ever know where you were when you first saw a fistfight, or when you tried to do the right thing but you weren't believed? Whose life will be altered by what country you feel an affinity with, even though you have never been there, or why you prefer Magritte to Monet, how you react when criticised, how many minutes it takes you to brush your teeth, or that you wish you had done that when the opportunity came up because it never will again? Who will remember that you spent a long time writing that to them and it hurt that they never replied, or that vodka makes you darker, or why you believe in the power of this but ridicule the power of that, or that you always sleep on your left side first, or why you were crying under the swing when you were five, or that apples make your mouth itch, or which colour calms you, or that you have always been scared of clowns, or that you spent years learning to do something you now have to unlearn, or that summer rains make your stresses dissolve?

Honestly, nobody. Not really. Not unless it affects them. Not unless they really love you.

Do all these miniscule personality tics and tiny deeds and small sufferings and high hopes add up to anything? Yes, in that they matter in the moment, to the person and often those around them, and the moment is all we've got. No, in the grand scheme of things, in this huge universe we find ourselves floating in; they are, we are, insignificant. It all just depends on how you want to view life; as important, or not.

Not many people will care about the details of him. Some will, yes; but things resonate for different people in different ways. We observe the traits of others in the context of our own. And perhaps my list of things I am remembering about him right now is mine and mine only. And so it is even more insular. Others have their own lists, their own encounters, their own perceptions. But my list feels important to me. And if I don't write it, it will be gone. And there will be more, so many more things that I don't recall now. That will reappear throughout the rest of my life, triggered by who knows what. In the days and months to come, as I struggle to understand what has happened, I imagine my mind will be clearer, my memory sharper, my perspective less skewed. I will remember more. But for now, for today, there are certain instances and fragments flowing through my mind.

Who gives a damn about them? Me. It mattered who he was. And I don't want to forget a thing.

Today's list:

him cupping his hands around his mouth to make an owl noise when conversation ran dry...

him cutting into someone else's sentence, with no preamble, no discernible segue, making me lightly wince at his social skills, when he had a newly learned fact to share...

him showing Papa Ping the 'Hendrix chord'...

him calling basic chords in their basic inversions 'Jesus chords'...

me cutting his locks, reluctantly, on the terrace in the sun, and him not letting me, as I giggled, take a photo of his back all covered in hair...

his exasperation at inane online comments referencing his changing hair length rather than the guitar lick he was demonstrating: "I cut it, it grows back, I cut it, it grows back. What's the big deal?"...

his thinking house plants were pointless...
his love for old buildings, things with history, documentaries...

his off-the-cuff fantastic cartoon drawings and bubble writing...
his actual writing, left-handed like me, but with a curious twisted hand position around the pen...

his long baths, his messy showers, his need to be clean...
his many-times-daily brushing of his hair, and his at least bi-annually telling me I was using the wrong hairbrush for mine...

his hatred of smoking, and his informing in no uncertain terms what would happen healthwise to those lighting up in front of him...
his contempt for 'oiks', and white van drivers, and in particular oiky smoking white van drivers...

his tears and dreaminess on the rare occasions he listened to music whose soul moved his...
his dismissal of cheap, badly-played rock as 'dowdy dowdy'; his older-than-his-years antipathy towards rap: "it's just shouting"...

his obsession with his cars, and our names for the different ones over the years: 'swoop', 'pimpmobile', 'custard', to name but a few...
his seizing upon a missing detail, a badly-executed job, a cutting of a corner in something that he was paying for, and steaming over it for days...

the always even temperature of his body: never hot, never cold...
the time it usually took for him to thaw and others to warm to him...

his tasting of and loving roast chestnuts for the first time only a year ago...
his excitement when any bar we visited specialised in mojitos...

his mild dyslexia and his annoyance at himself for it...

his seeing into other ghostly realms and sensing presences...

him calling me his 'puddle', because he got the same, inexplicable, strangely drawn feeling when he saw me as he had got as a small boy staring into one...

His saying "so..." whenever he was about to speak; his calling people 'dude' despite being in the wrong decade, or 'chap' despite not being that posh...

his laughing at my endless lists despite needing them himself...

his amazement at my calendar brain when it came to *his* engagements, and his inability to actually write anything in the Musicians' Union diary he received every year...

the enormously long and loud blowing of his nose, his crazy sneeze...

his shuffling, wobbling, painfully slow 'old man walk' he decided to do on random occasions to make me or us laugh...

his shouting "boys! Get off!" any time he heard that I went out, did a gig, or was anywhere where other males might be...

his saying that he didn't have a choice to be with me or not, it wasn't something he could choose; it just was...

And that is only a fraction of him. A fraction of a life lived. A fraction of a life cut short. A fraction of us. But this fraction matters. This fraction is now recorded.

enclosed and heavy spaces

26th October 2016

I walk, lugging a bigger suitcase than is strictly necessary, into the train station in Manchester. I feel so exhausted. And so anxious. Biglittlebro dropped me here, knowing my fears of being alone right now, alone amongst the throng. This seems like a far bigger journey than it actually is; a couple of hours are morphing into interminable weeks in my mind. Everything hurts. The case pulls on my every muscle; the stairs leading up and over to the platform I need are Everest-like. So weak. I feel tears forming. All things are hurdles. Insurmountable – until I fight back, pathetically, flimsily, but enough to do whatever I have to do.

The train pulls in. I wait for the others to press inside, and finally haul the suitcase up into the carriage. There is nowhere to put it, and it is far too big to go into the luggage racks above the seats. It is hot. How can it be hot? This is late October in England. But I am sweating. I hover, stickily, near the doors, wondering what to do with my case, how to manoeuvre myself into my seat. The air clags. Maybe I can open a window. But no: there are none to open. It starts to rise, the icy yet feverish panic. I am in an enclosed space and I need to run.

A lady with a trolley stuffed with coffees and unhealthy snacks arrives. I mumble something about there being no air, and she kindly tells me I can wait on the platform until the train leaves in a few minutes, that she will let me know when it is about to depart. She must have recognised my wide eyes and nervous tone for what it was.

I breathe outside. Look up at the station ceiling. Watch others passing me by who are almost certainly not panicking, and feel envious. The trolley lady gently calls to me, and says to let her know if I need anything. I reluctantly step back in, push my suitcase as far into the side of the overflowing luggage space as it will go, and take my seat. I am hemmed in by the window, and to my side is not the slimmest person I have ever seen. He has already won the armrest war that I have no inclination to fight, and is on track to fill up the entire table with sugary and salty accoutrements. Opposite is a father and small, I assume, daughter. She looks excited. Being stuck inside a long electric tube obviously enthrals her. I try to think back to when it would have thrilled me too: climb inside my younger skin, my eyes wide with wonder instead of fear. It works enough to bring my breathing back to normal, and to be able to step outside of myself and see the drained, shaky specimen I have become. Come back, seven-year-old me.

Serendipitously, at that moment I receive a text from A, a longtime friend of F's through his regular band. She has been checking on me since it happened, sending messages, organising flowers to be delivered to me by a group of friends, and being unbelievably sweet. It has been surprising, discovering who keeps in constant contact: often the people you least expect and know the least turn out to be incredibly supportive.

She also suffers from claustrophobia, and as I sheepishly explain I'm only on a train for less than two hours, not a long haul flight, and yet I'm feeling so anxious and hemmed in and wrong, she sympathises. She comes up with a phrase that will probably see me through many journeys to come: 'it's a doddle'. It's only a short ride, you can relax, read, look out of the window, you can do it. It's a doddle. The word makes me laugh enough to do it.

Papa Ping and Pickle meet me at the station. He saw me ten days ago or so, and says I look a lot better. I try to act vaguely normal; I *am* genuinely pleased to see them, of course, but I am apprehensive about how I will be, arriving in the town where Ping lives. The last time I was here I was with F. Each first moment in a place containing memories will pierce me, I know.

Sure enough, as we drive past rolling hills and along winding roads under expanded, pearly skies, time's well fills up and spills its everything around me. Tear ducts open their watery gates. I sense him, these views summon him, and all the times we drove around here together splinter my skull. Papa Ping puts his hand on my knee, Pickle on my shoulder from behind. We pass the garage; I see him buying petrol and a Cadbury's fudge. We pass a charity shop where he nearly bought a jacket last year, a pub we drank in once. We cruise past pavements we walked together upon, see the castle ruins he admired, and pull into Ping's cul-de-sac.

As I enter through the door, I see him the last time he arrived here, heaving an even bigger suitcase than I am carrying into the house, greeting Ping, holding me so tightly as we rub noses and kiss. He is there in the kitchen, eating, chatting, looking at his phone, chopping vegetables with me. He is there on the sofa in the living room, eating, chatting, watching TV, playing the guitar. He is outside in the garden, adjacent to the woods, eating, chatting, smiling, walking around with hands clasped behind his back (a posture we called 'chrysanthemum hands'). He is there in the spare bedroom, and my brain shuts down. I cannot imagine him lying here next to me, I just can't. My mind refuses. Too raw, too impossible, too bruising. The double bed, one half empty. The two pillows, one that will be undented in the morning. I will need to consciously, if my refusing mind falters in that regard, push him out of bed and onto the floor and roll him down the stairs and out of the door and into the street and out of the town and far far away to be able to ever sleep here again.

Outlines. Silhouettes. Shadows. Shapes of his spirit. Heavy spaces where he was. Where he should still be. How do I live around them, knowing them, feeling them, weeping for them, remembering his everything?

this is how it feels to be broken

25th October 2016

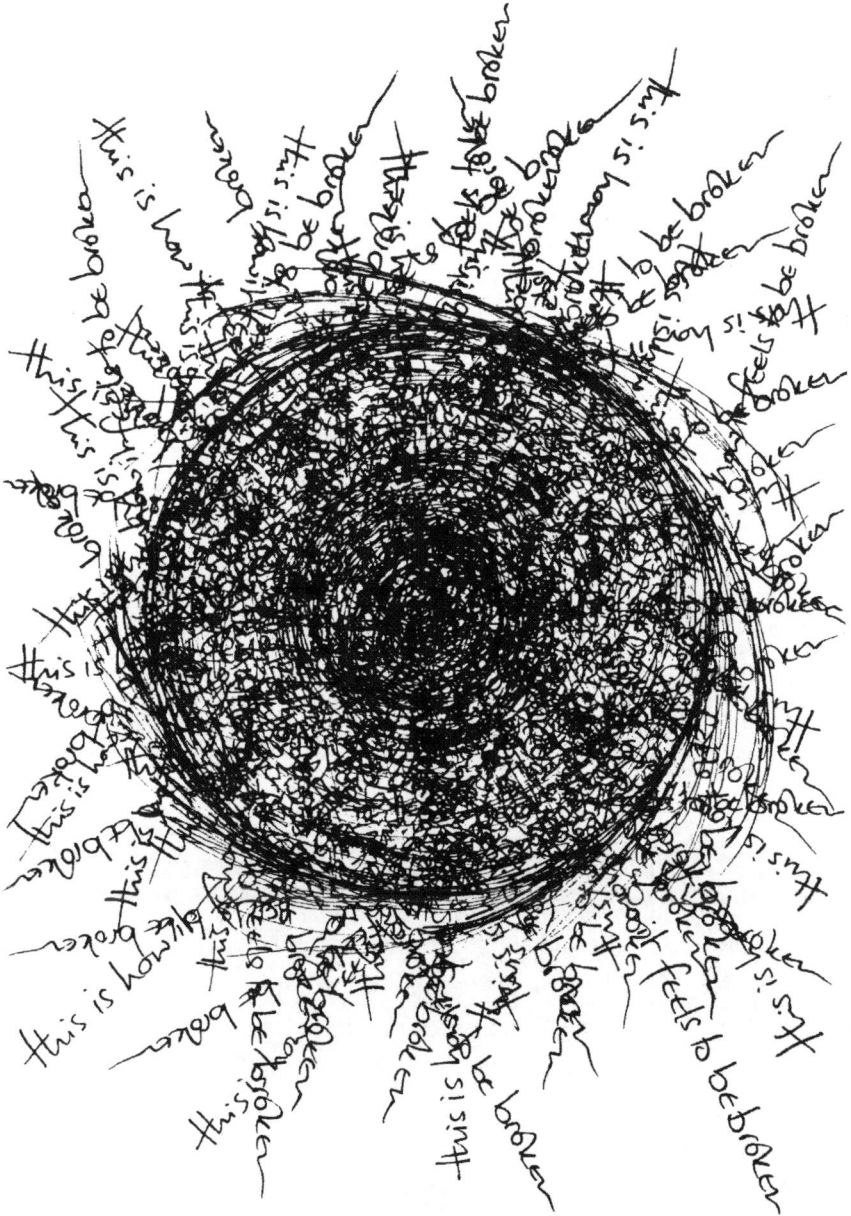

the robin, and other stories

One of my best friends in the world, SD, had got close to him in recent years. They played in the same band, and shared long car journeys, where they discovered their shared traits, and shared views on the world. They understood each other. They called each other 'twin', and pronounced it 'twiiiiiiiiiin'. She is devastated.

She had a dream last night. She was in a pub; he was there with her, and so was I. She kept saying to me, "Can't you see him? He's here." But I couldn't.

SD lives in a house that the two of us visited so many times. I even stayed there for quite a while, about twelve years ago. It is full of memories of us, in good times and not so good. She is moving out of it in the next week or so. Ever since it happened, a robin has appeared every day in the garden. Each day it gets closer. She thinks it is him. She wonders if it will appear in the garden of the house she is moving to.

The other day she was driving, with her little son A in the back. She didn't touch anything, and yet suddenly out of nowhere one of his album tracks started playing. She was unnerved, and started to cry, and had to answer A when he asked why she was so upset. Believing in being honest, even when the truth is painful and hard for a child to comprehend, she told him what had happened. A said, "I will remember him forever in my heart." He is eight.

They were close, they had a connection. She senses things. Maybe she is sensing him; maybe she is getting messages from him in some way, letting her know he is still around. Maybe even letting her know so that she can let me know. She believes that, and I would love it to be true. I only wish that I could believe it, and sense him, and that I could get those messages too.

high jump

23rd October 2016

Whenever we walked somewhere together, and the pavement narrowed to make way for something, a lamppost, or a tree, he would either wait a second to see which way round I would go, and then follow me, or, if we were holding hands, would gently but firmly pull me around the side that he was nearest to. If we were crossing a field or some wasteland, or a car park, or any large space, he made sure to use the same route as me to bypass whatever might otherwise block our way.

Sometimes, before I knew why he was doing that, or even remarked upon it, we would move past the obstruction on opposite sides, and he would have to come back around and pass it on the same side as I had.

Strange behaviour, I thought, once I noticed him doing it; cute, but strange. It took him a long time to be able to tell me why.

Eventually he told me that it was because he didn't want to have to jump all those distances, all the multiplied heights of objects we had walked around on the opposite side to the other, to get to me in the next life.

I always smiled, even laughed at him for doing it.

Now, as I pass lampposts and trees on my slow, unsteady way down sodden streets, the memory of it makes me dissolve into the puddles at my feet, and I wonder how far I will have to jump, should he prove to be right.

creature comforts

22nd October 2016

A package has arrived for me today. It is from L, who had said she was sending something. I open it up eagerly, to find a soft, warm, purple blanket; I wrap myself up in it immediately, and feel loved, and thought about.

These comforts. Small and big. A fluffy blanket from a best friend. Huge hugs. A snoozing cat at my side as I try to sleep, taking over the entire bed. Glasses of milk. Love. Homeopathic tinctures delivered via a friend of a friend of a friend, to help me through. Warm food. Caring messages. My hand being held. My hair being stroked. Smooth, precious stones. Sitting by the fire. 'Soft friends', as we always called soft toys in my family; I have a small monkey and a little leopard from M: two big-eyed unidentifiable but identifiably cute creatures from E, one blue, one white: Biglittlebro's ancient, well-worn teddy: another tiny bear that arrived with flowers from A and friends. I take a different one of these creatures with me around the house each day, and sit in the living room holding them tightly.

I have become a child. I can only cope with the simplest of things, and I just require warmth, food and shelter. I need looking after. Why do we regress in times like these? I am aware of my inability to be normal, and vaguely adult, and aware of my need to cling onto something comforting at all times. I see myself. But I don't care.

I have been sleeping with some of his clothes, and his smell, since I arrived back in England. The bed is not comforting me, and I don't want to linger in it. I prefer to cling to real human beings, not lie next to vacant fabric. I now wonder if filling the bed with his things is filling me with too much extra sorrow. I wake early, too early, and pad around downstairs, waiting for Biglittlebro or E or Hispeed to get up; when they do, I follow them around like a lost kitten. This early rising is, of course, unusual behaviour; I am ordinarily the last to rise, but everything is unusual now.

I make a decision, a huge endeavour. Today I will change the sheets. I will put his clothes somewhere else for a night, and see how I feel. I will not lie in the blackest of energies, as I have been doing. I need to be clean of these first three weeks without him, the worst weeks of my life. The next three weeks will also be hideous. And the three after that. And who knows how many months and years after that. But I feel the need to start again, somehow, rid myself of this malign mantle, and start to sew a new one, thread by thread. To the naked eye it will appear just as dark, equally as heavy, identically drenched in melancholy. But I will know it is less so. Only by a thread, but less so.

limbo

'The body has been released into the funeral parlour'.

What a statement. He's not a body. He is him! He is my F!

And yet, not.

When is it that a person becomes just a body? Or worse, corpse. The second after life departs they are merely that, I suppose. The soul, spirit, essence, whatever you want to call it, has gone elsewhere, leaving the shell. The person you recognise, but without them inside.

The UK coroner is satisfied with the autopsy report from Spain, after causing me to panic unduly when it seemed as though I would have to be interviewed about what happened, and the possibility of a second autopsy was mooted. That wasn't the case in the end; G spoke to the assistant coroner, told him what had happened, and that was that. But I allowed myself to give way to ludicrous visions of court trials and interrogations, as if I had done something wrong. As if I was guilty. As if I did it. As if I killed him.

They call it 'survivor's guilt'. I survived. I am left here in this world, while he is not. We know there is nothing that we could have done. It was an accident. But no matter how many times I try to tell myself that, the slightest thing can make me feel panicky, and my survivor's guilt paints me culpable inside my own mad head.

And we have been in this hellish limbo for three weeks. One week before he was flown back to England, not knowing when the flight would be, and so not being able, Biglittlebro and I, to book our flights back either. Another two waiting for trudging bureaucracy to get on with it. Three weeks without a date for the funeral. Not that I am wishing for that day. But this uncertainty is not helping anything. I am, we are, anxious, unable to do anything, unable to try to settle into our hole-filled lives and learn how to deal with it, unable to start properly grieving, unable to make a date for our own memorial evening, our 'Northern Gathering' (we decided it should be after the funeral; equally as painful, but far more important to me and far more personal, it should be the most recent memory).

In Spain, as in many countries and in many religions, the funeral takes place within forty-eight hours of the passing, and quite often within twenty-four. This would all have been done with, this would have been over; this would not have been something that fills my every waking and unwaking moment with dread, jostling for first position alongside grief.

We are expecting a date any time now. A date we can hang our sadness upon. A date we can attempt to get through. A date we can hope to move past. Let it be soon.

residue

20th October 2016

What is left?
After so many years, what endures?
Our love, yes.

Emotions undulate, swing, consume, dim,
fluctuate, uplift, plummet, disappear.
High passions can wane,
evolving into a less dramatic but no less forceful sentiment.
Jealousy, anger and negativity can devour all that was good,
or translate it into a different language, one that trusts,
is able to calm and be calm.
These things are transformed by time or events,
or simply wear themselves out.
We had much time, and many events, some testing, along the way,
and yet this emotion, our love, never wore out.
And for us, time now stands still.
There are no more events to alter our course.

My feelings could fade,
although that is impossible to imagine at this moment.
Everything fades sooner or later,
in one way or another.
But I instinctively feel that this love, my love for him,
and his for me,
will remain exactly as it is, and as it has always been,
as if it is preserved in a huge, glowing jar that sits next to me at all times.
Over future years I might place it a little further away.
Or it might move itself to the corner of the room,
onto a window ledge,
or the terrace outside.
But always there, always near to me.

Frozen in time,
it will never wane,
or get worn away,
or metamorphose into a different creature.
It is and will forever be what it was.

But what else lingers?

The residue of what happened to him, how it happened.
That nightmare will stay with me for all time.
How could it not?

The residue of our shared history.
Memories, journeys, stories, feelings, happenings,
things that nearly broke us, things that glued.
Photos, drawings, notes, gifts.
Residual objects:
a few of his clothes, a few of his things.
Plectrums, his 'eggs',
that adorned every surface and now appear in surprising places.

The musical residue:
all the songs of mine that he played on,
all the songs of others.
Videos of him online, gigging, teaching, interviewing.
His name on album sleeves, on track credits.
Live recordings of concerts.

The residue of things I learned to live with,
and things I learned to ignore,
and what that changed within me.

The residue of the lessons he taught me,
and the knowledge he imparted.
The wisdom he gained and the insights he gleaned
that now rest in my awareness,
having absorbed them along the way.

The residue of unresolved issues.
Past doubts, rare fights, recent itches.
Can these now be erased?

The residue that others around me carry, of *their* memories, *their* feelings,
which they might share with me from time to time.
Thoughts of him could be carried on the breeze,
sometimes lightly brushing my flesh,
sometimes entering my mind forcefully
and squatting there for the rest of my days.

The moments when he should have made a different decision;
ancient residue is biting me hard right now, during these terrible weeks.
Lacerating years, tearing time backwards,
to the time he should have been transparent, instead of clouding the truth.
The fallout is hurting me unnecessarily, when I am already devastated.
I have become the powerless one, despite being 'the one'.
I don't imagine for a second that he would have wanted it this way.
But his weakness in this regard has left me reeling, and omitted,
and open to rage.

This is residue I can do without,
and am determined to let go.

As for the rest,
the residue of all the good things:
the happy times, the closeness,
the passion, the respect,
the laughs, the sharing, the music,
the understanding, the adoration.
And above all, the love.
This is the emotional residual matter that I will not let go of.

This is our residue.

sis and bro

She was in a bar. Undecided about which beer to drink. He appeared next to her, and let her know which one to choose. Second from the left, an ale with a black handle. He was wearing his black and white shirt. He seemed happy and at peace, but she knew they couldn't speak.

She called him bro, he called her sis. Her arrival into Biglittlebro's life, and consequently our family, around five years ago seemed to coincide with a change in him. Around those close to me (and they remarked upon it over the following years), he was more relaxed, and seemed very content to be a part of the tribe. In previous years perhaps he was more aloof, closed off.

I changed all the time. He fluctuated far less. But this was a definite, if imperceptible at the time, development in him. It's true that over the last decade he had mellowed, softened, become less scratchy, forced himself to keep his mouth shut in musical situations to keep the peace and not be the feather-ruffler, and generally had found a better perspective on life. But I think there is a large possibility that this new openness was enticed out further by E; she brought out the side that he often hid, and she understood it. She was (is) also the partner of one of our fiercely close lion clan. She got him, and he got her; they clicked. They had so many things in common: approaches to life and people, likes and dislikes, songs and bands they loved that Biglittlebro and I laughed at, an affinity with and love for animals, a sociable side but choosily so, exactly the same (unusual) glasses prescription, and a need for privacy and quiet, antisocial moments. An empathetic meeting of souls; her bro thought the world of her, and now she has lost him.

Like SD and her twin. I was warmed by these relatively recent, in the context of our timeline, close bonds between people I had a deep connection with. It was as if they understood why I was with him, and had stayed with him through all the years, despite not living in the same country for half that time. It was as if their bonding with him justified some ancient, difficult moments, and my passive acceptance of what our relationship was not. It was as if they saw through the screen he liked to put up, and opened the heavy door he tried to keep firmly shut, and saw what I saw.

As an aside, my friends in Spain only knew the relaxed version of him. He was different there, lighter, more open. Happier. I felt that there was something about England, and his life there, and the history of his life there, and his interactions with many people, and his career as a guitarist, and, my take on it, his inability to move forward and shift things in his life, that made him act in another way. Was that the real him, or the one in Spain? I'll never know. Like most of us capricious, complex creatures, he was probably both.

Like the captioned line drawings and paintings E does that I adore, she has a take on things, a way with words, and an honesty that captures the essence of things that I am sometimes flailing to express. *Her* essence is one I need so much right now. It will support me, hold me. Despite my plummeting into deep, dark holes and not seeing much of anything, I feel her there. I love being beside her on the sofa, or across the dining table, or knowing she is upstairs, or just out for a while and will be back soon. I am unexpectedly in her life for the time being, a newly-found stray plucked from the street, who waits eagerly for the owners to come home. I am dependent on her, on Biglittlebro, on Littlebigbro and his girlfriend K who arrived recently from their home in Portugal to be here for me as well. Her, their, life moves on, as it must. And they are accommodating me, and, far larger, my pain, into that life. A debt I can never repay. A love I will never forget.

She watched her twin sister go through the same thing as I am going through, exactly a year ago, and is now having to relive those emotions for yet another life taken too soon, and experience the fall-out from that, as well as living with her own grief. She cared for her sister, she is caring for me.

I love knowing that she will be there, and *is* being there, for me when I need her. She will help repair me. She is not blood, but feels like it. My sis too.

hour by hour

18th October 2016

hour 1

I crawl confusedly out of a dream, the first dream I have had of him since it happened. He was still alive but we both knew it was not for long. He was next to me, but we were silent; he didn't look my way. I blearily take in the room around me as my eyes reluctantly widen; I am restabbed, resmashed, returned to reality, and bury myself under the duvet as I remember.

hour 2

I lie in bed for a while once the tears shrivel, trying to read, trying to eliminate the images seeping into my mind from all angles. I fail. I make my way slowly and gingerly downstairs, afraid I will snap in two, where Biglittlebro and E are having breakfast. I want to give them space, to have time alone, but that is at war with my neediness, which wins in the end. They squeeze up the sofa to make room for me, and I feel a little better. We talk; I make my daily scrambled eggs.

hour 3

I shower in fear. I dress in a blur, in black, in the same clothes as for the last few days. I think how ridiculous all these ablutions are, these daily cleanings and polishings; how pointless. I stare in the mirror, wondering who I am now. Do I look as different on the outside as on the inside?

hour 4

I go to the local surgery to find out my blood test results; I am anaemic again. I trudge to the chemist's for my giant pills, the few hundred metres seeming miles. I think fleetingly of going to the juice bar, pretending to be normal, pretending to read the paper, but the idea of being alone makes me curl up inside; I walk to Biglittlebro's studio instead, and hope he is free for a minute.

hour 5

He isn't free but the other studio room with the piano is. This is the second time I have been here, alone with these black and white entities that beckon gently. The first time I played other people's notes. Today I find my own combinations. Something is stirring; a pattern is emerging. I notice my face is wet, but keep pressing the keys. My fingers trace, over and over again, an inversion of the chord of A minor which modifies itself by one note each bar, gradually changing chord and key centre. It leads through harmonies and emotions, and I follow. This is for him.

hour 6

I feel drained. But simultaneously energised. This could be something I do. This could be something that will set in stone and musical form this moment. This could speak in a way that my mouth can't, about how I am feeling. This could be the thing that saves me. I will write an entire album, with him, and us, in mind, and dedicate it to his memory.

hour 7

Lunch with Biglittlebro, back at the house. I tell him my idea. He's happy that I have found the piano again, and that this album idea might help me to heal. He leaves to go back to the studio for the afternoon session, and I decide to try to be by myself for a while. I don't like it. But I get out the large piece of paper I am drawing on, and set to work.

hour 8

I started drawing a couple of days ago, and that brought peace, of a kind. The pen strokes move my mind away from what is dismantling me. They flow up and down, in curves, from left to right. I create a world where nothing like this could ever happen.

hour 9

Stupidly I move towards my laptop, when I should have just stayed glued to my pen. Even more stupidly, I Google his name. Why? Everything that comes up slices me in two, again. I am in so many pieces even the most ardent jigsaw puzzler would be stumped.

hour 10

Saved: Biglittlebro leaves work early, and we get in the van and drive to the airport. Pickle is arriving from Finland. She should have been flying to see me in Spain instead, and almost didn't come here, to England, after it happened, but I am so happy she decided to in the end. Both of us are.

hour 11

A sweet reunion. A new energy. She knew us when we were children and teenagers, when we had different names, different lives; we have changed, but she seems the same: ageless, beautiful, elegant, kind.

hour 12

I walk Pickle to her hotel nearby. The autumn colours frame her; the last rays caress her golden hair. She doesn't hold back in talking about him, asking, empathising. She tells me she has cried every day since her brother died, over a year ago. She is not religious, but spiritual; she believes he is still around. I usually feel evil in the air, not the benign, calming presence that the soul of a loved one might bring, allegedly. Maybe it takes time.

hour 13

Back at the house further reunions, with E and Hispeed. The surroundings are comforting, the ambience between us mellow, relaxed. Cooking and eating combines with catching up and consoling.

hour 14

I, and we, reminisce about our holiday in Finland, with him, a year ago. I remember lying on the wooden jetty with him, looking up at the silver birches. Some of us playing a frantic card game that made him mad. Sweating and giggling in the sauna, and running into the lake, hopping from one flat stone to another, laid out especially, until it was deep enough to swim. Driving along endless roads, with endless trees on both sides. Ambling by the port in Helsinki in the early evening. Visiting a zoo and watching the snow leopard cubs and the red panda for what seemed like hours but was not long enough. It all hurts too much, but the telling of it releases something of the pent-up pain.

hour 15

Biglittlebro walks Pickle back to her lodgings, and we settle into the sofa. I feel a little drunk from the wine we have imbibed; it numbs, it accentuates, in equal measures. The sides of the evening darken, and the lighter shade of grey that I was feeling for the last few hours loses itself in the night's grasp.

hour 16

E takes my hand, as we try to watch some lightweight film or other. None of our hearts are in it, but none of us are ready to sleep. Images flicker and twist, and plot lines trickle. We yawn, I teeter.

hour 17

We go to bed. I try to sleep, but my bed is full of nails. I try to read, but have become blinded. I lie there, swamped in hopelessness.

hour 18

I will never sleep again, it seems. Until I do.

entwined

17th October 2016

What happens now?
Were we so entwined that I cannot root elsewhere,
bud and leaf,
flower and push skywards?
Maybe.
Were we that enmeshed that this despair will never lift?
Probably.
Was my every waking moment filled with him before this?
No.
But it certainly is now.

Entwined through thought,
through touch,
through feelings,
through attraction,
through knowledge,
through words,
through distance,
through music,
through repetition,
through needing,
through years,
through airwaves,
through sharing,
through wanting,
through clarity,
through confusion,
through everything.
Entwined.

And now I am cut loose,
the familiar fronds binding us
and the seasoned knots holding us
and the resilient love filling us
all washed away
by the water that slayed him.

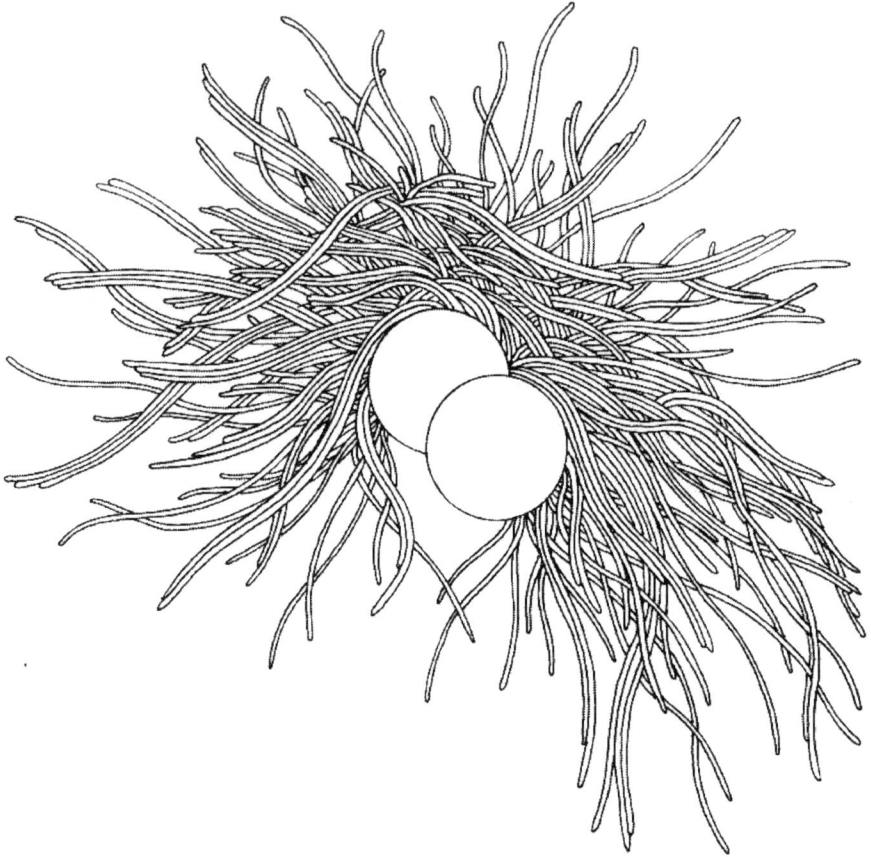

What happens now?

penned prophesy

16th October 2016

I always thought it was a girl. It always *is* a girl. The figures that appear in my etchings are resoundingly female.

This one materialised twice. Once as a detail in a large painting called 'some of this is real' (which I was working on exactly seven years ago), and again as a separate drawing a little later. I 'liked' the image, dark as it is. I called it 'too many to fight', which left it open to interpretation.

Now I am looking with fresh, though wretched, clouded eyes. It is not just dark, it is positively eerie.

The figure is not very feminine, in fact. Quite androgynous. The hair is the same length as his was that day.

What made me draw this, twice? Is this what they call a premonition? I am feeling utterly spooked.

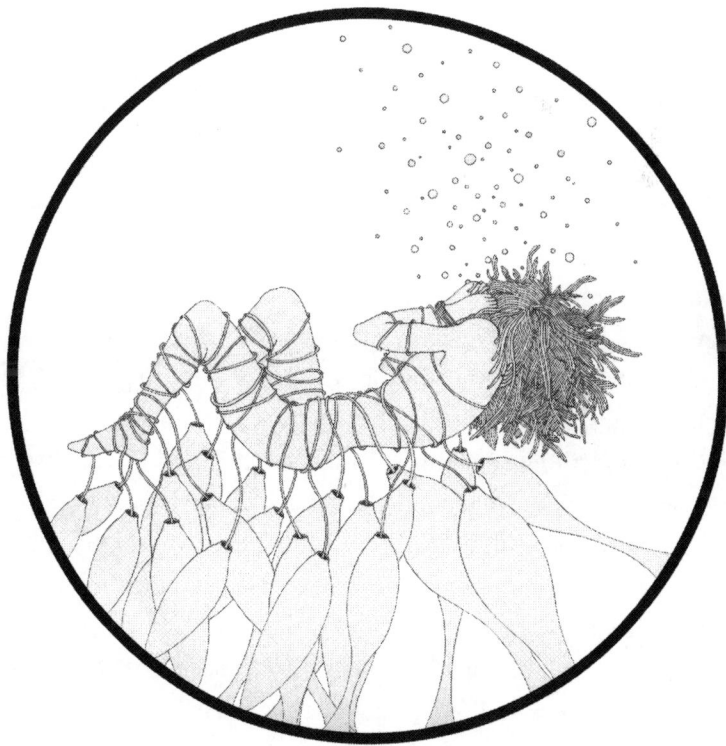

the creators

"We haven't done this since I was eight," I manage to force out, in a quarter-hearted attempt to be jocular. They look confused. "Us, sitting at a table, eating a meal together." "Oh. True." Small chuckles.

Not strictly true. There have been times in recent years when food has been consumed in this company, but always with others around. And to be completely accurate, I should have said, "Since I was two," before Biglittlebro came along, for it to be just us three. Either way, this momentous occasion seems to be something only I have thought about in those terms. But thought about it I have.

I am eating lunch with my parents in Biglittlebro and E's house in Manchester; the others are out at a wedding, so it is just us. Papa Ping has driven down for the day, Mum has been here since Wednesday. There is something so primal, so basic, so natural, about my parents, no matter what has happened in the interim between my being two years old, or eight, or whatever, coming to be with me now. It is probably a bit awkward for them, but they actually seem fine; I'm the one feeling uncomfortable, and I'm not sure why. Maybe it is the expectation of seeing them under these circumstances, and my worries about how to act; barring times of serious illness and family deaths, all other times with them since I left home have been happy, holiday times, where year by year our relationships developed in invisible increments from the parent-child dynamic to what it is now.

Or what it was. I am unsure about who I have become and who I will be from now on, and whether or not my changedness will alter my rapport with the rest of the world. I hope not, or, if it does, I hope it is somehow for the better.

Either way, everything is strange. I don't want them to feel bad, or ill at ease, and as they talk of weather, and old mutual friends and acquaintances, and changes in the area where they used to live together, I am relieved that there is no tension at all. At the same time, too much talk that talks its way around the space where he used to be makes me lose my mind. How can I tell them that, without causing upset? They are both there for me, specifically, and have made journeys to come and show their caring and support. Mum had a particularly convoluted and protracted expedition; she doesn't drive anymore, so has to take at least a hundred buses across the country to get here. I appreciate that more than I can say, and adore them both.

I am struggling with the small talk and the lack of reality checks, and the reason they are here never being alluded to, but I know it is out of love, and not wanting to upset me. I suppose that when something consumes you so utterly you cannot believe it does not consume those close to you equally, or that it will not be the only subject to talk about.

I am learning that people show compassion in different ways, and not always the ways that you expect. That how I would behave is not how others necessarily behave. And that everyone deals with things in the only way they can, whichever way that happens to be. Some are there in practical ways, helping to oil the cogs of existence and being a capable, dependable force. Others send messages, being unable to be there in person, or unable to express what they want to say eye to eye. Some are tactile, some not. Some check up on me frequently, some give me space. Some are happy to be quiet with me, and let things go their own way; others seek to distract, remind me of the better things in life through their stories or laughter. It's a good lesson, I think, and one I will probably appreciate more once a lot of time has passed.

How can my parents, who are not people who wail and beat their chests in times of sadness, suddenly become people they are not; more to the point, why should they? *I* am not even wailing or beating, and instead mainly retreat inside myself, closed off from the outside world, to deal with it (or not) there. I assume they are doing the same, and that also they want to be strong for me. They can see, hear and feel the despair and weakness in me and the destruction that this has wreaked; what goes through their minds when they see their firstborn like this?

In the afternoon I take a slow walk with Papa Ping, just around the block, which is far enough for me. He asks and I tell him more specifically what happened, and have to sit down on the brick wall surrounding a flower bed, overcome with dizziness, and a surge of nauseous disbelief. He holds my hand, and talks about his late wife, his consequent grieving, and the possibility of counselling for me. The subject matter is horrendous, but I am glad that he is going there and that we can finally talk about it all face to face.

Biglittlebro calls in the late afternoon. It is the first time he will be away from me for the night since he flew out to Spain soon after it happened. Two incredibly intense weeks at my side; I'm glad he gets some time off, to not inhabit this cheerless chasm with me, and be instead with E and friends at a happy occasion. It feels like a limb has been cut off, in my incredibly needy state, but he sews it back on with calming thread, and I will see him tomorrow.

In the early evening the three of us go out to eat. Papa Ping drives, even though it is not far; I am exhausted, and Mum finds walking painful at the moment. We spend an almost funny amount of time in the car park, trying to work out the ticket machine, and find the right change. I fleetingly imagine them still being together, which is difficult to do, so many decades having passed, and so many changes to them having occurred: but it is an interesting passing thought.

Inside the restaurant we are seated at a corner table. The walls are glass, overlooking the street outside, already closing in on itself with coils of darkness. The waitress brings the menus. How can such moments be happening? How can we be here, ordering food and drinks, surrounded by Saturday night diners, as if it is just another day? And yet we are.

I am trying desperately to keep it together. As we wait for the food to arrive, I sip my wine too quickly, grasping onto its liquid powers too eagerly. I am starting to overheat, although the temperature inside is not warm. I think that I should run out, away from everything, and flee everyone, especially myself. But where could I run to, where this ghastly fact is not the truth? Where he is still alive? Only into the past, and my time travelling skills are not honed to that extent. I excuse myself quickly, however, feeling the panic worms crawling insistently through my veins, and stand outside for a while, breathing deeply and erratically, crying, talking to myself.

I can't be normal. I just can't. I go back inside and try to explain that to my worried parents; that him not being mentioned is making me confused and upset, and that I am not good in confined spaces these days, but let's have another drink. The food arrives, and talk, still fairly small, but less so, resumes. I shed more tears, we imbibe more wine. I reference him here and there, hauling him into the air, knowing now that it has to be me that brings him into our conversation.

I feel nostalgic, ridiculously, for us as a family all those years ago. No doubt the rioja talking. They ordered the same dish, which surprised me, and through their anecdotes and similarities I see glimmers of how they must have been as a couple. Maybe now they have more in common than they did when they decided they didn't have enough; maybe all things come around.

Despite the perpetual chill that resides in me, I am warmed immeasurably by their presence, and by them having voyaged over hill and dale to be at my side, and doing their best to help and comfort, and simply by them being themselves, the amazing beings they both are. They don't quite know how to be with me, and I have no idea how to be with me, so in the end we are perfect company.

desconsol

A sleepless night. A lying-awake-full-of-horrors night. A night when I *almost* glimpse the last time I slept in the same bed as him, wrapped around each other dreamily, and *almost* feel how it felt, until it slips away, unable to stick. I don't think I'll ever be able to grasp it again, or grasp that that was the last time.

The Valerian I am taking doesn't really work, and smells disgusting. My face is creased in the shape of the pillow, my eyes sunken into my head. I study a photo of us together for a long while, as I wait for dawn to creep around the unclad trees, and wonder aimlessly what he would think if he saw my tormented, ravaged, tear-stained, aged face now.

I think, for some reason, about Barcelona, and all our shared memories there. My favourite sculpture in the city, despite being spoiled for choice, was always one in Parc de la Ciutadella, called 'Desconsol', created by Josep Llimona. I was so drawn to it, and spent long hours just sitting looking, alone with her, imagining feeling what she was feeling. I lived very nearby for quite a while, and the oval hedged space where the smooth white figure lay draped over roughly-hewn stone became my thinking spot, and escape. I felt her sadness; it spoke to me strongly, even though at that time nothing so bad had happened in my life.

I made a drawing, called 'gloop distress', based on this sculpture. In my work, she lies upon mountains, her finger in one of them; a different kind of stone.

I had forgotten that the plinth the real sculpture lies upon is surrounded by water.

Desconsol means grief: desolation: despair.

soul sister

She is so good for me right now. She's always good for me. I love her to absolute bits, and love her take on everything, her passion, her total individuality, her talent, her spirit, her inventiveness, her inspirations, and her ability to make me laugh. Even now, in this most heartbroken of moments, she can do that.

Mum remarks later that she has lightened and lifted me, and brought a much needed energy to all of us.

My soul sister L, my oldest and best friend, has journeyed all the way from the south coast to this northern city, and raises me up, at least some of the way, from the bottom of everything. I have known her for years longer than I knew him; we have shared so many experiences, lived through so much, recorded dozens of songs and played and sung on countless gigs together, travelled, holed up, dreamed mutual dreams, felt mutual disappointments, been manic, been down, hooted until we cried, existed in our own self-contained bubble in copious social situations, amused each other, listened to and spoken about the nuances of our lives forever.

She hasn't seen Biglittlebro or my mum for a thousand years, but it's as if it was, as they say, yesterday, so natural is her being with us all. After a short social while, we want to be just the two of us, and we leave Mum cooking up a storm for this evening's meal and leave the house.

She walks with me; we could have gone anywhere, and she had thought we might go to a park, but I am too weak. We get as far as the nearest bar, which seems far enough to me, and choose a wooden table outside. We need water and wine, and itchy ladies and chips, which she orders. And tissues, which she has brought, wisely.

We have spoken since it happened of course, but now we meander face to face through the maze that is trying to make even miniscule sense of it, and shoot off, as always, in tangents. I am not good at telling the story of it: it appears in teary rushes or muted hesitation, and the story of how I really feel now is impossible to write; she has endless thoughts, and empathetic input (she lost her mum only a few months ago), and manages to steer our conversation through and yet at the same time around the worst wounds.

Strange, and yet not, to see her here, in this branch of my family's stomping ground. Amazing to have her near; it doesn't happen often, the downside of moving abroad being the much reduced time with close ones back home.

She met him soon after I did, dragged by me to a music venue in west London, to watch him play. I had utterly fallen for him, and remember saying to her that I thought he was so beautiful, or words to that effect. I was trying to play it cool in front of him: him even more so in front of me, to the extent that she wasn't so sure about him at first. She was, is, protective of me, and I know would have liked me not to be so into him, with all that that brought, once we eventually got together. She never really knew him, I realise now, not like I wanted her to, and they had hardly seen each other in the last decade; initial impressions endured, and as much as I willed it to happen, they never formed the bond I would have loved them to have. You always wish those you adore to adore the others you adore, and it doesn't always happen.

It doesn't matter now. She is here for me, as she has always been, and I hope will always be, and sees the bits that I am in, and the pieces that are in danger of floating away in the October winds, and as we talk, and they begin to peel off me and start to fly up high above us, she reaches up and grabs as many as she can, and sticks them back on.

regression

No matter what comes before or after it, or how much time has passed, there's nothing quite like a mum hug. Some things never fade, some things never go away, and the need to be held and comforted certainly doesn't; when it is being held and comforted by the first person to ever do that, it is a fundamental, if unspoken, need.

But this is not a grazed knee or a bad dream; this is a fatally wounding very grown-up reality that not even the best of mums knows how to fix.

She is not her strongest self right now anyway; she had a mini stroke only a week before it happened. *That* message from Papa Dos, *that* phone call with Biglittlebro, already seemed scary enough, as the fragility and mortality of one we love twisted the air with 'what ifs' and scared wonderings. Thankfully her stroke was not serious, but she was very much shaken, and weakened, and is still today, as she sits on the adjacent sofa, quieter, slower. The fact that she still came, to be at my side, and to help Biglittlebro and his family as they help me is a testament to her lion love, and inner, incredible strength.

She busies herself with practical things once she arrives, that being mainly preparing the evening meal for us all. A fantastic cook, she takes her time throughout the day chopping this, boiling that, seasoning the other, and avoids the elephant in the room. Like everyone, she doesn't really know what to say; there are no words. I find myself in the strangest of positions of wanting to comfort *her*, make her feel better, assure her that it'll be alright, that *I* will be alright. But I can't. Not now. That's a promise I might not be able to keep.

Over the day, yes I talk about him, about what happened, but I can't formulate it properly, I can't express myself, can't throw certain combinations of words into the sunken air. She grabs hold of any microscopic particle of positive thinking, as is her way, and seems relieved any time I manage to talk of the future. I speak of Spain, and how I can never live there again after this. She looks disappointed; she loves the country, the language, the culture, the flamenco, the sun, especially the sun, and, as well as her own voyages and experiences, came to visit me countless times in both Barcelona and Órgiva, the Andalusian town I lived in before Las Negras. (I wish I'd stayed there; he would still be alive. Unless... we all have a pre-destined date to die...? I'm clutching.)

I succeed in articulating a recurring thought of mine at the moment: that my relationship with him never waned, never got old. Never died, never got mislaid. Never had the time to implode in a hail of hate or bored recriminations. We still loved, we still wanted. Our love died young, despite being quite old in the scheme of things. Mum's whole body appears to relax, and she beams: "That's the spirit, kid!"

All, *all* she desires for me, I know, is for me to be okay again. To dust myself off, give myself a shake, and start walking. Walking forward. To not be this etiolated wreck of a daughter, barely able to get up off the settee, clutching onto hot drinks and warm bodies, sobbing and shaking, shell-shocked and gutted, disappearing constantly into crepuscular, choking caverns. I am the needy, wailing baby she nursed all those years ago, but that time she knew I would stop crying eventually; I am not sure either of us know that now.

locations, hallucinations and medications

11th October 2016

Where is he now? I know, more or less, and I could pinpoint it exactly if I chose to; I have the name of the place. But that need is blocked by my own self-preservation; if I don't know exactly, if it is all a little hazy, there is more of a chance that it is not true.

Where is the news about the funeral? Why is it all taking so long? Torment upon torment, agony after agony. There seems to be no timeline; in any case, time is meaningless to me now.

Where is his essence? Is it circling me without me knowing? Is it waiting for a better moment to show itself, make me feel it?

Where is his love?

I force myself out, just for a few minutes; my body will atrophy, like my mind, if I never move. I walk up and down the street, a short way along from the house. The atmosphere is thick with white noise, the corners of my vision are snarling, the demon hounds on my scent, chasing away any leftover scraps of my former self. I glance upwards, towards a large dilapidated house, the windows broken and blocked up with cardboard, the small garden in tatters. In the window under the eaves, up high, I see him. His eyes, wearing his black glasses. Enormous, angry. Accusing. I lose my breath, falter on the kerb, have to look away. When I dare to look back up again I see it is just a shape in the bereft, dirty curtains, but the feeling stays with me. Was it really him? Was that his essence? I couldn't save him. We couldn't save him. He thinks it is my fault. And now his love for me has changed into hate.

I have to speak to S or G straight away, get their reassurance that there was nothing we could have done. I can't bear this cumbrous, cutting guilt that pins me down and slices me. I can't take this madness, for it *is* madness; I have been told often enough, and my logical mind knows, that it was one of those split second moments that no one can predict and no one can stop. I know that. I know that. And I know that I need help with this.

I trudge to the doctor's with E. It is so hot inside; I immediately feel trapped, and don't trust the electronic sliding door at the entrance which informed us that it has a fault and sometimes will not open, and to press the large button to the right if that happens. We will be stuck inside, and there is no air. The waiting room hems me in, with its depressing ambience, and as my palms heat and sweat, E holds my hands anyway. I grab my rescue remedy, the bottle already nearly finished, and pipette drops onto my tongue. I peel off layer after layer; my body, unaccustomed to this English autumn chill, usually has to be housed in multifarious cloths even inside, but here I am sweltering. I'm also aware that no one else is, and that it's because my nerves are shot, my balance in all things is off, and my emotions that suffocate my surface and pulverise my interior are ruling the roost.

Thankfully I am called after not too long an agonised wait. E says she will come in with me if I want, but at the last second I decide to go alone. Doctors always make me nervous, and lose my thread, but this is a new level. This is bizarre. Saying out loud to a stranger that 'my partner died'. The words flick venomously through the office, and land on his impassive, then, at least seemingly, concerned face. How many times will I have to utter that ghastly phrase? As I say it I almost laugh, it seems so ridiculous, and so impossible. This is not genuine; I am playing a role, I must be; this cannot, ever, be real. My mind explodes for the thousandth time, and screams for help; although to the doctor I know I appear calm, inside I am falling, falling, too deep, too fast, into that hole again.

I am here for three things. I need sleeping pills, for sleep eludes me every night: given, with stern warnings of their addictive qualities. I want to book a blood test to check for anaemia: noted. And I have to ask if my crazily sprinting heart rate, that is making me think I am going to die, is in any way normal: apparently yes; on the fast side, but it is regular. Chalk that down to circumstances, shock, stress, I suppose. And have I thought about counselling? Yes: a website address is given.

Where is he now? Please don't let him be those evil eyes I thought I saw. Let him be soaring free of all worldly anguish, peacefully gliding, watching over me with his love still intact, entering into another dimension I don't even believe in but want to know exists for him.

Where am I now? Lost. Buried in worldly anguish. Buried in vats of excruciating pain. Buried in denial, the first stage of grief. But also buried in caring arms, as E holds me tight, so tight.

shiver, forever

10th October 2016

Yes, it's cold here. But on the coast in the driest part of Europe last week it was colder. A maliciously warm breeze beckoned him into the water that froze his future, iced his life. That sea froze my life too, suspending it in tortured purgatory. The hot air chilled me, minute by glacial minute, as I stayed close to where it happened. The happy memories I had accumulated in the seven months I lived there got cubed, shoved violently into the past's fridge, and might never get defrosted. All is bleak. An arctic storm inside. I shiver, forever.

It took hours to get to sleep last night, even though the bed had been made up so cosily for me. I woke up several times, confused, then slapped fully awake, and after tormented shudders and attempts to shut down, eventually drifted off again, albeit temporarily. Now it is about six-thirty, and I have given up. I switch on the lamp, seeing the little circle of his guitar plectrums I put on the bedside table last night. They make no sense. I stretch my arm down, and grab the folder of photos of the two of us together. They make no sense. I stand cautiously, afraid my legs won't work, and take down the case from the shelf, and inspect his glasses inside. They make no sense.

What does it mean, now? There was no place I would rather have come to nestle and be protected against that which has already happened, but which continues to attack. I could not have stayed in Spain, and never want to see it again. My life was there, for almost nine years, but now what? I had just begun a new adventure, in a new area, and was content, and had no plans to leave, but now what? I have only just arrived in Manchester, and cannot in reality see further than the next breath, but already my over-active imagination toys with me.

How long will I stay here, what will happen, where will I go, how will I survive?

Biglittlebro has to work; he took off all last week to be with me, and has a lot of catching up to do. I trail along with him to his recording studio, content to sit near him quietly as he mixes and masters various projects for his clients. The wraith in the corner, I think to myself, doused in black material, hardly moving, heavy lids never able to shut, darkened eyes always on the lookout for the next nightmare. I reply to some mails, caring messages from various friends and acquaintances, with a few miserable words. In between working, he gathers me under his wing, makes me hot herbal teas, and we sit, unable to grasp what just happened, unable to fathom this new reality, struggling to comprehend this sudden geographical change.

My nephew Hispeed calls in after school, on his way to his mum's house, to see me. What a hug, what huge love from this beautiful, caring boy. We have always had a great bond, since he was tiny, and I instinctively know he will be there for me. He'll be back on Wednesday; it's too long, I can't wait for another hug like that one.

None of us really know how to be. We eat, sit together, talk, don't talk. I am held, I am stroked, my tears are given tissues. It is all unreal, every second of it. I think of other times here, where no one was stuck for words, where we laughed, chatted easily, joked, feasted, danced around and made videos of each other. With him. Before the gap in the universe, before the blank space on the sofa, before the chasm in our lives.

Biglittlebro and E find a picture frame, and ask me to choose one of the many photos I brought over to put in it, so they can have him there on the living room mantelpiece. I choose one that was taken a year or two ago, in Papa Ping's kitchen. I stare and stare at him, until his form becomes merely shades, angles, colours. Just an image now, just pixels on paper. I'll never stroke that beard again, or look into those eyes that stared back at me and spoke of so many things. Never kiss that mouth; never rub that nose with mine. Never get 'bundled', as he used to say, hugged and safe in his arms. The word 'miss' is not strong enough, not long enough, just not enough. There *is* no word for this feeling, for this desperate lack, for this crucified existence, for this anguished need, for this... nothing.

forced migration

M comes round earlier than he ever wants to be awake to pick us up from L and C's. They come out to say sad goodbyes; I have no idea when I will ever see them again. We drive out of Bayacas, down into Órgiva, across the 'Seven Eye' bridge and along twenty minutes' worth of winding road. Spectacular views I have driven past a thousand times seem alien and sombre, despite the brilliant sunshine, and as each kilometre is eaten up by the tyres I feel more peculiar.

Once onto the motorway, the A7 that reaches down from the depths of Andalucía to the heights of Cataluña , we see the Mediterranean down below. I thought I had had my last sighting of that four days ago, when we left Las Negras, but had forgotten that we would pass it on the way to catch our plane; worse than that, the most convenient flight ended up being from Almería, not Málaga. Backwards, backwards in time: forwards, forwards towards that piece of coastline.

We reach the airport, and I am bombarded by images of all the times I have been here in the last twelve days; picking him up, picking Biglittlebro up, picking J and B up. One sweet reunion, two tortured meetings. We are early, and loiter awhile in the tiny cafe. So hard to say goodbye to M, who has been a rock and a true, amazing friend, and I cry; as with L and C, I don't know when we will meet again. One by one, it feels, I am losing people. One for real, forever. Others merely for a long moment, I know. But all the goodbyes pain me, sticking small sharp shards into where the knife has already gouged too much out of me.

We have calculated that if I take a pill about an hour before take-off, I should be relaxed enough to not lose the plot when we board. We sit on the uncomfortable seats in the tiny departure lounge, and I occasionally pace, chanting, "Be calm, you can do this, be calm." We bought a crossword book, and Biglittlebro decides we should tackle it. It looks like a fairly easy one, but we are stumped on almost every clue. Where have they gone, our brain cells? We give up after a hopelessly head-scratching while.

An announcement: our plane is delayed, obviously, for at least an hour. Bang goes that pill timing. And really? I'm so frightened, so utterly terrified, of getting on, did fate have to make it even worse by prolonging the agony? We recalculate, and as we finally, after a seemingly interminable period of time, reach the aeroplane and find our seats, I take a second pill.

As the remaining passengers board, I can feel that I am acquiring the demeanour of madness. My pupils must be huge, my skin taut, my lips cracking. I grip Biglittlebro's arm, and say, "I can't, I can't." I am ready to run off the plane. He looks slightly panicky for a second, then tells me to start naming all the family pets we ever had. Genius; it immediately makes me smile at the randomness of it, and searching the past takes the place of the present hysteria. Somehow I half ignore take-off, although his arm might beg to disagree, and we are up. He keeps me talking, keeps my mind busy with something, anything, after all the animals have been exhausted. The pill doesn't come close to knocking me out, but I suppose it had some effect; I am slightly furry around the edges for a part of the flight. In any case, I don't run screaming down the aisle.

The touchdown is more than a relief. We are alive. I got through it, thanks to him. As we step off the plane into a biting breeze and that always surprisingly downcast sky over England, he tells me with a smile that Littlebigbro was on standby, in case I just couldn't get on the plane, to drive to Almería and take us all the way to Manchester in his van. Bearing in mind he lives in central Portugal, that just shows the beyond huge love that my brothers have for me. Whatever I have lost, I still have that.

unfamiliar familiar

8th October 2016

The last day here. Despite wanting to get out of the country, it is so peaceful in this place, and I almost want to stay, in this muted, dreamlike, curious limbo, the abundant green all around us sheltering us from the real. My mind has firmly shut down, and although I am aware of my surroundings, I cannot grapple with thoughts. The truth slides away from me each time any undernourished cogs try to whirr, and I decide to let it.

We need supplies, and M comes up to the house to drive us to Órgiva, the town I know intimately, whose streets I have trodden innumerable times, whose characters I have seen and greeted since 2010, off and on, whose bars, restaurants and shops I frequented for five years. In the last couple of days M shopped for us, but Biglittlebro and I decide to join him this time. I am vaguely curious, I suppose, as to how I will cope, seeing his shadow on those streets, remembering his pet names for and opinions of those characters, hearing his voice echoing through those buildings. Thinking back to all the moments we shared here: *so* many moments. He recorded the guitars for his album in my house here; I can hear the notes reverberating between the mountain ranges, bouncing off in all directions, as we drive down the hill towards the town. The sea lies behind the mountain facing us, and I attempt to erase it. If I can't see it, it doesn't exist.

We park outside the supermarket, whereupon I am seized by panic. I cannot possibly go inside, be near other people. I might meet someone I know; I will *definitely* meet someone I know, because you always do here. It's that kind of place. And there is no way that I can answer a casual "how are you?" with anything less than a howl. Biglittlebro reassures me that I don't have to come in, and that I can just stay here in the car. He goes inside with M, but that leaves me alone, and that can't happen. That can never happen again. I will be locked inside the car, despite the windows being open. I have to leave the door ajar, my foot holding it, to feel safe. Everyone I see seems out of a horror movie. Every stray dog winding its way down the road scares me. I want to run after Biglittlebro and M, but am frozen. How can this place that I called home for so long, and loved, fill me with such terror? All is so familiar, but rendered unfamiliar by something that happened nearly two hundred kilometres away. I imagine all places will be filled with demons; all unknown people will terrify me. The whole world is a spine-chilling space that will suck out the scarred and scared lifeblood I still have in me.

Such a relief when they appear, and Biglittlebro reassures me again. He is having to do that a lot, and probably will need to for a long while yet.

In the late afternoon, we decide to have a walk. It's such a beautiful day, and I can feel Biglittlebro itching to move, do something; we have been static, physically, for a week. L tells us which path to take, down from their house alongside a tiny stream, up an incline, and from there as far as we like, through woods, or down another hill and around back to the village of Bayacas.

How odd to stroll, to work my legs, to breathe this pure air and fill my lungs with it. How peculiar to watch my feet on dusty earth, kicking stones. A tremor of remembrance shakes me, but for once a good one. The memory of walking, striding out, stretching my muscles, feeling my body as part of nature, flowing with it, setting the mind free. I did it so much in Las Negras, and in fact wherever I have lived, be it in the city or the countryside. It is natural for me, and is where I do my best thinking.

This time, however, I have no intention of letting myself think. And I'm not so much striding as shuffling, my muscles have disappeared, I have no flow, and I feel no part of anything. We get about five minutes along and I am too drained to go further. A pathetic attempt. But, nevertheless, an attempt.

It takes me a long time to cool down. It is not really very hot, but even that tiny exertion has caused me to boil over. Perhaps tomorrow, as we are leaving for distinctly chillier climes, I will have to change the costume I have worn since the day after it happened. S already gently suggested I should get out of the dark blue dress a few days ago, but it was not dirty, and it isn't now. I have barely moved for seven days, and despite the late summer heat I have not sweated: I am ice. Until this moment. The dress, worn day in, day out, for some reason slightly comforts me, and perhaps has become an emblem of the pain that has become a part of me, and I just don't care if I wear it forever. Only October in England will dictate, and direct me to a different part of my wardrobe.

The evening passes, with less people than the night before. We need to be restful, and to try to sleep early, or the challenge of tomorrow will be even tougher. Biglittlebro still manages to cook a fabulous meal for the three of us, and we still manage to talk of things other than the thing. L and C come round for a while; it means so much that they have housed us here, and cared, and supported us.

So: mañana. The end of Spain for me. The continuation of this infinite inferno, this demented despair, this horrendous hell, this wailing wreckage, this bewildered bereavement, this terrified trauma, this monumental misery. The beginning of a new chapter.

time, and the last flight

7th October 2016

Time stands still. I realise it is Friday; it is after five o'clock, but before half past. A week ago at this moment, he was gone. But straight away I tell myself not to make this into a thing. Not to make every Friday for the rest of my life into that. Not to make between five and five thirty the time to dread for all time. It is just time. Time that, broken down into days and hours and months and centuries, means nothing in itself. They are markers, nothing more, these sun-made and man-made calendars.

Conversation darts around the room, the animated brew of languages jumping from one pairing or tripling of friends to another, as people change their tongue to suit. Everyone here speaks at least two languages, many three. Beer and wine flow, Biglittlebro concocts yet another tasty dish, and it almost seems like just another fun social gathering, of the kind we often had when I lived in Órgiva up until a year before now. Underpinning the pretend jocularity, of course, is the intense sadness that permeates the air, that twists and writhes in corners, that collects in webs upon the ceiling and under chairs. But this is the human way; an attempt to make things seem normal in order to cope with the abnormal.

Laughter is ringing through this shared space when my head suddenly cracks open; I frantically and repeatedly ask the time. Everyone looks puzzled, and someone finds their phone and tells me. I clutch my sides, subconsciously look up, and start to shake. I tell them that he will be in the air now, flying, or rather, being flown, back to London. Although the flight path goes nowhere near us, as he is going from Alicante airport, about four hundred kilometres from here, I sense him above us, see his face, picture his – no, I can't. I go blank. My being cannot bear to visualise too much. Yet I imagine all the passengers on the plane, a normal, commercial aircraft, sitting there completely unaware that he is lying below them. How many flights that I have been on have had an occupied coffin in the hold? Until now I had no idea that this could happen. How do they bring it on without anyone seeing it?

He flew so many times: with bands to play gigs, for holidays, but most of all to come and see me. Hundreds of flights throughout his life. His second to last flight ever was ten days ago. He arrived at Almería airport a wreck; the departure time was at 'evil o'clock', as we called it, and he hadn't slept at all, apart from a little nap on the plane. I drove up to collect him; I'll never forget how he looked then. He was sitting on the kerb in his denim jacket, small and sleepy, and my heart melted; as he stood to take me in his arms, he felt less than before, and vulnerable. This wasn't his strongest moment, his most sassy look. He was exhausted, not just from the lack of sleep, but the last months of work-related stress. We kissed, held each other, inhaled us again. It wasn't often that I felt protective of him, but this was one of those moments. Back at my place he took a shower, then wrapped himself in the towel and fell asleep on the bed. He appeared so cute, young and fragile, and I remember I took a photo of him lying there. I wonder if I will ever be able to look at that photo; the association will be impossible to bear. Three days later he was covered in another towel, for a different kind of sleep: one from which he would not wake groggily, make our little 'MMMmmmm' sound and open his arms for me to climb inside them.

sanctuary

Another confusing wakening. Jolted into the incipient day by what sounds like hordes of dogs barking crazily, I can hear running water, and birds. Where on earth can I be? It is dark, but the tentative wormings of nascent light through a crack in the door begin to point out enough of the room to remind me.

I turn over to see Biglittlebro lying there, also foggily awake, likewise woken by the howls of these persistent hounds. I nestle into him, as I have done for the beginnings of the last four sleeps, until he gets too hot and restless. He apologises, again, laughing, for his inability to spoon me through the night, knowing how much I want him to. He's a fiery creature, not like the frosty, flimsy slip of transparent gauze I have become.

We lie there for a listless, desolate while, clutching onto the disappearing tails of dreams, clinging onto this gentle, deceitful half-consciousness, both afraid to emerge fully into the morning, and therefore into the real, cruel world. Finally we have to move and, cursing the dogs, get up.

I am in a haze, as always. My head weighs more than this little holiday house, my legs are filled with sodden stones. He is more energetic, being generally better in the mornings than I am anyway, and opens the shutter doors from the open-plan kitchen and living room area onto the tranquil, luminous view outside. He makes coffee, and we drink it on the terrace, gazing around, bemused as to how we find ourselves here, in these epic and, now the dogs have calmed down, peaceful surroundings.

The place belongs to L and C, close friends of mine, and his, for the last five years or more. This cute cottage where we are staying is attached to their house, and is normally filled with guests: holidaymakers from the colder corners of Europe. In the only stroke of luck in the past days, it happens to be free just when we need a bolthole, somewhere to burrow, and be still, and wait for the news about when he will be flown back to England, so that we can then make our own flight plans. So generous of L and C to offer this to us, but that's the kind of people they are.

It is an oasis in the scorched lands of post-summer Andalucía. The rush and babble of the acequia, the stream used for the ancient water irrigation system put into place in Moorish times, gives rise to a lush, verdant garden which is atypical of these parts. The luxuriant air kneads our aching beings, as we wander slowly, amongst flourishing plants and olive trees, oranges and lemons hanging from branches, a prospering, cared for allotment on the bank below.

A lead-heavy lethargy sinks wearily upon me, upon us, as we think back, and try not to think back, over the last days. There is now nothing left to do; all logistics, in this country anyway, have been taken care of, and I have had to confront things in that short space of time that perhaps could have been left for future moments, in an 'ideal' world. It feels like everything is falling away, that hasn't tumbled like angry scree in a gale already, leaving a husk, a shell, a barely moving mass that contains the remains of who I was.

We talk, in little more than whispers, exhausted from so many words having had to be expelled before. I have no idea what we talked about, even a few minutes later, as my head whirls in some kind of space, a vacuum, a void into which all past happiness has been sucked. All is dense, sombre weight, pressing down on us, causing what from the outside would appear to be a relaxed state, as we lie or sit on loungers amongst lightly clucking chickens, our eyes fixed on the towering trees above us that dance softly in the negligible breeze, the warm sun on our upturned faces. My body and mind are closing: closing down, closing in, closing off.

Biglittlebro writes a post on my behalf for those who might not have heard, on the book of face; I never use it for personal things, but for this I will make an exception. There are so many people who I know slightly, or even quite well, and who knew him, and knew us together, that haven't been contacted by us, and that should know about this; I am incapable of stringing any words together, so he does it, and beautifully. I find myself checking replies too often for a while, desperate to connect, needing caring messages, wanting, wanting. But I then stop; each message, however lovely, proves yet again that he is gone, really gone. That he is now 'the late...' He has become the recipient of R.I.P.s, someone in the past tense.

That is something I cannot take; immediately after it happened, the tense changed. Is becomes was. 'Ed' ends the verbs instead of 's'. I trip over my sentences; correct myself when I say 'is', or the equivalent, then grimace, and mew, "How can he be in the past?"

And yet, he is. He is past. He has passed.

As friends arrive in the evening, to comfort, console, show their compassion through our togetherness, I can merely cherish those that are 'is'es, hold on to these present, and implore the universe to not strike them down as it struck him, and to let them remain part of my, of our, future.

tearing out togetherness

5th October 2016

It is time to leave. Leave this place, with its terrible memories, the stain upon this once inspiring, beautiful area too deep to ever scrub clean.

Early morning, and S and G are leaving first; this tears me apart inside. How can we be separated, the three of us who have shared this true nightmare? I hadn't realised how much I needed them at my side, and can't let go, but I must, however much it hurts. They will still be with me, I know, any time I need them. B and J will also be en route for the airport, back to their lands, no doubt utterly reeling from the intensity and anguish of these two days.

That leaves Biglittlebro, M and I. And a difficult task. How to pack up your life, how to fit it into three suitcases, not knowing how long you will be staying where you are going, only knowing that you are never coming back? The only returning I could ever do, and this seems impossible right now, would be to collect all my possessions, in some far-off future world existence, when I might be starting a new life somewhere else. But how can I possibly contemplate that? So, for now, I just need to get the hell out of here.

My mind is blank; all I know is that I need photos of him, of us together. Real photos; of course I have a few on my laptop, and thousands on memory sticks and hard drives. But I need paper, tangible memories, in my hand. The thought, however, is easier to fashion than the action.

Meanwhile, as I gear up for this, Biglittlebro searches around the one room that is my studio apartment for ideas, making suggestions in his gentler than gentle way. He builds up piles of objects, and starts wrapping up things in winter clothes that seem ridiculous in this heat. ("We'll take your clarinet, right?" "Why? I'm never going to play again!" "I'll pop it in just in case. And your sax mouthpiece?" "Ditto." "Well, it's only small. You should take some drawing pens." "I'll never be able to draw!" "They're tiny, and you will one day. And your soundcard, in case you want to record?" "As if!" "I think there's room, let's take it." Etc).

So adrift am I that I cannot contemplate, even for a nanosecond, using the tools of my trades, the things that made up who I used to be only a few days ago; or wanting to create, to make music and art, to lose myself in my passion for inventing and concocting and constructing the real out of dreamed ideas.

Even though all I want to do is lose myself, forget who I am and forget what has traumatised me to the core, enter the maze of oblivion and blindfold myself to the images that have wallpapered themselves to the inside of my brain with poisonous glue, and most of me *is* buried deep under sorrow's rubble, a small piece of me is here, is present, and needs to do this.

I open the wardrobe containing, among other items, all my photo albums that date up until 2008, when I moved to Spain. I search for the one of the year I first met him, flailing, inwardly wailing, pulling out books with such angry force, whisking through the pages, feeling my life flash before my eyes. I see my family and friends, and me, growing up, changing, ageing; I blink confusedly at reams of times, travels, gigs, holidays, as he appears in photo after photo. There he is, arm around me, in a London pub, one of the first photos of us together; there he is, kissing me on a mountain top; there he is, laughing with me by a river in Italy. There he is, there he is, there he is. Was.

I tear them out of the albums, these captured essences; I have turned into a robotic fury, a numb machine, unsticking, wrenching, snatching, throwing onto a growing pile of what we were. Biglittlebro, and M, who is busy cleaning the flat, both stay out of my way: in any case I am hidden behind the wardrobe, sitting on the floor, uncommunicative, not yet rocking, not yet losing it, but in sight of it. They know that I just have to get this over with, and pad around quietly dealing with their self-allotted tasks.

Finally it is done, I can take no more. I get up off the floor and hurl myself outside, beyond the tiny terrace and the wooden gate and onto the road, but not far enough that I can see the sea down below me. I feel mad, utterly insane. I don't know how to exist, how to process the fact that the face I have just been looking for, and at, has disappeared from my life.

Somehow we get it all finished; the apartment is presentably clean, the things I am not taking, in other words almost everything, are left where they are, and M assures me he will drive over here often to keep an eye on it all, water plants, air the place, make sure my artwork is not moulding from the winter damp. The car is loaded, and it only remains to say goodbye to my sweet, kind landlord and lady, I and R. On the way up the few steps to the side of my flat, towards their house, their dog Romeo blocks our way. 'Sticky', as I called him, because he was, sprawls lazily in the sunshine, and I stop to stroke him and say bye.

He knows. In some elemental, animal way he knows. I sit next to him, and he immediately puts his paw on me, something he has never done before. I start to cry, and I really feel that I am not imagining the tears in his eyes also. They had such a bond; every time F would come over to see me, he couldn't wait to see Sticky, and pet him, sit in the middle of the road playing, invite him in for water and any scraps we might have lying around, and have him, contented, at his feet as he sat on the sofa. I love Sticky too, such a lovely soul, and now my loss, our loss, is all too apparent in the eyes of this creature.

Farewells, embraces, feelings of love towards two people I have only known for seven months, but who have shown themselves capable of such caring, such empathy. I will miss them.

Driving down the hill, for what I hope will be the last time in my life, I cast a final, shuddering glance at that blueness that annihilated him. Kilometre after kilometre, its waves crash less upon my shore, its spray that stings my heart diminishes, as we drive and drive, away, to somewhere safer, somewhere inland, somewhere just not here.

they touched his skin

I storm down into my apartment, survey the surroundings as little as possible, and grab his suitcase. I march back up the stairs, through the garden, into the apartment, and crash it onto the floor.

I am cold, so cold. Icy. Fuming. Just do it, I say to myself, get through it.

What about *these* trousers? Or *these*? Which are more suitable? And what does that even mean?

Not shorts, I suppose. I'll go with the first pair of trousers.

What about *this* shirt? Or *this* one? I snarl and thrash through the items, quickly, so quickly. I choose the second shirt; black. As if he is at his own funeral.

And socks? Really? I look through his collection and want to choose the most vividly coloured stripy pair, but go with blue.

I am furious. Furious at the world. Furious that he is dead. Dead! Furious that I have to do this. Or rather, that I want it to be me that does it; someone else could easily go through his case and pick a few clothes out for him to be viewed in. But for some stupid reason I have decided that it is my job.

Mission completed.

I look up from the floor into the flustered faces of Biglittlebro and my friends, and smile bitterly.

"Stage three of the grieving process," I announce, "anger. Tick."

S tries to make light of it later, laughing that she thought she'd better guard the kitchen knives, I was so angry.

I was. I am.

A little later, with the suitcase still lying in the corner of the room, I go through it again, slightly more calmly. I want to take a couple of his things. I have a feeling that that will be all the material memories of him I will be left with. Because I had moved to this place relatively recently he hadn't had time to leave clothes, or guitars, or shoes, or effects pedals. Mainly stuffed with holiday beach wear, these are slim pickings, considering this is what I will be left with for the rest of my life. I choose a vest, a pair of his glasses, all the plectrums, and one lone stripy sock.

Waiting for news. Of the autopsy. Of what will happen then, and when. I need to get out of this malevolent place, but cannot leave the country until I know that he has been flown out of it. How can I leave him here alone? So we wait.

I give his sister and brother one of his plectrums each. It is just a little token, to keep in their purse or wallet or wherever, but I tell them that music was him, guitar was him, and each of these little picks had been touched by his fingers, and amazing music been made with them. I think they appreciated it.

A call comes in the afternoon to his brother B. He and his sister J met this morning with the man from the insurance company that takes care of all the arrangements, and were told it could take a while before all the paperwork is done, and therefore before a flight can be organised. It could even be weeks, he warns; you never know, dying abroad brings a lot of complications and a lot of red tape. The insurance man told them that he has the things that were on him, his jewellery, and that if I wanted them, he would meet me that evening, out of hours and as a favour, to hand them over. I want them so much, yet I don't want them, because to see his necklace in my hand and not around his neck will make it real.

We arrange to meet at 7.30, near a town I have never heard of, an hour's drive away. We are to follow the motorway until a certain junction, turn off there, go past a roundabout and a garden centre, and he will be waiting at a yellow service station. It seems fairly straightforward.

I feel like I am in a bad film, as Biglittlebro, M and I set off. M drives. I don't think I will ever drive again. We are speaking French, which somehow makes it even more surreal, even though I speak that language with M all the time. I am so tense, I can hardly breathe. They manage to make me feel less so.

The exit number we were given doesn't correspond to what we are seeing on the motorway; we turn off where we think it must be. Pretty soon we are heading towards a line of toll booths and signs to a city very north of here; this can't be right, but there is no way to turn around. We take the ticket, and roar up a different motorway, exasperated but almost amused, willing a turn-off to appear soon. It does, we exit, pay pointless euros, and turn around. Back to the junction we missed, which is easier to spot from this direction. Down winding roads, to a roundabout, with no garden centre in sight. We see a garage, but it is not yellow. We're now pretty late for the rendezvous, and call the guy apologetically. He tries to figure out where we are, thinks he knows, and directs us from there. Off we set again, round the same roads, round the same roundabout, searching for this stupid petrol station. We find a yellow one finally: but he is not there. Another call, another apology. He tells us to wait there, and he will try to find us.

The film has turned into a black comedy.

Finally he tracks us down, and is not angry as I thought he might have been. In fact he is very lovely, and kind. He hands over an envelope containing the items, and asks me to check that they are all there, hard as that might be to do, so that he can tick them off on his list.

- Silver necklace that he bought when we were in New York fifteen years ago and has worn forever since: check.

- Two silver earrings, that he wore on his right ear for as long as I can remember: check.

- A brown leather bracelet I bought for him: check.

- And lastly, and for some reason this gets to me most of all, his leather ankle bracelet: check.

It is too much to bear, but I hang onto the side of the car to stay vertical.

The man also tells me that they have done the autopsy, and he has brought a photocopy of the verdict for me, even though he shouldn't have really.

'Death by drowning'. Simply. Obviously.

There, written in black and white.

It happened.

Back at the apartment I tell everyone about the autopsy result. One is confused, another almost angry, sure that there must have been something else: a heart attack, a blow to the head, a broken neck. Not just drowning. All of us are shocked at how shockingly easily it can happen, never mind that it happened to him, and I think we all wanted another explanation. I tell them that he had been having tightness in his chest at times during this year, but, as usual with him and anything medical, he hadn't checked it out; I too was thinking it could have been a heart attack. Does it matter, in the end? We have to trust those that do this for a living to know their job, and all our speculation amounts to nothing more than talk. He is gone, that's all there is to say, and if they say it was death by drowning then it was.

This is the last night with us all here. S and G are, devastatingly for me, as our living through this horror story together feels like a union that should never be broken, leaving tomorrow; J and B are too. They have jobs and lives back home, however hard that is for them to contemplate right now. M is still here, I and R pop round; endless food is eaten, endless alcohol drunk, stories related. I am desperate to find similarities between B and him, surprising brotherly traits and things they liked, but don't find so much; just flickers of genetics and flashes of shared histories.

To anyone looking in, for most of the night it would appear that this was a happy occasion, filled with laughter and conversation; they would have to watch closely to see the occasional leaving of the room, or a pair of eyes filling, or a voice breaking. How do we do this, us humans – carry on, keep going, find ways to remain living and walking and talking and being? In a way I hate us for it, but love us too.

For most of the evening, despite the moving of my mouth and apparent interacting, I am far away; I can only think of the envelope containing his jewellery burning a hole in my bag, in my life, in my heart, and of him lying somewhere cold, not wearing them.

the eyes

I am staring into his eyes.

Mesmerised.

Unable to look away.

He is looking at me through the face of his older brother B, who, along with his sister J, has just walked through arrivals at Almería airport.

He had once said, years ago, that they looked alike, and I had girded myself for an apparition, a carbon copy of him. At first glance there is nothing: not the build, not the walk, not the hair, not the face. Until I find his eyes.

I stare for too long. It is probably uncomfortable for him. An almost eerie sensation, and yet it floods me with warmth, and ridiculous hope that maybe he still exists. For a moment I allow myself to think that it has all been a particularly hideous, detailed dream, and that they truly are *his* eyes and this is really him, looking at me again.

I miss him I miss him I miss him
and
it
is
killing
me

J is in bits. Her adored baby brother, gone; she grapples with this horror, helpless under its heavy truth. B seems numb as we, seven of us (M and I are also with us to help translate), make our way to the tanatorio (crematorium) in the city of Almería. I wonder what he is thinking; he is as inscrutable as his brother in this regard.

A big, modern building on the outskirts of the city: a large entrance hall, a cold floor. The oxygen in here is made up solely of woe; how many families, partners, friends have stood here knowing that somewhere in the vastness of its rooms lies their loved one?

Questions at reception, a wait, a lot of pacing, then an office, crammed with all of us and the overly-officious man in charge. Options and prices are discussed. Details of insurance requested. I have to hand over his passport, and kiss it as it leaves my hand. The word 'cuerpo' (body) circulates the room too many times to bear. Phone calls must be made, arrangements arranged.

B takes charge. I cannot do anything, as I am not 'family'. But perhaps that is just as well; I barely even know my name right now.

More pacing, more calls, more waiting. I focus on the ceiling, and the long, superficially cheerful fronds of probably fake leaves hanging down from it. I count floor tiles. I cling to Biglittlebro, to M, to S. This is what surreal looks like.

It is done. He had life insurance (which I knew, but it had to be proved). Everything is covered and all will be sorted out. We flee this deathly building and move into the plain, cheerless bar nearby.

What room was he in, which part of the tanatorio?
How far from us was he lying?
Does he still look like him?
My thoughts twist my cells, wringing all the life out of them.

If he could see this grouping of people! That's all I can think. His brother and sister who haven't seen each other in years having to make their way together to another country to deal with *this*, the worst of things. My brother, my friends, my landlord (also a friend now, of course). Worlds colliding. Would he be smiling, watching us interacting, pleased it is not awkward? Or horrified, crossing his fingers that ancient secrets and family embarrassments he might have kept from me will not slip out, he who compartmentalised so well?

The collective relief is palpable. Nothing, *nothing*, will make this any better, but it is at least a small comfort to have this out of the way. It went more smoothly, in the end, than it might have done, and one of the myriads of tensions that now live in all of us rolls a little way down this mountainous nightmare.

I can see that it suddenly hits B hard. His numbness breaks; now the business side of it is out of the way, he can feel it for what it truly is. We talk, all of us, tentatively weaving around he who is not here; the subject is too intense, the past hours too bizarre, and we are feeling our way blindfolded. I am incredulous that B and I are only finally meeting like this, for this reason, and am saddened by life's sick sense of humour. J I have known almost from the beginning, and see my despair mirrored in her, this lovely, warm person who took care of him as a mother would when he was small. A melting pot of personalities, though in this moment thoroughly subdued, we all approach conversation from our very different angles, but we have, of course, a strong feeling of solidarity. We all miss the same person, and not one of us can believe.

A flimsy façade,
this anaesthetised me,
deprived of self,
still upright,
still conversing,
but
inside
cowers
a hollowed, stricken, lacerated
imprint,
amazed that the attached mouth continues to move.

I don't envy J and B, who have booked into a hotel in Las Negras, having to be so close to where it happened. I for one cannot possibly descend down to the village ever again. It's bad enough just knowing it's there; it's hideous enough hearing the sea's contented whispers and bullying, contemptuous taunts. They go off to check in and get their bearings, guided to their lodgings by S and G, and the rest of us drive up the hill.

The afternoon passes somehow, in the usual shocked fog and piercing pain, and endless warm teas with sugar. Sometimes I look up, wondering if he is hovering above us all. Above the water that took him. I want to tear through the fabric of the air, fight my way through its timeless tunnels and reach for him, touch him, pull him back to us.

I finally manage to speak on the phone to a few people, family and close friends; I knew that they were there any time I wanted to talk, but have had to build up to it. So hard, so hard. So impossible to formulate phrases. Each call drains me more; each flood of tears linking our voices two thousand kilometres away solidifies the pain.

If I am a painting, I am Munch's Scream
and yet
if I am a piece of music, it is John Cage's 4'33.

Early evening: J and B arrive, and we all begin to get to know each other. In this place normally reserved for good times and happy holiday feelings, the whole scene has the dark irony of illusion. The apartment with its terrace and views, the weather, the sun loungers outside all collude in their lies, spinning webs of turmoil in and around these ostensibly innocent surroundings, these apparently normal, sociable evening. R keeps bringing round food, the sun keeps shining. We gather and share this story and that, times before these dreadful moments we could never have anticipated, and we scatter to various corners, to shed private tears. My body feels pummelled by evil spirits, the ghosts of our love chased away.

I am nothing. Broken. Shattered. Aching. Splintered.
I am a scream. I am silence.
Nothing.

la negra

2nd October 2016

This time I know where I am when I wake up. This time I know the arms around me are not his. The valium knocked me out for a few short hours, mercifully, but now awake my withering, inconsolable, woebegone brain won't stop howling. My demolished, wailing, dissolved heart won't stop breaking.

My Biglittlebro arrives. His hug as he comes through arrivals is bigger than the moon. He was only here a few weeks ago, for a short holiday with me. Who would have thought he would be back so soon, for such a reason? I climb inside his arms and never want to leave. I have the feeling, at least momentarily, that he will make everything alright again; he has that effect on me. But I know, and most of all *he* knows, that even for him that is an impossible task.

I have lost the person that, apart from my family and my oldest best friend L, I loved the longest.

How can that be? Images of him lying there punch me, punch through me, punch the wall I lean against, crack the plaster, shatter the brick, gouge holes out of the entire building, slay nearby trees, blast into nothing the surrounding mountains, flatten the whole area, blow up the whole country, implode the whole universe into a weeping ball and toss it away.

Multilingual times. English, Spanish, French, German, Dutch/Flemish. Around the kitchen table, on sofas and chairs inside the apartment, outside on the terrace, flow the voices of my friends, back again to comfort me, to cleave the growing pile of misery, cut through with love, gently persuade my ears to listen to their tones of caring, of concern, and to subconsciously remind me that I am alive, though seemingly only barely, and they are here beside me to prevent me from collapsing irrevocably.

For the first time in decades, the monthly hell arrives and I barely even notice. What is that pain, compared to this? Trips to the toilet, or trips to the shower, are more painful because of my separation from Biglittlebro and the others; to be alone is to feel more frightened than ever before in my life. I cannot explain the fear, but it hovers over my trampled, bruised spirit and from time to time swoops down to smash my face into invisible rocks.

I dare to go down to my flat. M is staying in it, as I cannot. Biglittlebro and I will sleep up at the apartment, in the spare room. How can I be in my place, with F's things still scattered around, with his smell still loitering, with a dent in the sofa where he was sitting only two days ago, with the breakfast spoon and bowl he used still on the side, with his towel still slightly damp from his last morning shower, with his brush holding its few strands of his hair, with his laptop and phone on the side, his portals of communication, lying locked, or drained of battery, never to be communicated with again?

But I need underwear. So I move as fast as I can, which is slowly, with Biglittlebro at my side, entering into this home of mine, frozen in time. Time before, time after. My soul spins, and I see him, almost. Not an apparition, but it is as if the air moulded itself around him where he sat, or stood, or lay, leaving transparent casings that only I can see inside of.

I spy the sneakers I was wearing that day, and the dress, and hurl them into a binbag; I will ask M to drop them off at the rubbish bins next time he drives down the hill. They are drenched in suffering, steeped in catastrophe, immersed in evil agony, and I cannot look at them, never mind wear them again.

Quirks of his are brandished, sayings of his are wielded by Biglittlebro and I, at different times, perhaps to defend ourselves from the truth; by keeping his ways and his words alive, we keep him alive.

We remember his sneeze. His ridiculously hilarious impossible sneeze. It had to be heard to be believed. It was so extreme, and comedic, it melted me every time. How can I never hear that again?

I remind Biglittlebro that only a couple of weeks earlier we had spoken of the family songs, a new tradition of ours. Using his studio in Manchester and mine in Spain, we had concocted crazy ditties for different family members, one a year, and all of us had added vocals. F's part had always been at the end, and each time it was completely off the cuff; he put on a plummy actorly voice and spoke, improvising randomly and very amusingly about the person. It was the best bit of the song, if only for its sheer stupidity, and never failed to make us all cry with laughter. I had asked Biglittlebro who we would 'do' this Christmas, and he replied that he thought we should leave it this year. How did he know that we would have to? And can we ever do one again? I doubt it – it would be too heart-wrenching to not have him, in his posh alter-ego, rounding off the song.

We use words he used, and that we used together: phrases only he uttered: speak of his opinions on this subject or that. We must not forget. We must not forget. Already I can feel him slipping away from me: hour by hour elements of him become hazier: his face comes and goes, and I don't want to lose it, but it is overlaid with the face I saw on the beach, the lifeless face which I want to forget. Which I must forget. Which I must forget. Which I without doubt will *never* forget.

We talk of recent times spent in each other's company, incredulous that that was that, that despite assuming there would be more times, more sneezes, there won't be.

I cannot breathe.
S tells me I can. Biglittlebro tells me I can. G tells me I can.
Everyone tells me I can.
I cannot.

In the 'pictures' section of my laptop, and probably everybody's, two photos from each folder are selected at random and shown, as if they are the first two pages of an album. The first folder I have saved in this section is from June. The top photo chosen at random is of him wading out into the sea.

I and R come round in the evening to join us; again, she has been cooking all day for us. Unbelievable kindness. Into the evening, he decides to tell the gathered group the story of how Las Negras got its name. I hadn't thought of this macabre coincidence until now. Years ago the village of San Pedro, in the next bay, lost all their men; one day the fishermen went out to sea, and every one of them drowned. The women moved their settlement, in order to survive, around the cliffs, and named the new, tiny village after the colour of their mourning garments. I get as far as the word 'men', my stomach contracts and head convulses, knowing what word he is leading up to, and sprint out of the room. M follows me, knowing, too, what he is about to say, and comforts me.

Of *course* he was speaking unthinkingly, not making the connection, and just eager to chat and share stories about the area; there will be many moments like this one, I am sure, where the 'd' word rears its gruesome head, and no one will mean to upset me, in fact would be horrified to think they have inadvertently done so. It is probably said more, this 'd' word, than I have ever realised; I think of all the idioms that will never be able to leave my mouth again: we drown our sorrows, drown our troubles, drown out the noise, drown in self-pity.

But what can I think, now? The legend has become my reality. The tale is now a present day actuality. Now I too am one of those women who lost their man at sea; la negra.

unable to breathe, unable to comprehend, unable to be

I wake up in his arms, gradually coming to. Strange, we are the wrong way round; I'm always on the left hand side of the bed, but I seem to be on the right. And he feels different, smaller; he doesn't hold me the same way, or smell the same. I open my eyes and don't know where I am. I am facing a wall I don't recognise, furniture I have never seen. I turn to ask him where we are, and instead see S, the one spooning me, and G beyond her, and the world inverts.

I choke on the evil air that has descended upon this world.
I tremble violently; sit hunched over clutching myself like I will break.
I *am* broken.
I am broken.

no, no, no, no, no, no, no

G is covered in bruises and gashes. Last night seems utterly unreal, entirely imagined. If only; the state of his cut and bashed body proves otherwise. I, and we, think backwards, rolling the memories around, attempting to make sense of them.

The stunned drive, urged on by the more compassionate policeman, up the hill to my flat: the hopeless searching for his passport, and not finding it anywhere: the final spotting of it on a shelf next to his wallet, some loose change, and of course a few plectrums: the handing it over to the police once we are back down next to the ambulance, there on the clifftop, with him lying below, covered: people all around, peering over the edge, hushed and drawn, in that human moth to a flame way, to a scene of devastation: G on a stretcher in the ambulance, wearing an oxygen mask as he has been constantly coughing and choking since he went in the water, legs bleeding, pale and wide-eyed: the helicopter that couldn't land anywhere near us, the cove being too small, and it anyway arriving far too late, looming large in the nearby car park: a woman medic giving me two miserly pills to 'help calm me', and me being generally shocked, apart from the shock of everything else, at the lack of caring support given to us: G being driven off, leaving only S and I, two out of the four that came to the beach only an hour or so ago: being told which hospital G is being taken to, and that we will be able to pick him up later, they are just taking him as a precaution; instructed to go as quickly as possible to give a statement to the police. And with that final order we are simply left to deal with it all ourselves.

Our drive to the Guardia Civil station in San José, the largest place in Cabo de Gata: the surprising hug and not so surprising commiserations from the officer there, summoned back to work by this event. (This 'event'! This is not an event. This is the end of my world.) The mumbled, jumbled words that crawled out of my parched mouth: his caring demeanour but incomprehensible (to my ears that roar and screech and block all sense), Spanish: S's tight hold of me throughout: the struggle to explain the unexplainable: the ridiculousness of the fact that the photocopier would not work, and then had no ink, so we would have to come back the following day just to sign the copies he needed to make for their records: the worst call I have ever had to make, to Biglittlebro, to tell him what happened, and just blurting out 'F's dead!', the words collapsing my mind, and his.

The next drive, to the hospital where G had been taken in the ambulance, to pick him up: the winding, black roads and the torturous, black thoughts: the befuddled receptionist, telling us there was no one by that name there: the horrendous phone call to D, F's bandmate for years, to let him know, and to ask him to somehow let his family, his kids, know (I have his phone, with all his numbers inside, but it is locked, and I don't know his password): another person at reception saying that they had tracked down G, and that he was at another hospital, even further away (what incompetence, how uncaring, to make us have to search the whole area in the state that we were in. I have absolutely no idea how S managed to drive at all).

Yet another drive, almost to the city of Almería, but using a crazily circuitous route, as even I, knowing the area fairly well, am completely lost: the rude, snappish receptionist when we finally find the second hospital, telling us in no uncertain terms that visiting hours were over and that was that: me pleading with her, but getting angry too, informing her that G was not staying overnight, we were there to collect him, and having to play the 'sympathy card', already, telling her what had happened: her finally relenting, perhaps seeing the deranged look in my eyes, and saying we had five minutes only: being directed down a corridor and into a room with around ten people in various states of disrepair lying on their beds: spotting G at the end, looking so small and scared, helplessly incapable of communicating in this foreign tongue: us holding his hands, and waiting for someone we could talk to: me leaving the room and howling in the corridor outside: finally speaking to the doctor in charge, explaining G didn't speak any Spanish (a fact he must have noticed), but that we were here to take him back with us: being told that if I asked if he felt okay and he said yes, then we could: he felt 'okay', in the sense that he wasn't seriously injured, but obviously in no other sense of the word: holding each other up as we made our way to the car park: S speaking to F's nephew, who sounded like he was being unnaturally strong and mature for a twenty-two-year-old.

The last drive of the night, back to the apartment in Las Negras: speaking to Biglittlebro again, and calling another couple of friends: a blur, an utter blur: valium: S spooning me, stroking my hair, trying desperately to comfort me as I shake and weep, unable to breathe, unable to comprehend, unable to be: I apparently suddenly stop moving, and appear to not be breathing, I am so still: S is petrified that I, too, have died, and has to check my pulse to make sure.

Yes, I was alive. But barely.

J and J arrive. The last of my friends to see him alive, just the night before, and the first to reach me, as they were staying in Las Negras last night. They heard the helicopter; they heard that someone had drowned. Not for a moment did they think it would be him. We were supposed to see each other last night for dinner and drinks, but they had decided to hole up in the hotel and switch off their phones, so never thought anything of us not meeting up, never wondered where we had got to.

S and I somehow get back into the car, and she somehow drives twenty kilometres, accompanied by J, who comes with us to help translate, my normally okay Spanish having been rendered obsolete. My English is not much better.

The officer on duty is cold, ultra-formal; a stark contrast to the one last night. The photocopier now has ink. My statement is printed, and I sign. J tells us he will talk to the policeman, and S and I leave the building, huddle together outside, as my body wrenches and bucks, my mind a hollow hell, my face contorted and ravaged.

As he joins us outside, on the fortress-like outcrop that is the Guardia Civil station, we are surrounded by the sea, this murderous entity that seems to sneer at me, taunting and flaunting its power; J explains the procedures that we have to follow in the days to come.

Being the wonderful person, and nurse that she is, S sets about being the carer, the protector, the rock. She cooks and cleans constantly, she tries to feed me. The only thing I can face is hot tea with lots of sugar. I hate tea. I hate tea with sugar. But right now it's all I want, all I can cope with. She has the brainwave of cooking me scrambled eggs, which need no chewing, something I am incapable of doing, and I manage to eat a bit. She holds me, hugs me, rocks me, talks to me, kisses me, calms me as I wail, assures me that I can breathe, that I will not die. G is utterly traumatised, as all three of us are, but is doing better than I am; no doubt she is doing the same for him, looking after him too.

Who will look after her?

Other friends begin to arrive, most driving over two hours to be with me. It is all a total haze. My best friend M is there as soon as he can be; others soon appear, and gather around, incapable of accepting what has happened, shell-shocked and stricken, encircling me, holding my hand, holding me close. A, from the flamenco group I have been playing with this summer, gives me a huge bear hug and tells me "eres fuerte" (you are strong). I am not. I have never been less so.

Phone calls, terrible phone calls, are made by S to my close friends in England, to her family, to his band members. G liaises with a couple of people in F's family. Everything is filtered through them, except my calls to Biglittlebro, who has told all my family, as I asked him to. He is booking a flight and will arrive tomorrow morning. I can't speak to my parents, to anyone, except him. I can't form the words, can't utter the sentences. Can't hear their pain, can't hear mine reverberating through the airwaves into their pained ears.

G goes back down to the beach, S tells me later in the evening. He wanted to be there, to try to understand what happened. I don't know how he did that. He said it looked completely different to how he remembered it. The angles had changed; the perspectives. The water was lower, and he could see all the rocks that were not visible yesterday. I *really* don't know how he did that. I never will.

My landlord and landlady, I and R, cut short their holiday in Córdoba when they hear the news, and arrive back in the afternoon. They envelop me in embraces, and do absolutely anything and everything possible to make it easier. R cooks huge amounts of food for the growing group of friends, and brings it round to the next door apartment shyly, not wanting a big deal to be made, leaving quietly with a small, sad smile when we thank her over and over again for her kindness. They offer beds for my friends, or to find apartments nearby for them to sleep in. They are there for me, and us, in a way that is incredible. Even through the wretched fog that suffocates my every moment, I am so grateful to them, and always will be.

It's not possible. It's not possible. It's not possible.

Somehow the sun rises and sets. Life in the village below goes on as normal. The sky scorches, the heat blazes. I sense rather than look at the sea; it is visible through the apartment's window, from the terrace, but I look anywhere but there. I feel its intensity; I have more hatred for it than anything before in my life. So innocently beautiful, lapping at the stony beach, home to happy holidaymakers, lifeblood of many of the villagers, background to endless photos, inspiration to all who gaze upon it. Yet it has destroyed him, destroyed me.

Valium again. S's tight spoon, again. Eventually, eventually, my sobs and shudders give way to short-lived sleep. And it is still not possible. And tomorrow, again, and I imagine for all time, I will be unable to breathe, unable to comprehend, unable to be.

one wave, one day

30th September 2016

It was a day like so many others.

The desert light scorches the mountains around my cave-like apartment, but this converted garage tucked into the hillside collects little of it. The strange moonscape is lit from above and, seemingly, below, with its red earth, once ignited from within, still bearing the residue of violent explosions and millions of upturned years. It is the end of September, and in this part of southern Spain autumn won't show its burnished, slightly apologetic face for many long weeks to come.

Down below, the fishing village of Las Negras sits looking out across the ocean to Algeria. To the left of it is the shadowy form of 'monkey rock' (my name), a huge cliff guarding the bay; its simian profile has increasingly obsessed me, giving me a feeling of calm, awed insignificance in the face of nature, and a sense of protection. To the right of the village rocks jut out, dividing the beach into Playa de las Negras and the beach of the campsite in the next cove, Playa Caleta.

Up above us, two of my best friends, S and G, no doubt already up for hours, will be impatient for us to join them for a morning drink, or at the very least lunch. They are renting the holiday apartment attached to my landlord and landlady's house for a week. I have been overly happy since their arrival; the combination of them getting to know my new home in paradise, and the out of context gathering of the four of us, have culminated in good times, holiday spirits, and I wish it could continue for longer than the next day or two.

I awake first, as always. Spooning throughout the night, turning from one side to the other but constantly attached, we do this well. We are peaceful, we are silent, and utterly content in this sleeping state, unlike many other couples who desperately want to stay conjoined as dawn approaches but the overheating or itchiness of one prohibits it. We said, often, how lucky we were to have that, to know those moments, when even unconscious we are bound together. Beneath the light blue, I feel his steady heartbeat, listen out for occasional tiny sighs. He is always amazed how I can be completely buried in bed sheets, given my propensity for claustrophobia, and how I breathe so quietly he has to check I'm still alive. But he's not much noisier. I lift my head out from under the soft cloth, and prop myself up on my left elbow. I like to look at him. After all these, many, years, I find him beautiful. I trace his exquisitely shaped right eyebrow with my blurry morning vision, searching for the grey hairs he often proclaims are taking him over. "It's finished! Pointless!" has been his vain refrain for countless years, as the silver and white creeps over his beard, through his hair and onto his chest. I spend happy minutes, each time we meet, plucking his twelve or so stray greys from his body, as he harrumphs at the passage of time and, I suppose, the loss of his flawless youth.

I know he'll sleep for a couple more hours yet, but want to study him some more, so slide gingerly and vaguely gymnastically over his side, so I'm facing him. He stirs. I venture a small "MMMmmmm," our greeting over the phone, in person in the mornings, or whenever and wherever during the day to get the other's attention or convey love. It is sweet, babyish, and it warms me more than I can express, not least because I know only I get to see this side of him. The sound makes me feel connected to this other being in this random world, and that is only ever good. I link my legs through his, hug him to me. Innumerable minutes are spent on his long lashes, his perfect nose, and the only sign of ageing on his face, a frown line at the top of it. His mouth, slightly pouting in repose, is as kissable as it has ever been. I lean in and skim his lips with mine, not to wake him, but because I just want to.

I feel something resembling sadness, remember why, and cling to him more tightly. It's our last day on this trip; tomorrow he'll fly back to London, and we have no concrete plans for the next time. It has only been a few days, slotted in between his new job at a guitar college in the northwest of the city, and a gig with his rock covers band the next night. Every time we get to this point, when we know we'll be torn apart again, yet again, and have to lock the door to extreme emotions or we won't get through it, I appear to be the needy one. I talk about it more, I am more insistent on booking the next flight, I am more like a sulky child. Paradoxically, when we are separated again, it is usually him who seems to feel it more, often sinking into almost-depression as he despairs about how far apart we are, about living in the UK, and how it's too long since we entwined.

My head twinges, and I remember the previous night's fairly impressive alcohol unit count. Gin and tonics, cava and red wine slosh wearily through my veins, as I wince and smile. It had been a great night. The four of us were joined by two other friends of mine, J and J, a couple from Órgiva where I used to live, and despite communication barriers and fairly drunken translations, we managed to cover life in general over the course of many, progressively hazy hours. In the very nice apartment overlooking the twinkling bay, the heat of late summer soporifically smoothing the city dwellers' stresses, we bonded, we shared, we laughed. We made plans to meet for dinner the following evening, down in the village, where J and J are staying for a couple of nights.

I have a relatively recent job, teaching piano using Skype. Connected to students from Kuala Lumpur to New York, Saudi Arabia to Switzerland, I do a few hours a week, which, incredibly, pays my rent in this beautiful place. The late morning and lunchtime is spent coaching children and adults through jazz, pop and classical styles, scales and improvisation, and I am happy to finish the last, fairly annoying class, and bound up the steps at the side of my studio flat to reach the rental apartment. I pass my landlord, a lovely, calm, generous Belgian, and he laughs at my speed to reach my friends.

We have a leisurely, delicious lunch on the terrace. It is hot enough to bask, to feel the immense difference between the air here and what it would feel like in England right now. We eat salad, fresh bread, and sample a special cheese, a favourite of G's.

"Guess what?" I ask F, smilingly. When he can't guess: "There's one lemon cornetto left!" How banal, but this was the last thing he ever ate, and I can't forget it. We had spent many years searching for this elusive beast; it would appear in one supermarket, garage or little shop after another, in the various places I had lived in Spain, only to disappear. His quest was completed in this village supermarket's refrigerator, where there seemed to be a limitless supply. His excitement at such things bemused me, but who could resist the huge grin that appeared on his face whenever one was spotted, and therefore many were bought.

Could he, would he, did he ever think for a moment that the taste of citrus flavoured ice-cream would be the last taste he experienced?

It's not long after lunch before he insists we go and swim in the sea. There is a place near the campsite, taking a high path around the headland, where the rock formations and churning waters in a huge cave make for incredible viewing; we want to take our two friends there, but first he wants to swim. They are reluctant, feeling relaxed in this place, and happy just to stay, dip in the pool, and enjoy the sun loungers. I am ambivalent; I want to show them the rocks, but not so bothered about a swim. But he is convincing; he has a force, and an excitable spirit when put into play, and soon we all agree. A quick swim at Playa de Las Negras, a short walk to the rocks, then dinner with J and J.

We gather swimwear, towels, the usual stuff, and drive down in their hired car to the stony parking spot above the beach. The sky arches across continents, blisteringly azureous, beckoning us down the steep incline to the sea below. The beach is almost empty, although the nearby bar is quite full; it is a Friday, out of season, just after five o'clock, and save for a couple of nudist sunbathers, free of people.

"What's the flag doing today?" he asks. When he had been here with me for most of August, looking at the flag was a daily pastime. Often red during that summer, with day upon day of strong winds (unusual even for this windswept region, apparently), he hadn't taken them very seriously. We hadn't, however, ventured out far at any time, preferring to keep close to shore. In any case, you had to wade out a long way to be out of your depth on that beach, further than I would ever go voluntarily.

I always had a healthy fear of the ocean. I am not comfortable in the water. I have bad memories of swimming lessons in school, my technique laughable even to the coach. I feared unknown monsters, and wouldn't happily go out of my depth. My fear was often illogical, steeped in folkloric nightmares and primeval dread, but it was very present. I am not particularly weak, but I never felt powerful in this state, and respected the waves enough to mostly stay out of their way. I used to swim underwater in my younger, more fearless years, but as an adult any games involving being ducked, or pushed down under the surface, rendered me helplessly frightened.

He, too, had a deep respect for the sea. He was quite a strong swimmer, but he didn't like to go out of his depth either. I remember one instance, in a calm bay on the Costa Brava in the north of Spain, where we were alone in an incredibly epic, fantastically stunning piece of water. We had clambered around the rocks surrounding the main beach of the town, and discovered this paradise. I swam around merrily between rocks, and climbed up onto an especially high stone. I saw him suddenly panic, even though the water wasn't deep, and the distance short between places to get out. I have never, as far as I recall, seen him spooked like that. When I got to him, drawn by his fear, he couldn't or wouldn't explain why he was scared, but scared he was. He had felt out of his depth, but the ocean was so calm, and I was so near, I didn't understand his anxiety. Now I wonder about premonitions.

We descend the tiny pathway, between spiky shrubs and loose stones, and walk along the beach. To the right someone has created the symbol for Almería out of stones. I take a photo. And I take the last ever picture of him. Really it was S that I was photographing; she is in the foreground, but I also capture G to the left a few metres on, and him even further, so eager for a swim. His last pose.

There are waves, but not crazy ones; not even close to surfing waves. He reaches the end of the beach and rounds the corner into a little pebbly cove, laughing as one breaks on him, soaking him.

I only started swimming in this cove a month ago, when other friends visiting from Switzerland discovered it, and found a nice, comfortable, almost sandy 'walkway' into the water between rocks. Before that, I had avoided it; I can't say why I was nervous about swimming there, but I was. As I said before, I was nervous in general about the sea. But there were other places, back along the beach towards the village, where you had to wade out at least ten metres to be out of your depth, and I stuck to those. In August, when he was here for nearly the whole month, we used to come to this cove, lie on the stones and throw them into the waves. We played the game where one person throws one high into the air, and the other then hurls another after it, to try to hit it. He made the rule that we couldn't leave the beach until we hit. It is harder than it seems, and long, giggling moments passed before we were allowed to escape, wander back along to the nearest bar, sit on its terrace on its white fabric chairs, and order two mojitos.

He is like a puppy. Bounding, bouncing, happy. He is onto the cove's tiny beach way before us, and his shirt is off. I am still walking around the big rock separating the two beaches, slipping on stones that rise and fall with the water, as he runs into the sea. One step, two steps, three, four, and he is swimming. I smile, then turn around, putting my bag on the ground, taking off my dress, in no hurry to plunge in. S and G are also in no rush. I turn back around, and see him out there, the waves carrying him.

He prided himself on an ability to be logical, calm and pragmatic if a situation or problem arose; he would assess the circumstances, think clearly and find a solution. In all the time I knew him, apart from that one time on the Costa Brava, I never saw him climb onto even the first rung of the ladder of panic, the rungs of which I am rather familiar with, and indecisive flapping was not in his nature. He might be more emotional *afterwards*, a long time afterwards, but in any potentially dangerous or volatile moment he was unruffled. He would know what to do, and was confident in that. And I believed that too. If he was in trouble, he would get himself out of it using reason and rational thinking.

As I observe him out there on the shifting water, a little further out than expected given the very short time he has been in there, there is no reason for me to have the intense feeling that there is something wrong. And even if there is, if he *is* in trouble, because he is the best person to deal with a bad situation then of course he will deal with it. He is swimming around absolutely normally, but I grow increasingly frightened; it is only a matter of seconds, but suddenly I know with more force and certainty than I have experienced at any time in my life that he is in danger. That he is not okay. I feel it rising in me, every pore is vibrating, my mind is yelling. It is clear, even though at the same time everything is starting to cloud and haze.

S and G think that I am having one of my panic attacks that I told them I sometimes have. "He's alright," they say, but I am shouting, "He's *not* alright, he's *not* alright," even as they try to placate me, pointing out that he is absolutely fine, he is just having a nice time in the water. At that moment, although I can't swear to this, I sense him; I feel like he looks my way, or his spirit calls me, and tells me, "No. No, don't come in the sea, it's too dangerous. No, I'm not going to make it." Either, or both. Or neither. Whatever, within this split second, my brain makes several lightning-fast leaps; if I go into the water I know without a shadow of a doubt that I will die: he is twice as strong as I am, and a much better swimmer, and I can see by the way the waves are moving now that I wouldn't even reach him, and that even if I did I would have no power to pull him back in: I know I have no phone signal in this cove, as I have been here before: I must run to get help.

Time is rushing through my ears; my lungs weep; my legs push aside hope step by step. I cry out something to the naked man who had just entered the cove, and now hurtle along, tripping over every stone, trying to catch my breath. Another naked sunbather, a woman, is the other side of the big rock separating the cove from the rest of the beach, and I shout to her too, imploring her to call the ambulance, the police, even though she probably has no signal either, and just looks confused. There is no one else on the beach. When my mind made its snap decision that the best possible thing I could do was to find help, it didn't know that there would be no group of strong men that had just arrived on the other side of the cove, or no people with boats that could push out quickly into the water. There are no lifeguards, lifeguards who were there all summer, up until two weeks ago, who could have saved him. Nobody. I tear up to the nearby bar, looking down upon myself, no longer really me, but a player in a drama. It must have taken me about a minute to reach it from the moment I left a bemused S and G, and I race to the counter and yell, call the police, call the ambulance, quick, *now*!

By the time I get back, he is gone. I don't know that for sure, but it is like my premonition earlier; logic doesn't come into it. I just innately know.

I miss the moment. The moment my love was downed, drowned, and the moment our lives were shattered.

But G tells me later what happened during the two or three minutes I was gone.

They can't understand my panic, and if anything, as I race off hysterically down the beach, they are annoyed at him for causing me worry, and making me so upset. They start shouting and waving to him to come back in, but he doesn't seem to hear or see them, is not looking towards the beach. S says she will go into the sea and try to reach him, but G stops her, seeing how strong the waves had suddenly become, probably whipped up by the wind. It never crosses G's mind that he could be in difficulties, as he is still swimming and floating around in a normal way, but he is drifting and swimming further out, and towards the line of rocks jutting out that mark the far side of the cove. G walks to the beginning of the rocks, to try to get nearer to him to get his attention, and starts clambering over them. The waves get stronger, and now he is disappearing from sight every now and again as they rise and fall. He is floating, in a sitting position, head above the water, as he gets further out but closer to the rocks, and then suddenly G loses sight of him, as one wave takes him down. When he comes up, he is face down, arms stretched out.

It all happens so fast. G sees the water is bringing him in towards the rocks he is on, and once he reaches the nearest place to him he jumps in, half wading, half swimming, with the waves crashing over his head, and gets hold of him. He rolls him over, and he is unresponsive. The sea keeps moving strongly this way and that, and G has his arms wrapped around him, but can't get hold of him properly, and is screaming for S. The naked man (now wearing swimming trunks) is on the rocks, coming to help. G drags him some of the way back to shore, until the other man reaches him, and together they pull him up over submerged rocks towards the stony beach, with S running towards them to help.

That's the point at which I return, to see them dragging him in; I run into the water too, the metre or so that is left, and we heave him up onto the beach. His shorts are being pulled down by being hauled along, and what is it that makes me pull them up? Even in that moment, that horrendous moment, I see myself doing this, I suppose out of a sense of respect, decency, privacy for him, even as I know he is not there anymore.

S is a nurse, a cardiac nurse no less, and there can be no doubt that no one could have done more to try to resuscitate him than she did that day. She does it forever. Another man, who had followed me in my sprint back to the cove, along with many hazy others who arrive bit by bit, takes over from her for a while. G is lying against a large rock nearby, choking, crying, retching, having swallowed too much water; he is bleeding from the sharp rocks he bashed against as he went in to save him. I am saying, "It's not possible," over and over again, or crying his name, as I see him there, his eyes open but unseeing, white froth pouring out of his nostrils, his chest being compressed repeatedly, and him *not* spluttering back to life in some kind of miracle. This is real. All of this is real.

Two policemen arrive at a run, too late to do anything, but anyway without any equipment, oxygen, anything that might have helped to bring him back. More curious people arrive. S keeps trying, the other man keeps taking turns. The naked man disappears. G keeps choking, I keep staring blankly, keep saying, "It's not possible," unable to absorb the truth of it even though it is plain to see. The police do police things. Time passes; at least, I suppose it does. Eventually, after what seems hours but isn't, the ambulance crew show up. They set to work, but S tells us not to get our hopes up. She has seen this kind of thing too many times before, and knows it is far too late. She has gathered the two of us from our separate rocks we were clinging to, and has sat us together, huddled in towels, shivering and quaking, to at least be at each other's side, as she speaks to the medics. We say nothing. What is there to say?

One wave. One moment. He was fine, until he wasn't. That, to the humble human eye, was the truth of it. And I have to say that you could not have two more intelligent, practical and sensitive humans than S and G, who saw nothing amiss, and only reacted to my hysteria, rather than what was in front of them, which was nothing. Nothing was wrong. He was fine. It was an accident, a terrible, fast accident. Not for a second did he gesture to them, wave his arms for help, or shout, as you surely would in that situation if you thought that you were in trouble. It was sudden. Something that, despite my sense of foreboding and connected intuition, just happened. In an instant. And no one, except the sea, which is just moving water, is to blame, and no one could have ever predicted it.

There is nothing to be done. The medics can't save him any more than we could. It is over. He is over. The three of us, glued in horror, stuck together in pure, incomprehensible grief, traumatised beyond repair, shudder as the stretcher bearing the man I have loved for so long is carried past us, the sea behind him surging towards and away from our eyes that will never unsee, the malicious breeze blowing our former lives away. It is not even crying that we are doing; it is something beyond tears, something deeper than weeping; something far more primal than mere sobs are convulsing our souls, and changing the shape of our hearts forever.

postscript

It's nearly two years since it happened.

I am still living in Órgiva, in Spain.

His scarab beetle bracelet has never left my wrist..

I often put on the black, now frayed, jumper, but also wear colourful clothes.

I haven't been in any water except the shower, and maybe never will.

I got a cat. And then I got another. Barnabé and Mitsuko, adorable creatures. And they *did* make things so much better. He would have loved them.

'The hunter of small happinesses' was released on September 30th, 2017, the day the blog finished, a year after it happened; I'm still hunting.

I'm recording a new album of songs, using some of the words from this book, and exploring new thoughts and feelings fuelled by this loss, this love.

I've completed commissions for new artwork, taken part in exhibitions.

I'm thinking about the next book I will write.

I went back to that beach very recently; it seemed impossible that this could have happened there. It looked so different. I felt numb. I launched a message in a bottle to him, to us, into the water, with my details inside in case someone discovered it one day, and I was contacted within an hour.

The hauntings still haunt, but less so. The tigers still growl, but more quietly.

His tree died, but has been replaced by a bigger, stronger one, and the daffodils flowered again in spring.

I have times of raw fragility, dark days, and tears that overwhelm in any situation, but nevertheless I can smell future smiles, taste future joys.

My panic rises and falls, but I am controlling it more and more, and will conquer it one day, I promise myself.

I'm trying to get me back, but I am forever changed; this me is different.

The hole he has left has not shrunk, but has been papered over with self-enforced sociability and schemes, and projects new and old, and kittens, and small voyages with friends or family, and large love from my circle.

It still makes no sense.

I still don't understand how he can be gone.

I still miss him more than I can ever say, and I'm sure I always will.

But I have hope.

all artwork by mix amylo

(all fineliner on paper unless specified)

photos by mix amylo except:

14   the hunter of small happinesses – Biglittlebro
44   frozen sound – G
160   spiralling – G
166   the final touch – Hispeed
227   betula pendula – E

The album 'the hunter of small happinesses' is available at
www.mixamylo.com
and
mixamylo.bandcamp.com

Contact – info@mixamylo.com

Thank you always, my circle of love – you know who you are.

To those who followed my blog, and wrote to me along the way with virtual hugs, thoughts and encouragement, thanks for taking the journey with me.

And huge thanks to Sarah, David and Julie who helped me to make this book happen.

26625343R00187